DISCARDED

CIRCULARITY AND VISIONS OF THE NEW WORLD IN WILLIAM FAULKNER, GABRIEL GARCIA MARQUEZ, AND OSMAN LINS

CIRCULARITY AND VISIONS OF THE NEW WORLD IN WILLIAM FAULKNER, GABRIEL GARCIA MARQUEZ, AND OSMAN LINS

Rosa Simas

The Edwin Mellen Press
Lewiston/Queenston/Lampeter

Library of Congress Cataloging-in-Publication Data

This volume has been registered with The Library of Congress.

ISBN 0-7734-9249-6

A CIP catalog record for this book
is available from the British Library.

Copyright © 1993 The Edwin Mellen Press

All rights reserved. For information contact

The Edwin Mellen Press
Box 450
Lewiston, New York
USA 14092

The Edwin Mellen Press
Box 67
Queenston, Ontario
CANADA L0S 1L0

Edwin Mellen Press, Ltd.
Lampeter, Dyfed, Wales
UNITED KINGDOM SA48 7DY

Printed in the United States of America

DEDICATION

To the New World of Marisa Angela

born

in 1992

CONTENTS

Chapter I
    Circularity, Linearity and America 1

Chapter II
    Voices of America 21

Chapter III
    "Ripples Spreading on Water" 39

Chapter IV
    A "Design" 71

Chapter V
    A "Gyrating Wheel" 95

Chapter VI
    A "Spiral on a Square" 129

Chapter VII
    "The World is Round" 171

Notes
    Chapter I 181
    Chapter II 187
    Chapter III 191
    Chapter IV 195
    Chapter V 197
    Chapter VI 201
    Chapter VII 205

Bibliography 207

CHAPTER I

CIRCULARITY, LINEARITY and AMERICA

Gabriel García Márquez began his 1982 Nobel Prize acceptance speech with the name of Antonio Pigafetta, the Italian adventurer who accompanied the Portuguese explorer/navigator Fernão de Magalhães (Ferdinand Magellan) on the first voyage to circumnavigate the globe between 1519 and 1522. True to his lifelong fascination with "our chronicle legacy," García Márquez calls the travel diary Pigafetta wrote, *Primo Viaggio Intorno al Mondo*, "one of my all time favorite books."[1] This historic voyage, of course, proved the long-held yet previously unconfirmed theory that, in popular terms, "the world is round." Round "como una naranja"[2] ("like an orange") José Arcadio, the precocious Buendía patriarch created by García Márquez in his famous 1967 novel *Cien años de soledad* would add. Linked to this actual physical experience of circumnavigation, the observation that "the world is round" signals a paradigmatic shift in popular world-view, a shift which coincides with the expansion of European perspectives through exploration of the American continents, a shift so significant that the Spanish historian Gómara was prompted to label the discoveries "the biggest event since the Creation of the world, excepting the incarnation and death of him who created it."[3]

It is highly significant that the physical location of human existence is newly confirmed to be a round world, i.e., that Europe elaborates "another more complete idea of our planet and cosmos,"[4] at essentially the same time that Europe also encounters and colonizes this "Nuevo Mundo" of the Americas, a "New World" seen as an infinite of field conquest, a limitless frontier, a world of new beginnings and unbounded possibility. As circumnavigation and exploration of the globe "created" another world in the fifteenth and sixteenth centuries, the exploration and interpretation of the New World "created" America and led to what has been termed the "invention" of America,[5] a project and process which subsequent centuries have increasingly equated with a linear concept of progress. Yet, as the concept and experience of America near five hundred years of *actual* existence, circularity forms the structural design and informs the thematic concerns of three major twentieth-century novels of the Americas: *Absalom, Absalom!* (1936) by the North American writer William Faulkner; *Cien años de soledad* (1967) by the Columbian Gabriel García Márquez; and *Avalovara* (1973) by the Brazilian Osman Lins.

A discussion of the concept of America during these five hundred years of actual experience will reveal that *both* circularity and linearity have been significant and fundamental to perceptions of the New World and to the interpretation of America. In fact, the possibility of land to the west of Europe was first defined according to the circular paradigm, since the unexplored land was seen as offering to the Old World the potential for cyclical renewal. The tremendous emphasis on linear progress which has fascinated the Western world since the Enlightenment, however, has not only privileged the linear paradigm of America, but has also equated the economic and technological development of the United States with America. So pronounced has been this tendency that the Mexican thinker Leopoldo Zea, for example, has felt the need to affirm time and again that any consideration of the meaning of America "must include both Americas"[6] in order to be valid. As would be expected, a study of *Absalom, Absalom!*, *Cien años de soledad* and *Avalovara* will reveal significant differences between the human experience of North America and of Latin America. The fundamental circularity of these three American novels, however, also reveals significant similarities that delineate the common experience of the New World and of the phenomenon we call "America." Very briefly, the circularity of these texts expresses the simultaneity and redundancy of human experience; reduplicates the dynamics of cyclical renewal and cosmic order; and contradicts the concept of linear progress dominant in the Western world and inherent to the traditional concept of America in the Modern World.

Before the exploratory navigations of the fifteenth century, according to the historian Edmund O'Gorman, the prevalent concept of the world and of the universe limited human existence to the *orbis terrarum*. This so-called "Island of Earth" was dependent upon Christian belief and tradition, which attributed spiritual significance even to the fact that the *orbis terrarum* was comprised of three continents, a terrestrial trinity made up of Europe, Africa and Asia. Reflecting the dominant prism of Christian orthodoxy, then, "medieval world maps showed a disk with Jerusalem at its center; radiating out from it were fanciful representations of the three known continents. The Garden of Eden and other locales from the Bible were then sketched at appropriate points."[7] Although geographers knew that the earth was an orb, the prevalent world-view formed by the Scriptures represented the earth as a flat disk in maps known as *mappaemundi*:

> The scripturally inspired plans were known as *mappaemundi*, Latin for "maps of the world." Almost all represented the earth as a flat disk, rather than the orb that geographers had long known it to be. The aim of the mapmakers, however, was less to convey geographical information than to express biblical concepts in schematic form. One of the most popular versions was the T-O model, in which the O was formed by an ocean ring encircling the three known continents of the earth: Asia, Africa, and Europe...The continents were shown separated by a T formed by waterways; the Mediterranean, dividing Europe from Africa, formed the upright, while Asia, depicted uppermost, lay over a crossbar composed of the Don and Nile rivers.[8]

The gradual realization that there might be land beyond, land separate from the *orbis terrarum*, ultimately implied a drastic shift in worldview, the first step of which was no less than the creation of an *orbis alter*, an *other world* which did not readily fit into the known world defined by Christian tradition and European thought. As the historian Wilcomb E. Washburn puts it: "The medieval world tended to conceive of a central land mass, an *orbis terrarum*, inhabited by humans and located in the Northern Hemisphere...The concept of an antipodal land mass, an *orbis alter*, tended to be denied by Christian writers since it was hard to conceive that the gospel had been preached in any such lands."[9] As exploration and circumnavigation of the globe proceeded, however, the old theory of the *orbis terrarum* as the only terrestrial space assigned to humans gradually lost credence, especially since further exploration and navigation proved this "other world" to be, not a mere island as was originally believed, but indeed a huge continent comparable to the three that made up the *orbis terrarum*. Along with the three known continents of Europe, Africa and Asia, then, there existed a fourth: America. The next step in this paradigmatic shift recognizes these previously unknown lands as equal to the *orbis terrarum* and labels this "other world," as the title of the text written by America's namesake Americo Vespucci indicates, *Mundus Novus*, a *New World* which exploration had added to the Old World, thereby expanding and making whole an earth recently experienced in circular terms. In a letter addressed to his patron Lorenzo Pietro di Medici, Vespucci explains:

> On a former occasion I wrote to you at some length concerning my return from those new regions which...we may rightly call a *new world*, because our ancestors had no knowledge of them, and it will be a matter wholly new to all those who hear about them. For this transcends the view held by our ancients, inasmuch as most of them hold that there is no continent to the south beyond the equator...But that this their opinion is false and utterly opposed to the truth, this my last voyage has made manifest; for in those southern parts I have found a continent more densely peopled and abounding in animals than our Europe or Asia or Africa and, in addition, a climate milder and more delightful than any other region known to us.[10] (Italics are mine.)

As this process of interpretation gradually made the concept of *new world* equal to the concept of *America*, these new lands became "an idea, an invention created by the spirit of Europe,"[11] as O'Gorman insists and the Mexican writer Octavio Paz reiterates. Emphasizing the difference between "universe" (the sum total of all that exists) and "earth" (the terraqueous globe) in relation to *world*, O'Gorman defines the latter as the "cosmic dwelling-place of man." Comparable to the Greek concept of *oikoumene*, the world is, then, "man's home within the universe," a physical location as well as a moral and spiritual order.[12] Related to the dynamics of circularity, especially to the creation of a whole form and the potential for unlimited expansion of the circumference, the physical location of human existence is made whole by the confirmation that "the world is round," at the same time that the exploration and colonization of the "New World" expands and redefines the previously static moral and spiritual order of the *orbis terrarum* by offering a new beginning and seemingly limitless expansion to Western Europe. "Rather than a fixed Ptolemaic universe," Western civilization began to interpret the cosmic dwelling-place of man (i.e., the world) as "an expanding cosmos," words that Sacvan Bercovitch employs in a North American context but which apply to both American continents.[13] Linked to circumnavigation, the dynamics of circularity set in motion the predominant world-view of the time by redefining the universe as "an expanding cosmos," and by transplanting Old World perspectives onto New World soil.

    The different perspectives which contemporary writers from both North America and Latin America adopt in order to describe this process of interpretation which created America, point to the fundamental difference which exists between the Northern and Southern portions of what was once globally considered the "New World." Once again, it is a question of location. When the Latin American Leopoldo Zea, for example, emphasizes the European origins of America, he points to the stronghold which the Old World, and later North America, have had over Latin America - "Tired of a world order over which he had had no say, the new European threw himself into the search of a new world where he could begin anew;"[14] the North American Russel B. Nye, on the other hand, emphasizes the New World origins of North America specifically, as he points to the independent self-assurance which characterizes a people which "knew very well that they were not merely Europe projected, but a new civilization with a separate future...The United States," Nye emphatically affirms, "was the result of a willed, creative act, by an identifiable set of people who deliberately set out to make a nation."[15] Although the passage of time has tended to emphasize the differences that these perspectives express, both continents of America, "this world of ours," as Juan David García Bacca puts it, "is invention, creation, improvisation, inspired thinking."[16] It is not pure coincidence that three significant creators of American fictions in the twentieth century should draw on the dynamics of circularity in order to elaborate their modern expression and invention of America. The interpretation of America as a "new world" within a "round world" is, after all, common to the whole hemisphere.

Along with this scientific and secular interpretation of America and redefinition of the world in circular terms, the New World was also interpreted in the mythic, and therefore sacred, terms of cyclical renewal and westward movement. Speaking of the Discoveries as "the mythic recreation of the world" and "a cosmology" which discovers anew "the unity of the world," José Lins López-Schümmer describes mythic time as "circular, reversible and significant" when he observes that "(a)ncient man conceived of human time in terms of nature, which is cyclical." He adds:

> Human life is the repetition of thousands, millions of cycles which end and begin again. Those repetitions are, moreover, significant. To ancient man, an object, an act was not real, did not exist in reality unless it was repeated; that is, unless it imitated a model or an archetype...By permitting time to turn upon itself, this archetypal repetition annuls and cancels time...Not in vain did Nietzsche speak of "eternal return." The conquest of history is eternity.[17]

So fundamental has been temporal transcendence to the concept and experience of America, that the North American critic David W. Noble was prompted to affirm in 1968 that "the central myth of our civilization" is "the transcendence of time."[18] Relating the myth of the New World to cyclical time, López Schümmer describes "the importance of the prophetic in the very genesis of the Discoveries" by saying:

> It is known that the enterprise that Columbus initiated was part of a vast endeavor which entailed finally capturing Jerusalem and realizing the unity of the world, universal christianization and the fulfillment of time. This fulfillment of time, inherent also to the legend of the island of Seven Cities, is intertwined with the origin of the universe, thereby closing the cycle of creation. Christopher Columbus' conviction was based on this belief, that earthly Paradise was located in the lands being discovered.[19]

Cyclical time was also significant on the other side of the Atlantic, in these lands being discovered. According to Octavio Paz, it was the Aztec belief in cyclical time which prompted Montezuma to acquiesce to Cortés, allowing a handful of conquistadores to topple a huge and bellicose empire. While explaining the perspective of the Aztecs, Paz describes their belief in cyclical rituals and observes that "Montezuma interpreted the arrival of the Spaniards...not so much as a danger coming from the outside, but as the end of an internal cosmic era and the beginning of another. The gods would leave because their time was up: but another time would return, and with it, other gods and another era."[20]

The great wealth which Cortés and his men discovered in the Aztec empire became, to a Europe "prejudiced in favor of Utopia and seeing El Dorados,"[21] one of many examples which seemed to prove that America would be the earthly paradise that had so long and persistently eluded the Old World. The legends of El Dorado, of the Amazons and of the Seven Cities of Cibola[22] are among the most popular terms which conjure up these long-held utopian dreams of an earthly paradise "West of Eden" which the New World seemed about to fulfill. Uniting these timeless legends of great wealth and earthly paradise with cyclical renewal and temporal transcendence, the location of this utopia traditionally pointed West. Roderick Nash states very simply: "The discovery of the New World rekindled the traditional European notion that earthly paradise lay somewhere to the west. As the reports of the first explorers filtered back, the Old World began to believe that America might be the place of which it had dreamed since antiquity."[23] Speaking of Thoreau's westward walk, described in *Walden and Other Writings*, Sacvan Bercovitch observes that "historically, the Westward movement signals a renascence of mankind." Thoreau himself relates this movement to the sun "as the great Western Pioneer whom all nations follow," while he considers "America's prospect of making real the utopian visions of the ancients."[24] John Crow, in his turn, attests to the enduring power of this myth when he ends his study of *The Epic of Latin America* by describing this westward course of civilization within which Latin America, he affirms, should be included: "There is a legend that the path of civilization, our civilization, has been ever westward. Originating in the fabulous gardens of the East, it has touched in turn Babylonia, Greece, Rome, western Europe and last America."[25] Finally, observing that the

"Westward course of empire implied a cyclical view of history,"[26] Bercovitch calls this perspective "the concept of *translatio studii*, the classical theory that civilization moves in a westward course, from Greece to Rome to Western Europe - and thence, according to certain seventeenth - eighteenth-century European thinkers, to the New World." He goes on to observe that "traditionally, in both its pagan and its Christian contexts, the *translatio studii* stems from the cyclical -providential view of history."[27] And so, the notion of earthly paradise and westward movement turned Europe's gaze "west of Eden."

Once Europe began to settle this "New World West of Eden," America as cyclical, westward renewal was gradually redefined, however, as it became firmly grounded in American soil. So firmly is it rooted in the land, in fact, that another twentieth-century writer of North America, F. Scott Fitzgerald, would end his portrayal of a moribund American dream, *The Great Gatsby*, by nostalgically referring to "a fresh, green breast of the new world," a maternal image which equates America to mother earth and to the cyclical renewal of the land through natural vegetation. While he contemplates Gatsby's, i.e., his own, shattered world, Figzgerald's disillusioned and naive narrator, Nick Carraway, acknowledges the overwhelming lure of this land as he traces the following image of "the last and greatest of all human dreams:"

> As the moon rose higher the inessential houses began to melt away until gradually I became aware of the old island here that flowered once for Dutch sailors' eyes - a fresh, green breast of the new world. Its vanished trees, the trees that had made way for Gatsby's house, had once pandered in whispers to the last and greatest of all human dreams; for a transitory enchanted moment man must have held his breath in the presence of the continent, compelled into an aesthetic contemplation he neither understood nor desired, face to face for the last time in history with something commensurate to his capacity for wonder.[28]

This "something commensurate to his capacity for wonder" sprang fresh and green from the American soil, while the "Old World" defined America as a land of unbounded potential and scope, a land for starting over fresh and anew. The "wonder" which the continents of America would inspire, though, soon proved to be of a different nature; i.e., while the "fabulous...enchanting regions" of Central and South America would inspire awe and wonder due to their seemingly fantastic terrain, the "grave, serious and solemn" terrain of North America would inspire a resolute wonder which counted on a concerted effort to tame such a harsh environment. In his *Democracy in America*, written as a result of his 1831-2 visit to the New World, Alexis de Tocqueville's words typify the European perspective, as he compares the two Americas:

> When Europeans first landed on the shores of the West Indies, and afterwards on the coast of South America, they thought themselves transported into those fabulous regions of which poets had sung...Every object that met the sight in this enchanting region seemed prepared to satisfy the wants or contribute to the pleasures of man.
>
> North America appeared under a very different aspect: there everything was grave, serious, and solemn; it seemed created to be the domain of intelligence, as the South was that of sensual delight.[29]

Fifty years earlier, the self-styled "American Farmer," St. Jean de Crèvecoeur, had transplanted European dreams of regeneration onto North American soil in the following "vegetative" terms:

> In this great American asylum, the poor of Europe have by some means met together...Everything has tended to regenerate them; new laws, a new mode of living, a new social system; here they are to become men: in Europe they were as so many useless plants, wanting vegetative mold and refreshing showers; they withered, and were mowed down by want, hunger, and war; but now by the power of transplantation, like all other plants they have taken root and flourished![30]

While North America defined itself in terms of autonomy and self-will, however, Latin America became more and more an extension of Europe; while North America increasingly defined itself as the life-blood of modern Western civilization, Latin America assumed the role of a mere branch grafted onto the tree of Western culture. Leopoldo Zea compares these two contrasting perspectives and experiences of America when he observes that the Anglo-Saxons very deliberately created a "new world," while the Iberian colonizers aspired toward mere imitation and repetition of the Old World.

> ...in America, the Anglo-Saxons were searching for the realization and fulfillment of a new world which could never be achieved in...the old European societies of feudal origin. Many of these men saw in America...a virgin world which could be molded according to the ideals of modernity...
>
> Such was not the case with the conquistadores and colonizers of the lands which would make up Iberian America. These, the Iberians, far from burning their ships and their past, as did the Anglo-Saxons in America, threw themselves into the venture of creating in the new continent a world similar to the one they had left behind in old Europe, in Spain and Portugal...Theirs was not to create a new world, but to reproduce the old in order to find the positions they could not achieve in the original.[31]

Contrary to this Latin American perspective, the settlers who shaped North America assumed a very self-conscious and independent stance toward their enterprise. Religious from the start, this "errand into the wilderness," as Perry Miller terms it,[32] sprang from the firm Calvinist tradition of the Puritans who set sail for the New World with the staunch conviction that they were a people in covenant with God, a people chosen to fulfill his divine plan here on earth. In the words of John Winthrop as they crossed the Atlantic in 1630: "...we shall be a city upon a hill. The eyes of all people are upon us."[33] So basic is this conviction of being "a chosen people designated for a special destiny"[34] to the North American psyche that, in referring to William Bradford's account of the Mayflower Pilgrims who settled in Plymouth, Massachusetts in 1620, *Of Plymouth Plantation*, Francis Murphy observes: "Bradford's account of a chosen people, exiles in a 'howling wilderness,' who struggled against all adversity to bring into being the City of God on earth, is ingrained in our national consciousness."[35] Prompted by a literal reading of the Bible, these early settlers of North America were rigid in their belief that God was speaking directly to them when in II Samuel 7:10, for example, they read: "I will appoint a place for my people Israel, and will plant them, that they may dwell in a place of their own, and move no more."

The new life that would spring from the soil of the United States, the national destiny of such a self-conscious people, was gradually but inexorably interpreted in linear terms, as the nation disposed of the indigenous peoples already on the land, and reshaped the circularity of cyclical renewal which governs the natural world into the linearity inherent to the concept of the North American frontier. In his famous and extremely influential study *The Frontier in American History*, the very words of Frederick Jackson Turner point to this reshaping of a land and its people, where the cyclical paradigm of natural "rebirth" is molded into the linear western progression of the North American frontier. Early in his work, Turner summarizes the peculiar dynamics which shaped the United States and illustrate his theory:

> Thus American social development has exhibited not merely advance along a single line, but a return to primitive conditions on a continually advancing frontier line, and a new development for that area. American social development has been continually beginning over again on the frontier. This perennial rebirth, this fluidity of American life, this expansion westward with its new opportunities, its continuous touch with the simplicity of primitive society, furnish the forces dominating American character...In this advance the frontier is the outer edge of the wave - the meeting point between savagery and civilization.[36]

However polemical Turner's theory, and especially his conclusions, may be, he certainly reached the nerve-center of the North American psyche, for the influence of the frontier, whether in a literal or figurative sense, has been "the strongest single factor in American history." The repeated process of 'beginning over again' on each succeeding frontier"[37] has so shaped the North American mind, that in 1977 William Humphrey would write about the frontier: "That word is charged with emotion for us; it could as late as 1960 still win a national election, without anyone even asking what it means."[38]

Viewed today by many as "a state of mind," "a complex process, always in a state of being,"[39] the frontier is presently seen by some in more universal terms. Studying the frontier experience of Latin America, Emilio Willems, for example, refutes some of Turner's conclusions, as he observes:

> Few anthropologists, I believe, would go along with the idea that, to qualify as a frontier, social life on freshly occupied lands should necessarily generate individualism, democracy, inventiveness, materialism, enterpreneurship, or whatever real or mythological traits are associated with North American frontier life. As an anthropologist, I refuse to impose ethnocentric criteria on a process the component aspects of which are fairly uncomplicated and truly universal. By frontier I mean an area of highly variable size into which migrants have moved to exploit some of its resources.

Resulting, according to Willems, in "large-scale miscegenation and cultural hybridization,"[40] the Latin American experience of frontier, as well as of conquest and settlement has been varied in nature due to the different types of indigenous societies which existed in the various regions of Latin America. John A. Crow explains that in the case of the centralized Indian empires of Mexico and Peru, "with their well-established agricultural economies and social systems, once the central power was overcome, the whole social structure gave up and accepted defeat." More similar to the North American experience of movement along successive frontiers, "in Argentina, Uruguay and Chile," for example, "the battle was against dozens of primitive Indian tribes who kept up a constant guerrilla warfare for many years...In this way there grew up in those countries a feeling of frontier." In the case of Brazil, explains Crow, where "there was no centralized empire, relatively few Indians, and during the early years little gold or silver, a frontier existed, but it was so vast that it could not serve as a great unifying factor."[41] These differences notwithstanding, Crow uses words which attest to the enormous impact that the concept of the frontier has had, - especially on the North American psyche; for, basic to human nature and to the concept of America, is the appeal of a new beginning, the promise of a "new horizon:"

> Many persons have spoken of Latin America as a "last frontier." In a world of industrialized might it is indeed a last great reservoir of unexploited wealth... It is a frontier behind which the old colonial economy persists, where in every region the mountain of tradition obstructs the march toward a new horizon.[42]

This cultural historian's words, in fact, belie his North American perspective, since the process whereby "starting over again" and again is recast in the linear mold of the frontier is not universal, but basic to the natural consciousness of the United States; because, just as its forceful public stance has made the United States equal to "America" in most people's minds, so this stance has made the word "frontier" equal in popular thinking to the North American experience of westward expansion. Moreover, along with this reshaping of cyclical renewal into the linear paradigm of the United States frontier, the North American psyche has also redefined the very word "frontier," which traditionally and in most other languages, means "a boundary line." Sacvan Bercovitch points out that the Puritan heritage of the United States shifted the meaning "from a secular barrier to a mythical threshold" when he explains that the American romantics'

> concept of the frontier is a measure of their debt to the Puritans. Traditionally, *frontier* meant a border dividing one people from another. It implied an acceptance of differences between nations. In a sense, the Puritans recognized those differences - their "frontier" separated them from the Indian "outer darkness" - but they could hardly accept the restriction as permanent. America was God's Country, after all, and they were on a redemptive errand for mankind. In effect, their motive for colonization entailed a decisive shift in the meaning of frontier, from a secular barrier to a mythical threshold. Even as they spoke of their frontier as a meeting-ground between two civilizations, Christian and pagan, they redefined it, in a rhetorical inversion characteristic of the myth-making imagination, to mean a *figural* outpost, the outskirts of the advancing kingdom of God. It became, in short, not a dividing line but a summons to territorial expansion...What in Europe signified history and restriction, came in America to signify prophecy and unlimited prospects.[43]

This "rhetorical inversion" stems from the Puritan tradition and heritage which shaped the United States and defined this part of the New World as a "utopia" expressing the "unfolding redemptive design"[44] of God. Grounded in Biblical tradition - leading from Genesis to Apocalypse - the concept of elect nationhood from which stems the experience of the United States, has also shaped the very concept of America into the linearity of Christian eschatology. The collective perception which cast the land in the linear mode of the frontier stems from these Puritan roots which, in accord with millennium tradition, awaited "the descent of New Jerusalem" at the end of time or prayed for a "final golden age within history." This historical linearity and eschatology of the Puritans' errand began, of course, with Creation and Eden, led to Canaan (Old Testament) and to New Canaan (New Testament), then to New Canaan in America and, finally, to New Eden (the Apocalyptic Second Coming of Christ and final fulfillment of time).[45] Accordingly, Puritan belief attributed special significance to the specific words and imagery of the apocalyptic Book of Revelation, the last book of the Bible. Relating the enigmatic visions of the author John to the discoveries of the New World, many believed that

> America clearly denoted the fourth and last of the round earth's imagined "ends." The apocalyptic number (see Revelation 6:2-8; 7:1) had been traditionally linked to the Four Horsemen as types of the spread of the gospel, each of the first three Horsemen representing one of the continents then known, and the fourth Horseman representing the last stage of time...During the last third of the seventeenth century, the New England Puritans seized upon these implications. They pointed out that *Asia, Africa* and *Europe* have, each of them, had a glorious Gospel Day, so that by the end of the fifteenth century, the Barrier *Solum* to the millennium lay across the Atlantic.[46]

While the discovery and settlement of the New World heralded a new era in sacred and secular history, the American Revolution confirmed, in the young nation's optimistic perspective, the divine destiny of a people who proposed for their national seal, among other motifs from Biblical history, the image of "Moses leading the chosen people from Egypt," as well as the symbol actually adopted, the eagle mentioned in the books of Isaiah and Revelation,[47] and in Exodus 19: 4 & 6, where they read: "Ye have seen...*how I bare you on eagles' wings and brought you unto myself...And ye shall be unto me a kingdom of priests, and a holy nation.*"[48] So ingrained is this rhetoric of divine mission and select destiny in the national consciousness of the United States, that a sense of being set apart from, and therefore misunderstood by, the rest of the unenlightened world, often attends it. The words of William E. Borah, "the champion of isolation who rose in the Senate on February 21, 1919, to challenge Wilson's Versailles speech," express eloquently the extraordinary fervor of a people who feel set apart by a unique destiny. "I do not want this Republic," he affirmed, "its free people and its institutions, to go into partnership with and to give control of the partnership to those, many of whom have no conception of our civilization and no more insight into our destiny. What we want is...a free, untrammeled nation, imbued anew and inspired again with the national spirit."[49]

Stemming from Puritan eschatology, and its preoccupation with prophecy and typology, as well as with the promise of religious fulfillment and salvation at the end of time, this fervor of elect nationhood fixed the gaze of the North American portion of the New World inexorably on the future. While the Old World of Europe examined its past in order to deal with its present, the New World of Puritan America looked steadfastly toward future spiritual fulfillment and salvation, as it grew into the New World of Yankee America, looking reassuredly toward future material success and progress. Such a collective identity, rooted in a prophetic view of history and nurtured by New World soil, soon grafted secular history onto sacred history, profane progress and fulfillment onto divine progress and fulfillment, in accord with an ever-"increasing tendency to redefine America's mission in secular rather than sacred terms."[50] This joining of wordly promise with Biblical prophecy and apocalypse transformed the linearity of Christian eschatology into the linearity of the North American gospel of material progress and success, "translated religious fulfillment from its meaning within the closed system of sacred history into a metaphor for limitless secular improvement."[51] The personification of this "idea of progress as an ascending line"[52] was/is, of course, the so-called "self-made man," thriving on open competition, upward mobility, and an increasingly progressive and secular view of history. Such an environment naturally selected the neat socio-economic linearity that molded his "rags to riches" story, the prototypical American success story. As Darwinian evolutionary theory "equated evolution with progress," belief in a "new race of men" became more and more prevalent and pronounced during the second half of the century, as the following words, written by Charles Norton soon after the Civil War, illustrate:

> I believe that we have really made an advance in civilization, that the principles on which our political and social order rest are in harmony with the laws of the universe, that we have set up an ideal which may never be perfectly attained but which is of such a nature that the more effort to attain it makes progress in genuine happiness more certain...We are getting rid of old world things and becoming accustomed to the new. We are forming new creeds, new judgements, new manners; we are becoming a new race of men.[53]

Indeed, social Darwinism reinforced "the deep and emotional attachment to the concept of progress"[54] that has characterized the colonial and national psyche of this portion of the New World - a "dominant Protestant mind" which, as Perry Miller puts it, "yielded itself to the vision of unchecked progress," to the "image of infinite progress...reinforced in the second half of the century by Darwinism."[55]

As he traces the development of Modernity, the Mexican thinker Leopoldo Zea describes the psychology behind this "new man," heir to "the first colonizers of North America who would become, by their actions and the ideas that motivated them, the most obvious exponents of the spirit we call Modern." Zea's words delineate the process whereby this "new man" discards the past in order to focus on the future, and "creates" that "something" available to each and "every man" - Progress:

> Having abandoned the past as justification for a present that he wanted to attain, the new man takes recourse in a new idea of his own creation to justify his future... Something that could begin with every man, with any man. Something that would not discriminate. Something that would be valid for all men without making distinctions. This something would be the idea of Progress.[56]

Not withstanding the "red men" that had to be done away with and the "black men" that had to be enslaved, not to mention the women who had to be kept in their place, this idea/ideal of Progress, supposedly available to "any and every man without making distinctions," prospered in the New World of the United States, virgin soil that could be molded into the linear ideals of Modernity. "In all fundamental aspects," says Canadian-born Berkovitch, "New England was from the start an outpost of the modern world," since it was a world where the emigrant Puritans "effectively forged a powerful vehicle of middle-class ideology: a ritual of progress through concensus...a 'civil religion' for a people chosen to spring fully formed into the modern world."[57] Stemming from a pronounced "tradition of expectancy"[58] and the beguiling promise of improvement, the middle-class culture of the United States is both heir to the linearity of Biblical sacred history and *the* most prominent descendant of modern middle-class ideology, an ideology delineated and shaped by the basis of Modernity: the linear paradigm of Progress. Indeed the sacred promise of the "city on the hill" erected on New World land was, from the start, the model of secular middle-class economy and modern culture. Such has been the "manifest destiny" of Old World ideals planted in the fertile New World soil of the United States, a nation which, from the time of discovery and original settlement, has read its destiny in its landscape and in its sense of mission.

As North America reached four hundred years of existence and experience since Columbus's famous voyage of 1492, Frederick Jackson Turner announced the closing of the frontier in the United States in 1890. "And now, four centuries after the discovery of America," wrote Turner, "at the end of a hundred years of life under the Constitution, the frontier has gone, and with its going has closed the first period of American history."[59] One hundred years later, as the Americas reach five hundred years of actual existence and experience in 1992, I have joined Latin America to the United States in order to attempt a more complete and comparative analysis of the American experience and the concept of America. With the characteristically predominant perspective of the United States, the historian Russell B. Nye has observed: "The central American myth has always been (the) myth of anticipation, of the search for opportunities, the quest for El Dorado, the unenclosed land of the frontier, the gold of California, the success story of Alger, the prospect of the open future."[60] No matter how frustrated the attempts and stunted the results, Latin America has participated in this myth, this search, this quest. In this study, I will follow a comparative approach that relates narrative structure and narrative discourse to cultural and ideological concerns, in order to analyze and evaluate the concept and experience of America in relation to the three novels that I propose *Absalom, Absalom* by William Faulkner, *Cien años de soledad* by Gabriel García Márquez and *Avalovara* by Osman Lins.

The literary expression of the American experience in English, in Spanish, and in Portuguese produced by these three noteworthy writers of the Americas, shapes their twentieth-century representation of America, *not in terms of linearity, but in terms of circularity*. As we have seen, the frontier concept, Christian eschatology and the ideal of modern progress have molded the United States and the very concept of America according to linearity. Given the prominence of this linear paradigm which defines America in the twentieth century, along with the linearity inherent to traditional storytelling (in any age), the fundamental and dominant circularity of these three important novels is indeed extraordinary and noteworthy. Briefly, this circularity reflects the aesthetic concerns of three self-conscious modern writers, representative of twentieth-century literary experimentation and creation. Reflecting the socio-cultural concerns of three novels representative of the three main languages and regions which make up America, this circularity also demonstrates the redundancy of human psychic perceptions of time in relation to human experience; reflects human desire patterned on the perception of cyclical renewal and cosmic order in nature and the universe; gives voice to America as collective collaboration and creation; and contradicts the idea and ideal of linear progress basic to Modernity and the Western world, and inherent to the prevalent concept of America.

Ending his chapter "Criticisms of the Frontier Thesis," James D. Bennett hopes for "a more realistic and comprehensive theory of American cultural development" than that of the frontier thesis, and makes the curious observation that "(t)his new theory will probably still be based on the great factor of population movement but it will not be simply westward movement but complex movement in all directions."[61] Nick Carroway in *The Great Gatsby*, decides "to go East" for, as he puts it, "(i)nstead of being the warm center of the world, the Middle West now seemed like the ragged edge of the universe."[62] In a de-centered modern universe, the twentieth-century literary expression of the Americas has certainly moved in "other directions." As Nick participates in and contends with the "ragged edge" of a linear world-view, so Faulkner, García Márquez and Lins contradict linearity by creating "visions of the New World" that are both shaped and invigorated, as well as stunted and "quagmired," by the dynamics of circularity.

Thomas Cole, an English immigrant who became North America's foremost landscape artist of the nineteenth century, painted his famous masterpiece "The Course of Empire" in 1836. In this five-panel painting we see in sequence, "a wilderness giving way to a pastoral society and then to a glorious civilization. But in the fourth painting new savages sack the great city, and in the fifth wilderness conditions are gradually returning as the cycle is completed."[63] As the image of infinite progress characteristic of the early nineteenth century was reinforced in the second half of the century by social Darwinism, the North American psyche resisted Cole's portrait of the rise and fall of a nationalism based upon the cycle of nature. "A few souls, like Thomas Cole," says Perry Miller of nineteenth-century America, "may still have nourished a lingering hankering after destruction...For most Americans, no doubt, the course of empire meant no such cycle of rise and fall, but the steady advance of American farmers and artisans across the continent."[64] However, while nineteenth-century America, intent on secular progress and material success, ignored Cole's portrayal of cyclical renewal and destruction, the twentieth-century reader of *Absalom, Absalom, Cien años de soledad* and *Avalovara* cannot but deal with and be aware of the dynamics and limitations of circularity, the traditional paradigm which shaped the original concept of America and which shapes these three representative novels of twentieth-century America.

CHAPTER II

VOICES OF AMERICA

The 1973 Comparative Literature Symposium at Texas Tech University considered the impact of the North American writer William Faulkner on world literature, yet only one sentence in one presentation, a talk by Robert G. Collmer entitled "When 'Word' Meets 'Palabra:' Crossing the Border with Literature," relates Faulkner to Latin American writers. While presenting a historical overview of the relationship between North American literature and Spanish American literature, Collmer mentions Faulkner's name in passing when he observes that "Latin American novelists, for example, the Mexican José Revueltas, the Argentinian José Carlos Onetti, the Mexican Juan Rulfo and the Chilean José Donoso, all would probably concur with the statement by the Cuban Lino Novas Calvo: 'I have Faulkner in my blood.'"[1] Yet, William Faulkner's writing has had a tremendous impact on contemporary Spanish American prose fiction, "an impact which began in 1934 with the first Spanish translation of *Sanctuary*," according to Harley Oberhelman.[2] So great has been this impact, in fact, that both critics and Latin American writers acknowledge the influence this North American writer has had on South American Literature. James E. Irby, as early as 1956, dedicated his master's thesis to this topic; John Brushwood speaks of the "the importance of Faulkner in the Latin American novel" in his 1976 essay of the same name.[3] Katalin Kulin, five years earlier, had emphatically affirmed: "The most direct influence, the one which is acting upon most writers, came from William Faulkner. Carlos Fuentes, Juan Rulfo, Manuel Rojas, Juan Carlos Onetti, Gabriel García Márquez are all indebted to this great North American writer."[4] Relating the affinity between the literature of Latin America and the Southern United States to the common experience of failure, the Mexican writer Carlos Fuentes observes in a 1976 interview:

> Until recently, American authors never had the chance to deal with a national failure. The American ideal of success has done a great deal to standardize American art forms. That's why I think that for many years the most original American writing has come from the South, where there had been a real sense of regional tragedy and where there was a need to reexamine the things that had been taken for granted.[5]

In another interview four years later, Fuentes echoes these words and adds Faulkner's name: "Suddenly there is the spectre of failure facing a country based on success. Then you can write *Absalom, Absalom!* and all the other great novels of Faulkner."[6] As early as 1969, in fact, Fuentes had related the name of William Faulkner to the novelists of the so-called "boom" generation in his famous study *La nueva novela hispanoamericana*.[7] Pointing toward technical considerations, along with thematic concerns, Gabriel García Márquez himself states:

> I feel that the greatest debt that we, the new novelists of Latin America, have is with Faulkner...Faulkner is present in all novels of Latin America; I think that...the great difference between us and writers before us is Faulkner; that was all that happened from one generation to another...That is to say, we were living our reality and we wanted to write about it, yet we knew that neither European nor traditional Spanish methods were adequate; and then we found that the Faulknerian method was perfect for recounting our reality.[8]

A year later he would state very simply: "After I read Faulkner, I thought: I have to be a writer."[9]

Exactly *when* García Márquez began to read Faulkner has, in fact, deserved special attention by those involved in influence studies. As early as 1949, a twenty-year-old Gabriel mentions Faulkner, along with Virginia Woolf, in an article written when he lived in the coastal town of Cartagena and worked for the local newspaper with a very universal title: *El Universal*. Discussing García Márquez's participation in a literary group from the nearby town of Barranquilla, Jacques Gilard explains in "García Márquez le Groupe de Barranquilla et Faulkner."

> In terms of the first mention of Faulkner, that occurs in an article García Márquez published in *El Universal* from Cartagena in July 28, 1949 (p.4) with the title *El viaje de Ramiro de la Espriella* (Ramiro de la Espriella's Trip). While speaking of his friend's departure, García Márquez says: 'Personally, we are going to miss de la Espriella...to talk about André Maurois, to discuss Faulkner and to agree about Virginia Woolf'...It seems that García Márquez knew Faulkner before becoming a member of the Barranquilla group and before establishing himself, some days later, in that town in order to become a journalist for *El Heraldo*.[10]

In a retrospective article, a personal friend Raúl Rodríguez Márquez confirms that it was during the Cartagena period that "with Gabito by my side I discovered Faulkner."[11] At the end of 1949 García Márquez actually moved to Barranquilla, where he worked for *El Heraldo* from 1950-1952. Most of his contributions appeared under the column "La Jirafa" ("The Giraffe") with the pseudonym "Septimus," a character in Virginia Woolf's novel *Mrs. Dalloway*. Four of these articles refer directly to Faulkner. The first is from 8 April 1950 and offers the young author's appraisal of recent Nobel Prize winners in the field of literature. Mentioning James Joyce and Pablo Neruda, García Márquez considers the merits of writers who had long been overlooked, and points especially to Faulkner whom he calls "the most extraordinary of modern novel writers." He then goes on to state his fear that Faulkner, like Joyce and Virginia Woolf before, will never be a Nobel winner.[12] A few months later, on July 19, 1950, García Márquez offers a commentary on the film version of *Intruder in the Dust*. Titled "The Master Faulkner in the Cinema," this article discusses brutality and destruction of temporal chronology in Faulkner's work, characteristics which offer special problems to the script writer.[13] Since Faulkner did in fact receive the Nobel Prize in that same year, the 13 November 1950 entry celebrates this unexpected event, while that of 15 January 1951 comments on a Paris interview in which Faulkner had stated that he was not a literary man.[14]

In spite of this evidence and in reaction to such critical discussion of "the influence of Faulkner" or "a Faulknerian period," García Márquez went so far as to deny ever having read the North American author before the publication of his first novel *La hojarasca* (*Leaf Storm*) in 1955, when he spoke with Armando Durán in a 1971 interview:

> Critics have insisted so much on Faulkner's influence in my books, that for some time they succeeded in convincing me. The truth is that I had already published the novel *La hojarasca* when I began to read Faulkner casually. I wanted to know just what the influence critics talked about was.[15]

Further confusing the issue and showing how problematic influence studies can indeed be, Márquez goes on to describe his 1961 "homage to Faulkner" trip, when he travelled by Greyhound bus through the Southern States "with his books tucked under my arm."[16] In conversation with Miguel Fernández-Braso, he says

> Many years later, while travelling through the South of the United States, I thought that I found the explanation that I had not found in his books. Those dusty streets, those sun-baked and miserable towns, those people without hope seemed very much like those that I invoked in my stories. I don't think that the similarity was a coincidence: the town where I had been was constructed in a great part by a banana company from North America.
>
> It's not that I mind the talk about Faulkner's influence, of course, that should be understood as praise because Faulkner is one of the great novelists of all times. But what happens is that I don't really understand how critics establish influence. In reality, a writer who is serious tries not to be similar to anyone; in fact, he tries to elude instead of imitate his favorite authors.[17]

Provocative though the question of García Márquez's acquaintance with and reading of Faulkner might be, the answer, of course, remains beyond literary production and illustrates, as already mentioned, the problematic nature of influence studies.[18]

Consideration of biographical similarities has been yet another approach utilized by previous critics, who usually begin by pointing out the similarity between the two regions where these two authors were born and raised. Octavio Corvalan sketches the parallels between Faulkner's Mississippi and García Márquez's Colombia with the following words:

> The South of the United States - the "deep South" of Mississippi, Alabama and Georgia - is socially and culturally similar in many ways to our South American world. If we were to reduce those characteristics to common abstractions, we could summarize them thus: from the beginning, there have been difficult racial problems to resolve; it is basically an agricultural region which follows an almost feudal system of land ownership with slave labor (more or less); the ruling classes resist structural change from the outside...world of capitalism and industrialism; there is a nostalgia for paradise lost, that is, a traditionalist attitude which refuses to adopt new patterns of life...; the two classes feel a rivalry that is equally passionate on both sides; it is a world of myth and profound spiritually nurtured during three centuries by the fact that whites and negro slaves (or Spaniards and Indians in our case) have lived side by side.[19]

García Márquez has himself referred to these parallels on various occasions, and extends the borders of his Caribbean to include the Southern United States when he discusses "fantasy and artistic creation in Latin America and the Caribbean" in a 1979 essay of the same name:

> That unbelievable reality reaches its maximum potential in the Caribbean, which, strictly speaking, extends (northward) to the South of the United States, and southward to Brazil. Don't think that this is an expansionist fantasy. No, it's just that the Caribbean is not only a geographic area, as of course geographers believe, but also a culturally homogeneous region.[20]

Personally, for example, both authors acknowledge the impact their grandparents had on their young minds, especially when they would spin convoluted tales of the past, tales which these artists, in turn, spun and re-spun into their own narrative creations.[21] Also among their ancestors, both include colonels on whom they modeled military figures crucial to their respective sagas. Harley Oberhelman brings together these parallel characteristics from the personal and cultural past of William Faulkner and Gabriel García Márquez, while referring to the literary creation of Yoknapatawpha County and Macondo, when he observes:

> There are frequent examples of exterior relationships between the two authors: both created fictional settings for much of their writing, settings based primarily on their childhood memories of life in provincial, rural regions washed by the nearby waters of the Caribbean and the Gulf of Mexico. These societies both bear the burden of a historical past interrupted by civil wars leaving memories that still shape the present.[22]

Drawing on these personal and cultural similarities, critics have also sketched out common themes and motifs: civil war which leads to social defeat and personal tragedy; societies ravaged by "yankee" and "gringo" intruders from the North; generations endlessly haunted by the ghosts of the past as well as by the specter of incest; families which generate and degenerate into obsessive, individual solitude; characters eternally burdened by the weight of human time and destiny; continuous yet doomed struggle against socio-cultural decline and decadence; and profound nostalgia for the natural harmony and balance which characterized the region(s) before economic and technological exploitation. Florence Delay and Jacqueline de Labriolle explain the sources of this profound sense of loss and longing in relation to the myth of a "golden age" through which both of these authors recall and recreate different personal and regional experiences of the past:

> ...nostalgia also resurrects the myth of a "golden age." For Faulkner this is the time before the destruction of the Indians and of the "wild," the time of the primeval forest (like that one finds in *The Bear*), while for Márquez it is the time of Macondo's innocent beginnings before anyone knew aging and death.[23]

While not a consistent textual analysis, this 1973 article - "Márquez, Est-il le Faulkner Colombien?" (Márquez, Is He the Columbian Faulkner?")-is an initial comparative presentation which considers central similarities and differences between the literary production of Faulkner and García Márquez. Commenting on the universal significance these two writers achieve through their regional stories, Delay and de Labriolle explain:

> While through a local story Faulkner expresses the fundamental drama of a ruined and alienated South, Márquez turns Macondo into a microcosm of Columbian reality expressing its present problems. Both find the root of evil to

be that accursed "solitude" which, through the regional, becomes characteristic of all men.[24]

Considering the treatment of time in the work of García Márquez and Faulkner, these two French critics also point out:

> Márquez himself takes on the project of Melquíades: "to organize the facts not according to the conventional time of men but...to concentrate a century of daily episodes so that they all coexisted within the same instant."...This is the old dream of *totum simul*, of a divine and transcendent vision, as Faulkner explained to Malcolm Cowley: "My aim is to put everything within one sentence, not only the present but also the past on which it depends and which catches up with the present at every second."

Referring to *Light in August* and *Cien años de soledad* within the text of their analysis, and to *Absalom, Absalom!* only in a footnote, Delay and de Labriolle continue by briefly describing the "suspension of time" to which Faulkner's words refer, as less an "eternal present" than a "presentation of the past"-"within the heart of Lena's journey" (*Light in August*) "or within Melquíades' room" (*Cien años de soledad*): "This suspension of time is less an eternal present...than a continuity of the past through the persistent phantoms within the two works."[25] Earlier, these French critics relate the treatment of time to "circular images," as they quote Ursula's observation about time going in circles in Márquez' novel, and then relate this circular image to the experience of Christmas, Lena and the Reverend Hightower in Faulkner's novel.[26] In this manner, Delay and de Labriolle touch on the use of circularity in Faulkner's *Light in August*. Within my textual analysis of *Absalom, Absalom!*, I will discuss the relationship between the initially linear image of the road and the circularity of human experience in *Light in August*, in order to show the development of these two images in Faulkner's work. Although Delay and de Labriolle take an initial step, they leave the road to understanding the functioning and significance of linearity and circularity in Faulkner and Garciá Márquez virtually unexplored, and, in fact, seem to take a step backward when they offer the following superficial appraisal of cyclical time in the work of these two authors: "And so both Márquez and Faulkner -

more often for the worst than for the better - present a cyclical conception of time."[27]

Almost ten years later, Lois Parkinson-Zamora would publish her essay on myth and narrative structure in the two novels with which I am primarily concerned. Entitled "The End of Innocence: Myth and Narrative Structure in Faulkner's *Absalom, Absalom!* and García Márquez' *Cien años de soledad*," this article, which appeared in 1982, is the first and only attempt at a textual analysis comparing works by these innovative and important twentieth-century writers of the Americas. Early in her discussion, Parkinson-Zamora very clearly states her position in terms of previous influence studies and relates her textual approach to the common theme of America:

> I do not want to explore this provocative question of Faulkner's influence on Latin American literature, for influence studies require incontrovertible evidence beyond the texts themselves. Rather I want to juxtapose one of Faulkner's novels to one of García Márquez pointing to similarities and differences in their thematic and narrative structures which may illuminate their common comprehension of America and their common mode of narrating its history.[28]

I completely agree with Parkinson-Zamora that "how we remember and how we create the past with our words and our literary forms" is crucial to an understanding of the thematic and narrative structure of *Absalom, Absalom!* and *Cien años de soledad*. However, while her consideration of "the nature of historical truth" and "the mode of narrating history" in these two novels focuses on linearity and the Apocalyptic paradigm, the close textual analysis that I propose reveals circularity to be the fundamental narrative structure and thematic projection of these two texts. Parkinson-Zamora, in her turn, goes on to explain the significance of Judeo-Christian Apocalypse, and then quickly discounts the circular/cyclical paradigm by saying:

> The word "apocalypse," which comes from the Greek word meaning "revelation," is the Judeo-Christian explanation of the nature and meaning of history. Apocalypse is eschatological, that is, concerned with final things, with the end of the present age, the Day of Judgement and the age to follow ... Unlike

oriental myth, in which history is projected in recurring cyclical patterns, apocalypse envisions history as essentially linear, irreversible and unrepeatable.

The close analysis of *Absalom, Absalom!* and *Cien años de soledad* that I propose will carefully study both linearity *and* circularity in these texts, not only in terms of how these basic geometric paradigms function but also in terms of what they signify. In order to more fully understand and appreciate the achievement of William Faulkner and Gabriel García Márquez, both *Absalom, Absalom!* and *Cien años de soledad* must be carefully analyzed in terms of eschatological direction and cyclical motion, *both* fundamental temporal paradigms.

In addition, my analysis will relate the narrative structure and thematic concerns of these twentieth-century novels to the concept of America. Parkinson-Zamora too considers the "history and myth of America" in her thought-provoking article, which she explains in the following manner:

> It is in *Absalom, Absalom!* (1936) and *Cien años de soledad* (1967) that Faulkner and García Márquez are most clearly aligned, for these novels are explorations of the history and myth of America. The histories of the Sutpens and Buendías reiterate the archetypal American experience of leaving the past behind and striking out to create an innocent new world in the timeless wilderness; they reiterate, furthermore, the equally American experience of discovering that the virgin wilderness can be the site of evil as well as innocence.

She then goes on to limit her analysis by focusing only on the eschatological direction of "an apocalyptic narrative perspective," as she puts it, when she observes: "Faulkner and García Márquez depend for elaboration of their essentially American tales upon what I will call an apocalyptic narrative perspective, that is, a comprehensive temporal perspective from which the various narrators view the beginnings and ends of the worlds that they remember and describe."[29] While her perspective is extremely pertinent and indicates a very much-needed but all too rare consideration of the technical and textual aspects of these narratives - for instead of studying external biographical data and/or listing general thematic tendencies, this attentive critic *actually studies the texts* - Lois Parkinson-Zamora's evaluation of the "essentially America [nature of these] tales" is limited in scope, as I have mentioned, because of her attention to linearity alone.

Also concerned with the American experience, Mark Frederic Frisch studies the "Parallels between William Faulkner and Four Hispanic American Novelists" in his 1985 dissertation.[30] This study, he says, "seeks to define the reasons for the parallels between William Faulkner and Eduardo Mallea, Agustin Yáñez, Manuel Rojas, and Gabriel García Márquez as well as the characteristics of those similarities. It emphasizes their common New World experience and in particular their conceptions of solitude, the community and nature and their inclination to experiment with the form of the novel." While listing parallel motifs, all of which "manifest a certain solitude which is characteristic of the New World," Frisch describes the technical experimentation of these five writers in terms of cinematic techniques:

> The villages which they create are often isolated and solitary, as is the New World, and frequently rural, suspended a bit in time and economically underdeveloped. These communities often get caught in the conflict between the past and the present in their struggle with the problems of technological change and the Industrial Revolution. Individual characters are often idiosyncratic figures who manifest a certain solitude which is characteristic of the New World. The conflict between the need to conquer and manipulate the vast natural world and the desire to live in harmony with it is one source of that characteristic solitude and is an important theme in many of the works. In order to distinguish themselves from the writers of the Old World they also take readily to innovation in the structure of the novel. This experimentation with narrative techniques and with the form of the novel frequently parallels the cinema, often emphasizes techniques, considers legends, dreams, myths and the imagination as valid raw material for the novel and suggests the autonomy of the literary work of art.

Both Frisch's attention to technical experimentation and concern with the central theme of solitude characterize my work. My analysis, however, begins with the texts themselves, major twentieth-century novels written by significant writers of the Americas. By first considering both narrative structure and discourse in detail, I analyze the specific texts as thoroughly as possible, in order to examine the relationship between the thematic projection of these works and "their New World experience." Frisch focuses on cinematic techniques and narrative experimentation in order to "suggest the autonomy of the literary work of art," as seen in the work of one North American and four South American writers. In my work, I am basically concerned with *how* a specific narrative is conceived and presented in its *entirety*, and *what* that literary representation expresses about the actual experience of America.

In an attempt to present an analysis that will be as representative of the American (North and South) experience as possible, I have chosen three novels written in the three major languages of the American continents- English, Spanish and Portuguese, three novels written by very conscientious and innovative creators of literary fictions and masters of the craft and art of fiction. Because these texts were written by three significant writers of the Americas - two are in fact, recipients of the Nobel Prize for literature - I feel that a comparative analysis of *how* they recreate and represent their stories and *what* these stories express about the American experience, will lead to a better understanding of both the differences between the various parts of this vast hemisphere and the similarities which, when taken together, constitute "American-ness." Finally, the three novels I will analyze were written and published during the twentieth century - in 1936, 1967 and 1973 - and represent the high point of each author's literary production. The close analysis of these texts that I propose will, therefore, also lead to a detailed consideration of the American experience in the twentieth century. In 1992, the concept of America reached five hundred years of actual existence. The original concept of America, when seen in relationship to the actual experience of America that those five hundred years has produced, forms and informs these twentieth century narratives of the Americas. How these novels represent and express the human experience of America in this century, will lead to a greater understanding and appreciation of the meaning and significance of America.

I would like to end this examination of previous comparative scholarship by proposing a new perspective for future comparative study. My point of departure is, as I have indicated, the narrative structure and discourse of three texts. For critics who are interested in William Faulkner's influence on García Márquez - or on Latin American literature, or even on twentieth century narrative - I would propose, therefore, a perspective that is based on literary technique and language, a method that actually begins with the analysis of narrative discourse. In order to describe the nature of this perspective/method, I will re-examine certain critics and writers who have discussed Faulkner and Latin American literature.

John Bushwood concludes his study of *The Spanish American Novel: A Twentieth-Century Survey* (from 1900-1970) by comparing what he terms "transcendent regionalism" with "traditional regionalism." His penultimate paragraph focuses on these two and draws the following comparison:

> The transcendent regionalism present in many novels of the past quarter-century probes deeply into the character of a region. It is not photographic; it is not even a painting. It is a collage, or a happening, or both. It produces the experience of knowing a region intimately. In order to produce such an experience, the author is increasingly conscious of making his work itself an experience - this is the reason for using narrative techniques that are sometimes difficult. Given this attitude on the part of the author, it is apparent that his real concern is for the creation of the experience, rather than for the fact of having portrayed a region. The activity required by the experience makes the new, transcendent regionalism a more intimate experience than is possible in the traditional regionalism of the oh-yes-I've-seen-that variety.

Drawing on this distinction, Bushwood ends his study by affirming that "there can be no doubt that, in general, the Spanish American novel in 1970 is still the voice of Spanish America - the voice, not the portrait - and more profoundly so than ever before."[31] These final words point to an emphasis on technique and language which I consider fundamental to literary analysis, be it comparative or not. Just as writers pay closer and closer attention to "voice," so should critics examine the phenomenon of narrative discourse more and more closely. Indeed, in order better to understand the literary achievement of William Faulkner in relation to that of Gabriel García Márquez, and also of Osman Lins, I would propose a careful consideration of *voice* in Faulkner's fiction and poetics.

In the second paragraph and second page of *Absalom, Absalom!*, Rosa Coldfield's haunted "voice" evokes the "ghost" of Thomas Sutpen, the "man-horse-demon" who invaded the "hundred square miles" of Jefferson with "his band of wild niggers" and the "French architect," in order to "drag house and formal gardens violently out of the soundless Nothing...creating the Sutpen's Hundred...like the olden *Be Light*." By mentioning the members of his family and how they contributed to the final outcome of the Sutpen House, this second paragraph already "tells" the reader the whole story of the rise and fall of the House of Sutpen. By including a brief description of Rosa's listener as "two separate Quentins" - "Then hearing would reconcile and he would seem to listen to two separate Qentins"..."the two separate Quentins now talking to one another in the long silence" - this second paragraph also presents to the reader the elements which make the next 376 pages necessary and *Absalom, Absalom!* in its entirety possible. Of these, the most essential is voice - which, of course, immediately demands a listener in order to exist and function. It is, in fact, Rosa's voice echoing in Quentin's divided consciousness - and his father's voice, as well as his friend's and even his own - which create and recreate *Absalom, Absalom!*. This dialogical process structures and constructs the novel out of voices which "haunt" the present "Quentin Compson preparing for Harvard in the South, the deep South dead since 1865 and peopled with garrulous outraged baffled ghosts, listening, having to listen, to one of the ghosts which had refused to lie still even longer than most had telling him about old ghost-times." The process whereby Rosa's voice flows and joins all of the other voices, creates the novel *Absalom, Absalom!*, as the following image of a stream (from paragraph two still) indicates: "the voice not ceasing but vanishing into and then out of the long intervals like a stream, a trickle running from patch to patch of dried sand, and the ghost mused with shadowy docility as if it were the voice which he haunted where a more fortunate one would have had a house."[32] As Faulkner evokes Rosa Coldfield evoking the figure of Thomas Sutpen, the narrative proposes the image of a ghost which is not "fortunate" enough to haunt a "house," but instead haunts a "voice." At the very beginning of this significant modern novel, then, William Faulkner indicates very clearly that his narrative perspective is based on "voice," that, as Brushwood puts it, "his real concern is for the creation of experience."

In 1985, ten years after Brushwood affirmed the vigorous and innovative voice of Spanish American literature, Mary E. Davis observes that Faulkner's "voice, at once quite eccentric and aware of tradition, haunts the narrative now being produced in Latin America, to the extent that a mention of Faulkner's influence is almost obligatory in the introduction of particular writers."[33] After mentioning general characteristics of Faulkner's literary philosophy and practice, Davis offers a very brief discussion of the "echoes of William Faulkner" in the writing of Gabriel García Márquez, the Mexican Carlos Fuentes and the Peruvian Marion Vargas Llosa. Due to its brevity, this ambitious article by Davis offers but a first step in the direction which I propose; because of its initial focus on Faulkner's voice, however, Davis' perspective is one that both benefits literary analysis and echoes the very concerns of the writers themselves. Carlos Fuentes, for example, observes that "the new writer in Latin America is undertaking a revision based on the lack of language, a fact which makes traditional denunciation a much more arduous elaboration: an elaboration of all that has been left unsaid."[34] García Márquez himself has given special attention to language and has on various occasions described his attempts at finding an adequate "lenguaje" with which to express the reality of his world. Wanting very much to "make his reality believable," yet realizing the he is dealing with a "disproportionate reality," he describes a Latin American writer's difficulty due to "the insufficiency of words" thus:

> Our disproportionate reality presents literature with a very serious problem: the insufficiency of words. When we speak of a river, the most that a European reader can imagine is a river the size of the Danube, which is 2,790 km long. It's difficult for anyone who hasn't seen it to imagine the reality of the Amazon River, which is 5,500 km long. In the area of Belém do Pará, you can't see the other side, and it's much wider than the Baltic Sea. When we write the word *storm*, Europeans think of lightening and thunder, for it's difficult for them to imagine the same phenomenon that we want to represent. The same is true, for example, with the word *rain*. In the Andean mountains, according to the description of Javier Marimier, there are storms which can last up to five months. "Those who haven't seen these storms," he says, "can't begin to imagine the violence. For hours on end, lightening bolts follow one after the other like falls of blood, while the air reverberates with the thunder echoing off the huge mountains."

> The description is no masterpiece, but it is enough to make any European tremble with fear....For this reason, it is necessary to create a whole system of words the size of our reality.[35]

García Márquez's preoccupation with "la insuficiencia de las palabras" prompted him on another occasion to relate his search for a "lenquaje" that would give voice to his reality, to the method with which his grandparents confronted their world and told their stories to the young grandson whom they raised and influenced so much. The mature artist and accomplished writer observes:

> My most difficult problem was to destroy the line separating what appears real from what appears fantastic. Because, within the world that I was trying to evoke, that distinction didn't exist...language was a basic problem, for the truth doesn't appear true simply because it is, but due to the way in which it is expressed. I had to live twenty years and write four preliminary books before discovering that the solution to my problem lay precisely within my problem: I had to tell the story simply, the way my grandparents used to tell stories. That is to say, in a fearless tone, with serenity and a conviction that will not allow any alteration even if the sky should fall, and that will not raise any doubts about what was said, even if it was extremely frivolous or very fierce, as if those old folks knew that in literature nothing is more convincing than conviction.
>
> The reduction of the marvelous to everyday proportions, which was the great find of the novel of chivalry,...helped me to resolve the problem of language, for, what was once true when told in one way, had to be true each time that it was retold in the same manner. That is to say, I had to tell the story simply, utilizing the same language that my grandparents had used. This was a very difficult task, recovering a whole new vocabulary and a way of saying things that is uncommon within the urban settings in which we writers live, a way that is on the verge of disappearing forever.[36]

In this alliance of the "fantástico" with the "cotidiano," then, García Márquez found his own "voice," as Delay and de Labriolle affirmed in 1973: "Through this alliance of the marvelous and the everyday, Márquez found his own personal register...a true Latin American voice."[37] This search for "a way of saying things that is uncommon within the urban settings" led him to the narrative methods of his cultural past - his grandparents, the "novels of chivalry" and "our chronicle legacy;" this search for his own voice led him also, to the narrative experimentation of twentieth-century writers - especially Virginia Woolf[38] and William Faulkner. According to García Márquez himself, Faulkner's art showed him how to give order and form to the elemental chaos of his Columbian experience: "The chaotic materials which entered into Faulkner's art were very similar to the basic material of Columbian life. Faulkner showed how that elemental turbulence could be managed and transformed."[39]

The "método faulkneriano" that Márquez described previously, is a narrative method concerned with voice in relation to order, with human and cultural expression given form and structure. As Thomas Sutpen willed the "construction" of his House, William Faulkner's voice(s) will the structure and form of his novel *Absalom, Absalom!*, of Faulkner's works, the one that has most captivated this famous Columbian writer.[40] The narrative technique which gives form to this important novel is basic to Faulkner's art, and is reflected in *Cien años de soledad* by García Márquez and *Avalovara* by the Brazilian Osman Lins. Overall, circularity is the fundamental structure of this important North American novel, as it is the fundamental structure of the two South American novels I am analyzing in this study.

While the second paragraph of *Absalom, Absalom!* appeals to the fluidity of narrative motion, Dorothy Tuck also describes the fluidity and motion of Faulkner's narrative technique and structure in circular terms:

> The idea of motion as a technical recreation of the fluidity of life can be said to be the basic determinant of Faulkner's style. The techniques through which this sense of motion is achieved in form are seen at their most elaborate and most successful in *Absalom, Absalom!*, although they are present in varying degrees in the majority of his novels.
>
> The traditional novel ordinarily operates on a linear basis in which characters are introduced, conflicts set up, and resolution achieved, frequently with due regard to chronology. In contrast to this, Faulkner's novels can best be seen in terms of overlapping circles, with a point of entry that is not, strictly speaking, a beginning, but simply a point in time in which the novelist has chosen to intercept his characters... The chronology may be reconstructed after the fact, but piecing together the events can convey only the facts of the story, not its essence as a recreation of life that Faulkner has given it. The circularity of narration, particularly in *Absalom, Absalom!*

has a very definite purpose to immerse the reader in the living flow of the narrators' consciousness of Sutpen and, by extension, to capture for a moment out of time a living image of the mind of the South as reflected in the characters of Sutpen, Miss Rosa Coldfield, Mr. Compson, and Quentin.[41]

Whereas Harley Oberhelman affirms that in *Cien años de soledad*, "more than at any point in his entire career as a writer, there is the evidence of the synthesis of his interest in Faulkner and the American South,"[42] Gregory Rabassa observes that: in *One Hundred Years of Solitude* García Márquez has written what well might be called the ultimate circular story."[43] In his presentation of "Osman Lins and *Avalovara*: The Shape and Shaping of the Novel," Rabassa discusses Lins' novel in relation to other Latin American novels, especially *Hopscotch* by Julio Cortázar and *One Hundred Years of Solitude* by Márquez, and proposes a closer look at "the structure of some of the new Latin American novels."[44] I agree whole-heartedly, but would expand that proposal to include the North American whose narrative "voice" made the technique and structure of a novel equal to its meaning. After Faulkner, that is, narrative discourse and form could never again be separated from thematic signification and projection.

The circularity which is fundamental to the narrative structure of the three novels I am studying, takes on different configurations, which I shall call - "ripples on water" in Faulkner's *Absalom, Absalom!*, "a gyrating wheel" in García Márquez's *Cien años de soledad* and "a spiral on a square" in Lins' *Avalovara*. Each of these circular configurations reflects the individual writer's voice which created it, as well as the collective cultural voice(s) which it recreates. Together, they reflect varying perspectives and experiences of the collective cultural phenomenon we call "America." Rabassa ends his essay by observing that: "For some reason, the new Latin American writers are the ones who have come closest to this essential understanding of the importance of collective creation in literature."[45] I would add the name of a North American writer to that group: William Faulkner, the writer whose art springs from the union of structure and meaning, the writer whose voice flows into and out of literature as collective creation. The circularity of *Absalom, Absalom!*, like that of *Cien años de soledad* and *Avalovara*, not only allows this process of collective creation and expression, but actually makes it necessary, since the circular structure of each novel draws into its circumference the many voices which together create the text and its circularity and meaning.

CHAPTER III

"RIPPLES SPREADING ON WATER"

Rosa Coldfield's "haunted voice" sets in motion the narrative discourse of William Faulkner's *Absalom, Absalom!*. This voice is, so the text tells us, "like a stream, a trickle running from patch to patch of dried sand," (8) searching for an appropriate, a sympathetic listener. Rosa's voice begins, therefore, by explaining to the young Quentin Compson that he has been chosen to hear her story of the rise and fall of the House of Sutpen, a story that recreates the rise and fall of the South, because he will be going North soon and may become a writer there; i.e., will see the South at a distance and may become a disseminator of her narrative. (9) Quentin, in his turn, muses that

> *It's because she wants it told...so that people whom she will never see and whose names she will never hear and who have never heard her name nor seen her face will read it and know at last why God let us lose the War: that only through the blood of our men and the tears of our women could He stay this demon and efface his name and lineage from the earth.* (11)-This passage is in italics in the original text, which uses both italics and regular print in order to signal a change in voice, however misleading these signals may appear at times).

Still wondering, Quentin asks his father on the next page: "But why tell me about it?" (12) While Mr. Compson's voice forms and expands later chapters of the novel, it appears here briefly in the first pages of Rosa's telling in order to explain to his son, as father and protector of the family/narrative line, that perhaps Miss Coldfield wanted to keep the story "in the family." "She chose you," Mr. Compson explains, "because your grandfather was the nearest thing to a friend Sutpen ever had in this county, and she probably believes that Sutpen may have told your grandfather something about himself and her...And that your grandfather might have told me and I might have told you. And so, in a sense, the affair...will still be in the family."(12-3) Indeed, Sutpen's family lineage runs parallel to narrative lineage in *Absalom, Absalom!*, as Thomas Sutpen, the determined father who tries to found his house and create a family, tells his story to Quentin's grandfather, General Compson, who tells Quentin's father, Mr. Compson, who tells Quentin. Focusing on the young Compson, David Wyatt observes that "Quentin seeks out, through narration, a genealogy into which he can assimilate himself."[1]

Preparing to go off to Harvard at the end of that "long still hot weary dead September" of 1909 when he hears Miss Rosa's and his father's versions of the story of Sutpen, Quentin Compson is the focus of narration in this novel. "Miss Rosa and Mr. Compson have an essential role to play in the total narrative structure," says Michael Millgate; "ultimately, however, the burden of recreation, interpretation and suffering falls inexorably on Quentin." Shreve, Quentin's Canadian roommate at Harvard in January of 1910, "participates in the task of imaginative reconstruction" which creates the second half of the novel; "but," says this critic, "final responsibility remains inescapably Quentin's."[2] Also focusing on the young Compson in relation to Miss Rosa, Mr. Compson and Shreve, John Irwin affirms that "Quentin is the central narrator, not just because he ends up knowing more of the story than do the other three, but because the other three only function as narrators in relation to Quentin."[3] Although some will observe, as has Deborah Robbins, that Shreve "dominates in the imaginative work of the later chapters" because of his active participation in retelling and recreating the Story of Sutpen, he is nevertheless "clearly dependent on Quentin for his narration."[4]

While Mr. Compson's answer to "Why Quentin?" springs from the linear paradigm of paternal genealogy, Miss Rosa's reasons interpreted within Quentin's mind, widen the narrative scope indefinitely, bequeathing the Story of Sutpen, as has been noted, to "people she will never see and whose names she will never hear." Such an expansive dynamic is in keeping with a character such as Quentin, of whom these first pages of the novel affirm: "he was not a being, an entity, he was a commonwealth." (12) *Webster's Dictionary* defines this word "commonwealth" as "a group of people united by common interests," a definition which applies to Quentin's role as the character that *brings together and unites* the different voices from the narrative past and present, a process without which, of course, *Absalom, Absalom* would neither exist nor function.

A novel which indeed unites a group of people around a common interest, then, *Absalom, Absalom!* reflects and gives voice to the collective creation and recreation of the story of Thomas Sutpen. "Representing creation as collaborative discovery,"[5] this Faulknerian novel is "a drama of incessant voices in which remembering becomes talking, talking in turn becomes remembering, and remembering, talking."[6] Given his central role within this dialogical process,[7] it is Quentin's haunted psyche that proposes the image of fluid circularity which graphically portrays the narrative structure and dynamics of *Absalom, Absalom!*; it is the young Compson who translates the linear image of rhetorical fluidity which begins this novel - Miss Rosa's haunted voice trickling "like a stream" - into the circular image of narrative fluidity which forms and informs this dialogical novel - the rhetorical image of "ripples" spreading on water. As Quentin and Shreve create and recreate the story in the last four chapters of the novel, their identities merge with and emerge from the previous narrators, prompting Quentin's consciousness to propose the dynamic image which reflects the narrative structure and rhetorical flow of *Absalom, Absalom!*. "*Maybe nothing ever happens once and is finished*," muses the beleaguered consciousness of this young decendant of the South:

> *Maybe happen is never once but like ripples maybe on water after the pebble sinks, the ripples moving on, spreading, the pool attached by a narrow umbilical water-cord to the next pool which the first pool feeds, has fed, did feed, let this second pool contain a different temperature of water, a different molecularity of having seen, felt, remembered, reflect in a different tone the infinite unchanging sky, it doesn't matter, that pebble's water echo whose fall it did not even see moves across its surface too at the original ripple-space, to the old ineradicable rhythm.* (261)

As this dynamically exquisite image of *ripples on water* joins Shreve's Canadian, and therefore "different temperature...and...molecularity," to Quentin's brooding Southern temperament, the rhetorical flow of the entire novel renders this ripple movement on a narrative level, for the telling of one narrative voice "sinks," and "moves on," and "spreads," and "feeds" on the telling of the next narrative voice, to which it is "attached by a narrow umbilical water-cord," the matrix of human imagination and consciousness. The following diagram offers a graphic representation of the rhetorical flow and narrative structure in this Faulknerian novel:

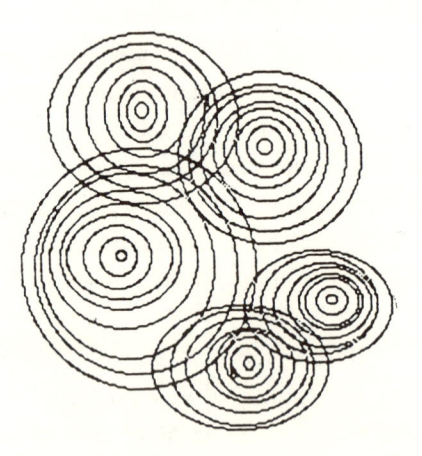

"ripples on water"

Described as "probably his greatest novel" by some and "perhaps the greatest American novel" by others, *Absalom, Absalom!* is generally recognized as "the most carefully articulated of Faulkner's novels."[8] It was written, of course, after this North American writer had experimented with narrative form and technique in his numerous previous novels. In *The Sound and the Fury* (1929), "the first of his novels to make the question of form and technique unavoidable,"[9] he structures the narrative as four voices, four circles of consciousness focused on an absent center, the departed sister and only daughter of the Compson household, Caddy. Multiple narration becomes refracted many times in "*As I Lay Dying* (1930), a collection of forty-nine interior monologues (from five words to eight pages in length), created by fifteen different characters (the seven members of the Bundren family and eight neighbors and strangers) all focused, once again, on a "presence" which is absent, the dead body of Addie Burden waiting in its coffin for final burial. Focusing on the family members, the dominant voices that create this novel, David Minter observes: "Like the Compson children, the Bundrens are held fast by the close-knit circle of their family... Within the larger circle of the family, each child forms a smaller circle...held and isolated... The problem lies at the center: possessing no principles of order and no capacity for life, the parents fail to spread order and love around them."[10] Two years later, and four years before *Absalom, Absalom!*, Faulkner would publish *Light in August*, the story of Lena Grove, a naive expectant mother, Joe Christmas, a drifter with part negro blood, and the Reverend Hightower, a spurned reclusive minister. Speaking of circularity in *Light in August*, and of this novel in relation to *As I Lay Dying*, Richard Chase relates the symbol of the circle of selfhood to the modern imagination and to the novel's three main characters.

> The symbolism that seems most profoundly organic with the action and meaning of the book is that of the circle... Three circles should be kept in mind; they are associated with the three main characters. Remembering the theme of solitude vs. society, alienation vs. community that we noticed in *As I Lay Dying*, we remember also that Faulkner spoke of Addie Bundren's aloneness as a circle that had to be violated in order to be made whole. Although this is a literary idea that Faulkner might have absorbed from many sources...the symbol of the circle of selfhood may be taken as an archetype of the modern imagination, and especially wherever Puritanism has made itself felt. Lena Grove's circle, then, since she is a kind of earth goddess, is simply that of the death and renewal of nature.
>
> The circle associated with Joe Christmas is the fatalistic repetitive pattern of his life; in actual symbolization it varies from the silver dollar the dietitian gives him to the pattern of his flight from the sheriff and his dogs. He wants, of course, to break out of his circle... One might add that his circle is also racial; he is doomed to oscillate helplessly between the white world and the black. If Christmas's imprisoning circle is imposed on him by circumstance, the Reverend Hightower's is

imposed by himself, forged by his own intellect and neurotic fantasy.[11]

Opening with the pregnant Lena Grove "sitting beside the road...thinking although I have not been quite a month on the road I am already in Mississippi, further from home than I have ever been before," and ending with her favorite phrase "My, my. A body does get around. Here we aint been coming from Alabama but two months, and now its already Tennessee," *Light in August* partakes of the traditional literary trope of *homo viator* on the road of life. Fleeing a stern and mean stepfather later in the novel, Joe Christmas, in his turn, "entered the street which was to run for 15 years.... He thought it was loneliness which he was trying to escape and not himself. But the street ran on."[12] Joe himself joins this linear image of the road of life to the circular image of selfhood trapped within the vicious circle of a hopeless existence. After he has committed the murder which makes him flee once again, he feels himself

> entering it again the street which ran for thirty years. It had made a circle and he was still inside it..."And yet I have been further in these seven days than in all the thirty years," he thinks. "But I have never got outside the circle. I have never broken out of the ring of what I have already done and cannot ever do." (373-4)

While Joe Christmas perishes within the vicious circle of non-self and Lena's complacent motherhood portrays the cyclical renewal of life, it is the vicious circle of Reverend Hightower's consciousness that sets circularity in motion toward the end of this novel, as this character's life itself comes to an end. Depicting the minister's approaching death, then, the text describes the circular patterns of his mind and consciousness as a wheel turning on sand. Gradually, then,

> thinking begins to slow now. It slows like a wheel beginning to run on sand, the axle, the vehicle, the power which propels it not yet aware. He seems to watch himself among faces, always among enclosed and surrounded by faces, as though he watched himself in his own pulpit, from the rear of the church, or as though he were a fish in a bowl. And more than that: the faces seem to be mirrors in which he watches himself. (538-9)

Finally, as this "sand clutched wheel of thinking" (541) becomes the collective halo of everyone the dying minister had known during his life, it also overcomes time, joins past-present-future and

> whirls on. It is going fast and smooth now, because it is freed now of burden, of vehicle, axle, all. In the lambent suspension of August into which night is about to fully come, it seems to engender and surround itself with a faint glow like a halo. The halo is full of faces...they all look a little alike, a composite of all the faces which he has ever seen. (542)

As Hightower's "sandclutched wheel of thinking" spins the refracted faces of the minister's personal past into the halo of death, Quentin Compson's "ripples spreading on water" graphically portray the narrative structure of the text and the rhetorical flow of the collective voices that together create the novel *Absalom, Absalom!*. Called a "verbal voluptuary"[13] whose style is characterized by a "flowing Latinate quality,"[14] William Faulkner struggles against the sequential nature of language and maintains the narrative discourse of this novel rhetorically fluid, by employing oratorical techniques and complex syntactical devices which tend to erase traditional divisions between sentences and paragraphs. Among these are: elaborate modification and qualification, especially adjectival phrases flowing into each other; verbals, modals and qualifiers strung together to function as nouns; series of nouns, verbals, phrases, and clauses in parallel structures; and an accumulation of paraphrasing and repetition, usually within lengthy paragraphs which, at key points in the novel, lead to a delayed climax. A demonstration of these techniques, along with an example of the appeal to the memory-evoking power of the five senses which recurs throughout the text, occurs with the first paragraph of the second chapter, a paragraph which reconstructs Thomas Sutpen's arrival in Jefferson in a dramatic mode; i.e., gradually sets the stage for the appearance of Sutpen into the life of Jefferson by superimposing references that echo this arrival of 1833 in the minds of the town then, and in the four minds/voices which together reconstruct the story in 1909 and 1910, as they construct the text for future readers. Characteristically, then, this paragraph overflows with references connecting Quentin's memory of Rosa's narration in chapter one to his father's version about to begin with this chapter two (1909), and to the atmosphere of the Harvard room where he and Shreve will, in chapters 6-9, retell and recreate (1910) "that Sunday morning in 1833" like so many other Sunday mornings in Jefferson, when "there the stranger was," whose actual name will only appear at the very end of this first paragraph, going "back and forth among the places of business and of idleness and among the residences in steady strophe and antistrophe: *Sutpen. Sutpen. Sutpen. Sutpen.*" (31-2) Just as Sutpen's name echoes in the minds of Jefferson's citizens during this paragraph, so *Absalom, Absalom!* could be described as Sutpen's name echoing in the minds and voices of the past and present.

Writing in 1939, only three years after *Absalom, Absalom!* was published, Conrad Aiken, says Dorothy Tuck, "was the first to perceive the basic purpose behind what is usually considered Faulkner's obscurity; it is an elaborate method of deliberately withheld meaning...a calculated system of screens and obtrusions, of confusions and ambiguous interpolations and delays, with one express purpose...to keep the form - and the idea - fluid and unfinished, still in motion, as it were, and unknown, until the dropping into place of the very last syllable.'"[15] Reflecting more current critical perspectives, partial to relativity, intertextuality and narrative non-closure, J. Hillis Miller's observations on this novel shun the very thought of a very last syllable. "The meaning of a given word or phoneme," writes Miller, "is relative to the surrounding words or phonemes, and those in turn are relative to it, in a perpetual self-sustaining round - though the word 'round' is misleading insofar as it sidesteps the tendency of the context in such structures to widen out and become virtually boundless. Where does the verbal context of a given word in *Absalom, Absalom!* stop, except arbitrarily?"[16] Quentin Compson's "ripples," it seems, would be a more adequate image to reflect the "widening out and becoming virtually boundless" of which Mr. Miller speaks.

Created from the fluid matrix of Faulkner's narrative style and discourse, therefore, the structure of this twentieth-century novel recreates the circular dynamics of ripples spreading on water, an image which repeats and widens the traditional depiction of the circle. According to *The Metamorphosis of the Circle* by Georges Poulet, the circle is "the most constant of those forms thanks to which we are able to figure...the place in which we find ourselves, and to locate within it what surrounds us. Its simplicity, its perfection, its ceaseless universal application," continues Poulet, "makes it the foremost of those recurring and chosen forms which we discover at the base of all beliefs and which serve, too, as a structural principle for all types of consciousness."[17] Earlier associated with the Godhead, the image of "enlarging circles produced by a stone falling into a pond" was interpreted during the Renaissance in humanistic terms. "Center of the world, like divinity," observes Poulet, "the human mind, again like divinity, can propagate its influence excentrically; and be likened therefore to the enlarging circles produced by a stone falling into a pond."[18] Seen as a representation of the human mind, then, the image of enlarging circles in water reflected the growing awareness of and belief in the expansion and diffusion of human potential and creativity which characterized the Renaissance. In *Absalom, Absalom!* the rhetorical image of ripples spreading on water actively reflects the dynamic process of human consciousness(es), enlarging and spreading and overlapping with each telling and retelling of the story that so preoccupies the novel's characters: the story of the rise and fall of the House of Sutpen. Reflected in the image Quentin proposes, this narrative recreates the evolving patterns of the human mind revolving around a fact/idea/sensation, working over a part of the story, speculating about it, rejecting one possibility, considering another, widening out with new information/speculation, echoing and overlapping with other minds, all participating in a fluid circular process which is virtually boundless. This image, therefore, takes on meta-literary reverberations as the various narrative voices come together to create the collective voice/ripple pattern of *Absalom, Absalom!*, at once a collaborative creation of literary recreation and a portrayal of human epistemological process(es).

Considered by many to be "Faulkner's most accomplished, moving and sustained meditation on the act of fabricating meaning,"[19] the novel *Absalom, Absalom!* is constructed from "circular ratiocinations"[20] revolving around and evolving from the organizing principle of the novel: telling and interpretation, which make retelling and reinterpretation necessary.[21] The fluidity of Faulkner's narrative discourse and oratorical style, as we have seen briefly, tends to make sentences and paragraphs run on and into each other. Similarly, the flow of Faulkner's narration also succeeds in erasing and invalidating traditional chapter divisions, which the text itself presents in order to organize the material, as well as to orient and guide the reader through the complex circular labyrinth of *Absalom, Absalom!*. So complex, nonetheless, did the novel's circularity still prove, that Faulkner himself appended a chronology of the chief events and dates, along with a genealogy giving the lineage of each of the principle characters. The fact that the very creator of the circularity which forms and informs *Absalom!* felt the need to add a linear sketch of the events the novel recreates, attests to the complexity of this narrative and to the difficulty many readers have had in penetrating its labyrinthine prose. A mere glance at these linear "visions" of the Story of Sutpen, however, serves to prove all the more readily just how essential and necessary circularity is to this novel. To guide and orient my own reader, I will refer to the chapter divisions designed by the author, in an attempt to demonstrate how the ripple pattern the novel itself proposes, is created and made to function within the pages of the text, and how narrative circularity oversteps and overlaps these chapter divisions. Not intending to present an exhaustive study of this text within what is a comparative analysis of three novels, I will cite representative examples of techniques and characteristics which together transform traditional narrative linearity into the complex ripple pattern of this circular novel.

Divided into nine chapters, *Absalom, Absalom!* takes the reader from a Sunday in September of 1909 in Jefferson, Yoknapatawpha County, Mississippi, to a cold Harvard student room in Cambridge, Massachusetts early in January of the following year. The first chapter is narrated from Miss Rosa Coldfield's "dim hot airless" Jefferson parlor "with the blinds all closed and fastened for forty-three summers," letting in only the smell from the wisteria vine blooming for the second time that summer on a wooden trellis outside one window, (7) as Rosa's voice recreates its particular version of the Sutpen story for the young Compson, and so initiates the process of telling and retelling that creates this novel. Chapters 2, 3 and 4 take Quentin and the reader to the Compsons' porch near twilight of that same day of story-telling in Jefferson, as Mr. Compson relates to his son what he knows of the story, while the odor of the father's cigar and the twilight full of wistaria, mingle with the smell of Rosa's wistaria vine within Quentin's imagination and memory; for, as the text echoes, "it was a summer of wistaria." (30)

The ripple movement of Rosa's voice begins her story of by affirming Sutpen, "He wasn't a gentleman. He wasn't even a gentleman," (14) an observation which will overlap with the spreading ripples of Mr. Compson's version when he puts it his way in chapter 2: "Yes, he was underbred." (46) Critics have observed that, for example, "Rosa explains in terms of demonic powers" what "Mr. Compson attributes to fatality,"[22] or that Rosa's version resembles a gothic thriller while Mr. Compson's stems from classical drama.[23] Although these distinctions hold in terms of the general flow and tone of their respective narrations, both voices overlap and widen their view and telling by echoing and intersecting and repeating each other through the ripple effect this novel creates. Extremely obsessed with how the demonic Sutpen "discovered Ellen" (Rosa's sister and Sutpen's future bride) "inside a church," Rosa's voice takes on the fatality of classical drama which characterizes Mr. Compson's voice, as the mind of the one surviving Coldfield repeatedly revolves around the fatal flaw which has tragically cursed her family and the South. At once interrogating the Gods and Fate, Rosa's voice sets the stage for the demonic drama which is constantly playing in her haunted mind, as she says of Thomas Sutpen:

> A man who to my certain knowledge was never in a Jefferson church but three times in his life - the once when he first saw Ellen, the once when they **rehearsed** the wedding, the once when they **performed** it - a man that anyone could look at and see that, even if he apparently had none now, he was accustomed to having money and intended to have it again and would have no scruples about how he got it - that man to discover Ellen inside a church. In church, mind you, as though there were a **fatality and curse on our family** and God himself were seeing to it that it was **performed** and discharged to the last drop and dreg. Yes, **fatality and curse on the South and on our family** as though because some ancestor of ours had elected to establish his descent in **a land primed for fatality and already cursed with it,** even if it had not rather been our **family, our father's progenitors, who had incurred the curse long years before and had been coerced by Heaven into establishing itself in the land and the time already cursed.** (20-1) -In quoting this passage, I have used bold-face type to

designate the words and phrases which especially exemplify my point, as I will do in subsequent passages cited from this text).

While Rosa's voice is haunted by accumulated memories and demonic fatality, Mr. Compson's chapters (2-4) tend to cast the story in the dramatic mode. His voice, as it overlaps with the elements provided by Rosa in the passage quoted above, takes her cue and stages a ten-page "performance" of this fateful wedding washed by Ellen's unceasing tears:

> It was in June of 1838, almost five years to the day from that Sunday morning when he rode into town on the roan horse. It (the wedding) was in the same Methodist church where he saw Ellen for the first time, according to Miss Rosa. The powder (on Ellen's face) was to hide the marks of tears. But before the wedding was over the powder was streaked, caked and channelled. Ellen seems to have entered the church that night out of weeping as though out of rain, gone through the ceremony and then walked back out of the church and into the weeping again, the tears again, the same tears even, the same rain. She got into the carriage and departed in it (the rain) for Sutpen's Hundred. (48-9)... He did not forget that night...she washed it out of her remembering with tears. Yes, she was weeping again now, it did, indeed, rain on that marriage. (58)

A few pages later, in chapter three, Mr. Compson describes his view of the name Sutpen had given his illegitimate negro daughter Clytie, who faithfully accompanied Judith, Sutpen's legitimate white daughter by Ellen, through childhood and adulthood. His explanation is based on classical figures and their roles, as is his description of Sutpen's ogre face, playing its role throughout Rosa's life "like the mask of Greek tragedy." "Yes," says Mr. Compson,

> Clytie was his daughter too: **Clytemnestra**. He named her himself. He named them all himself: all his get and all the get of his wild niggers after the country began to assimilate them... Only I have always liked to believe that he intended to name Clytie, **Cassandra, prompted by some pure dramatic economy** not only to beget but **to designate the presiding augur of his own disaster,** and that he just got the name wrong through a mistake natural in a man who must have almost taught himself to read. - When he returned home in '66, Miss Rosa had not seen him a hundred times in her whole life. And what she saw then was just the **ogre-face** of her childhood seen once and then repeated at intervals and on occasions which she could neither count nor recall, **like the mask in Greek tragedy,**

interchangeable not only **from scene to scene**, but **from actor to actor** and behind which the events and occasions took place without chronology or sequence. (61 & 62)

A lack of chronology and sequence is characteristic of *Absalom, Absalom!*, of course, as the text passes from "scene to scene" and from "actor to actor," for, in this case, Cassandra and ogres had also appeared in Rosa's chapter. Pages before, then, these classical and demonic elements had also been conjured up by Rosa's voice and by the third person narrative voice which joins the telling voices of the text and which Peter Brooks, speaking of this novel, labels "that transindividual voice that speaks through all of Faulkner's characters" along with "the individual's voices."[24] In the following example, the ogre-faced Sutpen haunts Rosa's childhood through the faces of Sutpen's and Ellen's children, Henry and Judith, the responsibility for whom casts Rosa into the abnormal role of caretaker, "a child who had never been young;" describing Quentin's imagination as he watches Miss Coldfield, the transindividual narrative voice also describes Rosa as living in an "ogre-world" and as performing a "Cassandralike" role, "profoundly and sternly prophetic." Watching and hearing her, therefore, Quentin's imagination places the minute aging Rosa within the scenario of a childhood "ogre-tale" in the following passage:

> "Yes," the grim quiet voice said from beyond the unmoving triangle of dim lace; and now, among the musing and decorous wraiths Quentin seemed to watch resolving the figure of a little girl, in the prim skirts and pantalettes, the smooth prim decorous braids, of the dead time. She seemed to stand, to lurk, behind the neat picket fence of a small, grimly middle-class yard or lawn, looking out upon the whatever **ogre-world** of that quiet village street with that air of children born too late into their parent's lives and doomed to contemplate all human behavior through the complex and needless follies of adults - **an air Cassandralike** and humorless and **profoundly and sternly prophetic** out of all proportion to the actual years even of a child who had never been young. "Because I was born too late. I was born twenty-two years too late - a child to whom out of the overheard talk of adults my own sister's and my sister's children's faces had come to be like the faces in an **ogre-tale** between supper and bed long before I was old enough or big enough to be permitted to play with them yet to whom that sister must have to turn at the last when she lay dying, with one of the children vanished and doomed to be a

murderer and the other doomed to be a widow before she had even been a bride, and say, 'Protect her, at least. At least save Judith.'" (21-2)

Indeed, the ripple movement of Rosa's voice assumes the repetitive locution of prophetic discourse throughout chapter one, but especially when she lists what she has seen, thereby providing the basic elements and events of the story once again. As discussed in a previous chapter of my analysis, all of these events and had already been presented in the very second paragraph of the novel, the paragraph on voice. Repeating these elements and events in the prophetic mode at this time, Miss Rosa Coldfield proclaims:

> **I saw** what had happened to Ellen, my sister. **I saw** her almost a recluse, watching those two doomed children growing up whom she was helpless to save. **I saw** the price which she had paid for that house and that pride; **I saw** the notes of hand on pride and contentment and peace and all to which she had put her signature when she walked into the church that night, begin to fall due in succession. **I saw** Judith's marriage forbidden without rhyme or reason or shadow of excuse; **I saw** Ellen die with only me, a child, to turn to and ask to protect her remaining child; **I saw** Henry repudiate his home and birthright and then return and practically fling the bloody corpse of his sister's sweetheart at the hem of her wedding gown; **I saw** that man return - the evil's source and head which had outlasted all its victims - who had created two children not only to destroy one another and his own line, but my line as well, yet I agreed to marry him. (18)

In terms of her experience and life, she is an augur not of the future but of the past, as the oracular past-tense phrase **I saw** indicates; in terms of the novel, however, she assumes the role of the Greek chorus in ancient drama, pronouncing enigmatic phrases which only future narrators will clarify; e.g. Why was Judith's marriage forbidden? Why did Henry, Judith's brother and Sutpen's son by Ellen, repudiate his home and birthright? Whose bloody corpse did he fling at the hem of his sister's wedding gown? Why did Rosa agree to marry Sutpen? Indeed, only future narration will clarify and expand these past events and the motives behind them; only the *circular* ratiocinations of future chapters will attempt to explain the destruction of Sutpen's and Rosa's *line*.

Appearing early in the text, these pronouncements establish Rosa as the one surviving voice that actually participated and "saw" the Sutpen story unfolding. Consequently, Miss Coldfield's voice recreates a very subjective and individual version of the story, which expands to paradigmatic proportions as it takes on classical overtones and recasts the fall of the South as the traditional Christian fall from Grace and God. Partaking of this expansive process and taking especially from classical mythology and drama, Mr. Compson's chapters (2, 3 and 4) attempt a more collective reworking and elaboration of the same narrative material which occupies and preoccupies Rosa Coldfield's psyche. With the spreading out of Mr. Compson's narration, consequently, Rosa is encorporated into the perspective of the town of Jefferson, watching its new citizen arrive, build his mansion and plantation and marry Ellen Coldfield, by whom he has two children, Henry who fled from home and Judith who never wed her brother's college friend, Charles Bon. "And then," when "something happened. Nobody knew what," (79) Rosa only ended up knowing as much as the town knew for, according to Mr. Compson, "She could have **known** no more about it than the town **knew** because the ones who did **know** (Sutpen or Judith: not Ellen, who would have been **told** nothing in the first place...) would not have **told** her anymore than they would have **told** anyone in Jefferson or anywhere else." (80) As the voices of *Absalom, Absalom!* **tell** what they **know**, and **know** what they are **told**, examples such as this of narrative markers indicating just "who told whom" and "who knew what" abound. This process of relating material from person to person results in both the repeated variations of the same elements and the overlapping of different minds reworking the same story which, together, create the circular ripple pattern of this novel. "According to what **Miss Coldfield told Quentin** seventy-five years later" (41) and "as **General Compson told his son**, Quentin's father," (37) observes the transindividual narrative voice, for instance, while Quentin's father repeats these same speech directives as he addresses his son: "**Miss Rosa didn't tell** you that?" (61) and "**I have this from something your grandfather let drop** one day." (49) While Miss Rosa "knows" her material from actual experience, the primary source of Mr. Compson's version is, as these examples indicate, the version of his own father, General Compson, Mr. Compson's father and Quentin's grandfather.

During these first four chapters, as well as the five to follow, then, *Absalom, Absalom!* is a circular labyrinth of voices revolving around repeated attempts to learn/know/understand. Given this epistemological preoccupation, the text is shaped by modals and qualifiers, as speculation and conjecture modulate and recast verbs and events through the repeated use of, for example, "might/may/must have," "perhaps," "maybe," "probably," etc, each time a particular segment of one mind's story overlaps with another mind's version. Referring to Rosa Coldfield after her father's death left her "an orphan and pauper," Mr. Compson's conjecturing in the following passage revolves around what she "may have known" and "might have done:"

> She **must have seen** Judith now and then and Judith **probably** urged her to come out to Sutpen's Hundred to live, but **I believe** that this is the reason she did not go, even though she **did not know** where Bon and Henry were and Judith **apparently** never thought to tell her. Because Judith knew. She **may have known** for some time; even Ellen **may have known**. Or **perhaps** Judith never told her mother either. **Perhaps** Ellen did not know before she died that Henry and Bon were now privates in the company which their classmates at the University had organized. (87)

In chapter four, as Quentin listens to his father telling of Bon's relationship to Henry and of Bon's letter to Judith during the Civil War,[25] Mr. Compson describes the extremely precarious epistemological process *Absalom, Absalom!* recreates and expresses frustration at the repetitive circularity of human consciousness, trying again and again and again, yet finding "something missing." In this passage, moreover, he comments on the "heroic proportions" people from the past take on with the passage of time, thus reflecting the enlargement of the characters to legendary status which is taking place as the ripple narrative enlarges and widens the text to the status of a novel. Finally, Mr. Compson's voice becomes a meta-narrative commentary on the difficulty of reading the novel itself, as he combines popular oral narrative ("old mouth-to-mouth tales") with written narrative ("faded letters exhumed from old trunks and boxes and drawers"), the stuff of which *Absalom, Absalom!* is made. Expressing a resigned frustration as "nothing happens," Quentin's father observes:

> We have a few old mouth-to-mouth tales; we exhume from old trunks and boxes and drawers of letters without salutation or signature, in which men and women who once lived and breathed are now merely initials or nicknames out of some now incomprehensible affection which sounds to us like Sanskrit or Chocktaw; we see dimly people, in whose living blood and seed we ourselves lay dormant and waiting, in this shadowy attenuation of time possessing now heroic proportions, performing their acts of simple passion and simple violence, impervious to time and inexplicable - Yes, Judith, Bon, Henry, Sutpen: all of them. They are there, yet something is missing; they are like a chemical formula exhumed along with the letters from that forgotten chest, carefully, the paper old and faded and falling to pieces, the writing faded, almost indecipherable, yet meaningful, familiar in shape and sense, the name and presence of volatile and sentient forces; you bring them together in proportions called for, but nothing happens; you re-read, tedious and intent, poring, making sure that you have forgotten nothing, made no miscalculation; you bring them together again and again nothing happens: just the words, the symbols, the shapes themselves, shadowy inscrutable and serene, against that turgid background of a horrible and bloody mischancing of human affairs. (100-1)

Chapter five, the middle chapter, plunges into the matrix of human life and memory, "the living blood and seed" in which, Mr. Compson says above, "we lay dormant and waiting." Almost entirely in italics, this chapter seems to give voice to Miss Rosa's version of her visit to Sutpen's Hundred on the night Bon was shot and of her engagement with Thomas Sutpen that "vintage year of wistaria" when she was fourteen; (144) at the same time, this transition chapter revolves around the dynamics' of human memory by echoing her narrative in the impressionable young mind of Quentin Compson, thereby preparing the reader for the young man's more active participation and recreation of Sutpen's story which will occur in January of the next year in Cambridge, Massachusetts (chapters 6-9). As this section plunges deeply into the memory-evoking powers of the senses, it gives life to Rosa's buried recollections of her repressed childhood and stunted coming of age. *"Yes,"* says Rosa of herself, *"not even growing and developing, beloved by and loving light,...so that instead of accomplishing the processional and measured milestones of the childhood's time I lurked, unapprehended as though, shod with the very damp and velvet silence of the womb.*" (145) Admitting her attraction to light, these words echo the "Be Light" pronounced at the beginning of the novel by Thomas Sutpen, as he commands his mansion into being through words which themselves echo the biblical command from Genesis: "Let there be Light." More significantly, though, these words contrast Sutpen's active "masculine" creative drive with Rosa's passive "feminine" procreative potential, nipped not even in the bud, as her own words will specify, but at the root. Comprising darkness and birth imagery, therefore, Rosa's element, as her dark airless parlor had indicated on the very first page of the novel, is "*not living but rather some projection of the lightless womb itself.*" (144) Her engagement at fourteen during "that vintage year of wistaria" recreated in this chapter, also presents a stunted view of the natural cycle of vegetation, as Rosa Coldfield describes herself not in terms of "*bloom, at whom no man had yet to look...nor do I say leaf,*" but in terms of "*root and urge...because the neglected root was planted warped and lay not dead but merely asleep forgot.*" (144) While Miss Rosa's "*warped chrysalis*" (144) existence of "*childhood's solitary remembering*" (167) encircles and envelops her, however, Rosa's "root/urge" to pass her version on to Quentin remains very much alive, as she too struggles with the insufficiency of words and with the limitations of human speech. Repeating in her own words the epistemological preoccupation and struggle which permeates this novel, she says in this middle section of the text: "*I will tell you what he did and let you be the judge. Or try to tell you,*" she adds, "*because there are some things for which three words are three too many, and three thousand words that many words too less, and this is one of them.*" (166)

Attempting to explain why Rosa agreed to marry Sutpen, then, this chapter expands the ripple movement of her voice in chapter one, obsessed with why "I saw...yet I agreed to marry him." Her voice, in addition, overlaps with Mr. Compson's version of her life from chapters 2-4 and with Quentin's own developing consciousness, since, while all of this has been occurring and recurring, of course, the young Compson's perspective has been spreading and widening out, as each voice he hears taps into his own personal memories, while "part of it...Quentin already knew. It was a part of his twenty years' heritage of breathing the same air." (11) This "air which Quentin inherits" in *Absalom, Absalom!* is permeated with the smell of wistaria, the sensory stimuli which set individual human memory in motion and which helps make of this text an intricate pattern of collective memory. As it plunges into the complex process and evanescent matrix of human consciousness and remembering, this middle chapter denies the very existence of memory in order to designate the senses as "the substance of remembering." As the scenes overlap and Rosa/Quentin recall the smell of wistaria from her parlor/at his father's porch/during her fourteenth summer, the following passage probes into the process of human sensory recall whereby this smell of wistaria will, at one and the same time, make its way up to Quentin and Shreve's Cambridge room later in the story/text, and provoke, as it has before in the novel, the vivid recreation of the Story of Sutpen. Evoking past tales and tales of the past, the passage begins whimsically:

> *Once there was - Do you mark how the wistaria, sun-impacted on this wall here, distills and penetrates this room as though (light-unimpeded) by secret and attritive progress from mote to mote of obscurity's myriad components? That is the substance of remembering - sense, sight, smell: the muscles with which we see and hear and feel - not mind, not thought: there is no such thing as memory: the brain recalls just what the muscles grope for: no more, no less: and its resultant sum is usually incorrect and false and worthy only of the name of dream.* (143)

The final words of the passage quoted above overlap with Quentin and Shreve's youthful and fanciful recreation of the Sutpen story within the chapters to come, where they sit in their Cambridge room "the two of them creating between them, out of the rag-tag and bob-ends of old tales and talking, people who perhaps had never existed at all anywhere," (303) words which openly acknowledge the youths' recreation as probably "incorrect and false and worthy only of the name of dream." While the scene of Quentin and Shreve sitting in their room overlaps with that of Henry and Bon in the New Orleans drawing room of Bon's part negro Haitian mother, the transindividual narrator validates the process whereby the young Compson and his Canadian schoolmate join to create their fanciful and romantic version of Sutpen's story (chapters 6-9). The text portrays the "four of them...in that drawing room of baroque and fusty magnificence which Shreve had invented and which was probably true enough" with "the Haiti born daughter of the French sugar planter...whom Shreve and Quentin had likewise invented and which was likewise true enough." (335) As if preparing for the news of Rosa's death and for Quentin's total involvement in the new England chapters to come, the narrative shifts abruptly from first to third person pronouns toward the end of this middle section, thereby signaling Rosa's physical disappearance and "foretelling" future tellings of her life:

> *They will have told you how* **I** *came back home. Oh yes,* **I** *know:* **Rosie Coldfield***, lose him, weep him; caught a man but couldn't keep him"...***I** *waiting for him because* **I** *was young still...and ripe for marrying in this time and place where most of the young men were dead and all the living ones either old or already married or tired, too tired for love...because now the town-farmers passing, negro servants going to work in white kitchens-would see* **her** *before sun-up gathering greens along garden fences, pulling them through the fence since* **she** *had no garden of* **her** *own, no seed to plant one with...if* **she** *had not become engaged to him* **she** *would not have had to lie at night asking* **herself** *Why and Why and Why as* **she** *has done for forty-three years...he looking at* **her** *daily with that in his mind and* **she** *not even knowing it. But* **I** *forgave him. They will tell you different, but* **I** *did. Why shouldn't* **I**? **I** *had nothing to forgive;* **I** *had not lost him because* **I** *never owned him: a certain segment of rotten mud walked into* **my** *life, spoke that to* **me** *which* **I** *had never heard before and never shall again, and then walked out; that was all.* (168-71)

As Miss Coldfield's individual voice "dies" at the end of this section, it projects a descending elliptical trajectory into nowhere for Sutpen's damned soul: "*He was a walking shadow...from abysmal and chaotic dark to eternal and abysmal dark completing his descending...ellipsis, clinging, trying to cling with vain unsubstantial hands to what he hoped would hold him, save him, arrest him...'Dead?' I cried. 'Dead? You? You lie; you're not dead; heaven cannot, and hell dare not, have you!* But Quentin was not listening," says the text, "because there was something which he too could not pass." (171 & 172) While the young Compson stops listening, this final page of chapter five juxtaposes Rosa's memory of going up to the Sutpen house on the night Bon was shot, with Quentin/Rosa's memory of going to the Sutpen house on the September night they discovered the fugitive Henry had been out there for four years "living hidden in that house." These are the final words of Chapter five, as the telling of that September afternoon and night in 1909 draws to a temporary close in Jefferson, Mississippi, only to be actively resumed four months later in Cambridge, Massachusetts.

A student at Harvard in January of 1910, then, the young Compson receives a letter from his father telling him of Rosa Coldfield's death and reviving memories of "that dead dusty summer." As chapter six opens with "snow on Shreve's overcoat sleeve" and with the letter "lying on the open text book beneath the lamp-lit table in Cambridge, then, that dead summer twilight- the wistaria, the cigar-smell, the fireflies - attenuated up from Mississippi and into this strange room, across this strange iron New England snow." (173) A Canadian from Alberta, Shreve has been called Quentin's "confessor" by some[26] because of the approximation of his name to the verb "to shrive," meaning "to hear the confession of and usually after penance, give absolution." True to his name, therefore, Shreve assumes the role of the outsider and queries his roommate: *"Tell about the South. What's it like there. What do they do there. Why do they live there. Why do they live at all,"* (174) basic questions around which, in effect, *all* of the voices of *Absalom, Absalom!* revolve. As these two young men join to create their own particular version of the Sutpen Story, the ripple pattern of their voices, as happens with all of the other voices, expands and overlaps with the previous voices of the text and of the narration. Since Quentin's beleaguered consciousness becomes more and more weighted down with the burden of Southern heritage it assumes, the experience of listening becomes overwhelming at times: *"You were not listening,"* he thinks, *"because you knew it all already, had learned, absorbed it already without the medium of speech somehow and from having been born and living beside it, with it."* (212) In contrast, Shreve's objective voice is robust as it parodies Rosa Coldfield's demonic tone by repeatedly interpolating or actually substituting the word "demon" for Sutpen's name. As he dramatizes this substitution, Thomas Sutpen takes on the role, in Shreve's version, of "this Faustus, this demon, this Beelzebub." (178) The young Canadian's expanding narration overlaps with the dramatic tone of Mr. Compson's voice, as Shreve's cool objectivity characteristically reduces Southern histrionics and Sutpen's Design to size: "So he just wanted a grandson," Shreve said. "That was all he was after. Jesus, the South is fine, isn't it. It's better than the theater. It's better than Ben Hur, isn't it. No wonder you have to come away now and then, isn't it." (217)

Two other voices which contribute to narrative creation and recreation in these New England chapters are those of Quentin's grandfather, General Compson, and of Thomas Sutpen himself. While, through the young schoolmates' fanciful and romantic version, the narrative ripple pattern of *Absalom, Absalom!* widens and spreads to the "might-have-been which is more true than true" mentioned in the middle chapter, Quentin and Shreve's "heart and blood of youth" (294) seem to follow a regressive linear pattern back to the origins of the story. This tension between the expanding ripple discourse and the regressive search for linearity and origins reflects the tension between the Derridian notion of "freeplay" and the "dream of deciphering a truth or an origin which is free from freeplay."[27] Along with the two young men and the transindividual narrator, Mr. Compson's voice resurfaces in these chapters, telling Quentin what his grandfather General Compson knew and did not know about, for example, Charles Etienne, Bon's son by an octoroon who appeared at Sutpen's Hundred "that winter, that December of 1871." (195) Some events and motives, admits Quentin's father, "your grandfather didn't know, even though he did know more than the town, the countryside, knew." (200)

Chapter seven moves furthest back in time, to Sutpen's birth in 1807 in the mountains of West Virginia, as he himself appears telling his life's story to General Compson, who tells his son Mr. Compson, who tells his son Quentin Compson, who tells his Canadian schoolmate Shreve in their cold New England room. As the young Compson retraces his narrative line, Quentin's, (and then Shreve's) telling continually overlaps with his father's and grandfather's versions, consequently, "Father said" and/or "Grandfather said" and other phatic variations indicating narrative sources appear over and over again in this text of retelling. For Sutpen's own telling of his story to General Compson, Quentin sets the scene: "All the time he was speaking he was sitting on the log, Grandfather said, telling it, making gestures to tell it with." (253) Gradually letting the doomed patriarch of Sutpen's Hundred speak in the first person, Quentin openly expands Sutpen's cryptic phrase about going to the West Indies by offering possible situations and events not given by the original speaker:

> "**He went to the West Indies.** That's how Sutpen said it: not how he managed to find where the West Indies were nor where ships departed from to go there, nor how he got to where the ships were and got in one, nor how he liked the sea, nor about the hardships of a sailor's life and it must have been hardship indeed for him, a boy of fourteen or fifteen who had never seen the ocean before, going to sea in 1823. He just said, '**So I went to the West Indies**,' sitting there on the log with Grandfather...saying it just like that day thirty years later when he sat in Grandfather's office...telling Grandfather in that same tone while they sat on the log...'**So I went to the West Indies.** I had had some schooling during a part of one winter, enough to have learned something about them, to realize that they would be most suitable to the expediency of my requirements.'"(239 & 240).

Sutpen's two telling scenes of the 1800's overlap with Quentin and Shreve's 1910 retelling in Cambridge, at the same time that the Story of Sutpen, which lacks "logical sequence and continuity" as it is created by many voices, takes on paradigmatic proportions and becomes the story of "Anyman." Spoken by Quentin to Shreve, the following passage exemplifies, once again, the meta-narrative tendencies of this novel:

> "And I reckon Grandfather was saying 'Wait, wait for God's sake wait' about like you are, until he finally did stop and back up and start over again with at least some regard for cause and effect even if none for logical sequence and continuity...and they (he and Grandfather) drank some of the whiskey and ate...and he telling it all over and still it was not absolutely clear - the how and the why he was there and what he was - since he was not talking about himself. **He was telling a story.** He was not bragging about something he had done; he was just telling a story about something a man named Thomas Sutpen had experienced, which would still have been the same story if the man had had no name at all, if it had been told about any man or no man over whiskey at night." (247)

Quentin's narrative line (Sutpen -- General Compson -- Mr. Compson -- Quentin Compson) is, as it turns out, limited and fails to pass on to the young Compson sufficient information, as he himself admits in the following exchange with Shreve:

> "Your father," Sheve said. "He seems to have got an awful lot of delayed information awful quick, after having waited forty-five years. If he knew all this, what was his reason for telling you that the trouble between Henry and Bon was the octoroon woman?"
> "He didn't know it then. Grandfather didn't tell him all of it either, like Sutpen never told Grandfather quite all of it."
> "Then who did tell him?"
> "I did." Quentin did not move, did not look up while Shreve watched him. "The day after we - after that night - when we--"
> "Oh," Shreve said. "After you and the old aunt. I see. Go on. (266)

At the end of this exchange, as the young men refer to Quentin's visit with Rosa to Sutpen's Hundred the summer before, Shreve's irreverent and playful voice undermines the narrative authority of Quentin's lineage. Characteristically, he treats traditional Southern figures in extremely relaxed and informal terms; if Rosa becomes "the old aunt" in the passage quoted above, Mr. Compson becomes "your old man" in the following:

> "Your old man," Shreve said. "When your grandfather was telling this to him, he didn't know any more what your grandfather was talking about than your grandfather knew what the demon was talking about when the demon told it to him, did he? And when your old man told it to you, you wouldn't have known what anybody was talking about if you hadn't been out there." (274)

It is, in fact, Rosa's request which allows Quentin to account for the fugitive white son, Henry Sutpen, missing since the night in 1865 when the son with part black blood, Charles Bon, had been shot. Only in the very last chapter of the novel (9) does Quentin recreate this climatic scene of 1909 which, we recall, had occurred at the end of the day in September that the young Compson had spent listening to Rosa and to his father. From Massachusetts now, Quentin's consciousness expands his narrative of that Mississippi day of wistaria, by evoking, once again, the memory provoking powers of the senses. Exhausted by their evening of lively and fanciful narrative recreation, both youths had finally heeded Shreve's suggestion to "get out of this refrigerator and go to bed." (359) Lying in that cold Cambridge room in January, Quentin begins to gradually warm up. At this point in the narrative, the density of sensual stimuli revolves around dust and decomposition, as the young Southerner's senses and memory recreate the scene, after being prompted by Shreve's crucial question: "Do you understand the South?"

> "I don't know," Quentin said. "Yes, of course I understand it."
> They breathed in the darkness. After a moment Quentin said: "I don't know."
> "Yes. You don't know. You don't even know about the old dame, the Aunt Rosa."
> "Miss Rosa," Quentin said.
> "All right. You don't even know about her. Except that she refused at the last to be a ghost. That after almost fifty years she couldn't reconcile herself to letting him lie dead in peace. That even after fifty years she not only could get up and go out there to finish up what she found she hadn't quite completed, but she could find someone to go with her and bust into that locked house because instinct or something told her it was not finished yet. Do you?"
> "No," Quentin said peacefully. He could **taste** the dust. Even now, with the chill pure weight of the snow-breathed New England air on his face, he could **taste and feel** the dust of that breathless...Mississippi September night. He could even **smell** the old woman in the buggy beside him, **smell** the fusty camphor-reeking shawl and even the airless black cotton umbrella in which...she had concealed a hatchet and a flashlight. He could **smell** the horse; he could **hear** the dry plaint of the light wheels in the weightless permeant dust and he seemed to feel the dust itself move sluggish and dry across his sweating flesh just as he seemed to hear the single profound suspiration of the parched earth's agony rising toward the imponderable and aloof stars. (362)

Indeed, the stars were just as aloof on that night in 1909 when Quentin and Rosa discovered an emaciated Henry in an upstairs room of Sutpen's Hundred, as they were aloof on the night in 1865 when Rosa discovered Bon's body in the same room, and as they are aloof on this night in 1910, while the expanding ripples of Quentin's consciousness overlap with previous recreations of rooms containing other morose, near moribund sons of the

South. The Jefferson chapters had closed with the juxtaposition of two room scenes; the Cambridge chapters close with three.

Referring to Quentin's relationship to his narrative/genealogical line, John T. Irwin establishes a cyclical pattern of repetition, revenge and substitution from father to son-who-will-one-day-be-father, to son...etc. As Irwin explains:

> In terms of a generative sequence of narrators, Mr. Compson, Quentin, and Shreve are father, son, and grandson (reincarnation of the father). Confronting that cyclic reversibility, Quentin realizes that if...for the affront of sonship...they seek to supplant their fathers, then the very fathers whom the sons wish to become are themselves nothing but sons who had sons in order to take that same revenge on their own fathers. Generation as revenge against the father, as revenge against time, is a circular labyrinth; it only establishes time's mastery all the more... And if for Quentin the act of narration is an analogue of this revenge on a substitute, then narration does not achieve mastery over time, rather, it traps the narrator more surely within the coils of time. What Quentin realizes is that the solution he seeks must be one that frees him alike from time and generation, from fate and revenge: he must die childless, he must free himself from time without having passed on the self-perpetuating affront of sonship.

Ending his thought-provoking study in this matter, Irwin seems to himself get caught in the "circular labyrinth" of his argument by offering here a psychoanalytical interpretation of Quentin's "motives" for dying childless in *The Sound and the Fury.* Two pages before, still focusing on the text instead of on a fictional psyche, Irwin finds that Quentin does indeed pass on "the affront of sonship" to Shreve, for Quentin realizes, says this critic,

> that by taking revenge against his father through a substitute, by assuming the role of active teller (father) and making Shreve be the passive listener (son), he thereby passes on to Shreve the affront of sonship, the affront of dependency, and thus ensures that Shreve will try to take revenge on him by seizing "authority," by taking control of the narrative.[28]

Indeed, as Shreve becomes more involved in the telling and retelling, Quentin thinks, "He sounds just like father...Just exactly like father if father had known as much about it the night before. I went out there as he did the day after I came back" (181) and, a few pages later, "I have heard too much. I have been told too much; I have had to listen to too much, too long...Yes, Shreve sounds almost exactly like father." (207) After these observations from chapter 6 occur, nevertheless, the ripples of Quentin's consciousness echo these same words in chapter 7, but this time with a significant difference: **both** he and Shreve are father, both are joined by the dynamic human ritual of narrative/literary creation when Quentin's psyche joins the observations about "sounding like father" to the image of "ripples spreading on water." (261)

Earlier in the text, Mr. Compson had depicted Judith Sutpen performing the essential existential act of "**passing from one hand to another**," an act she describes while she is herself **passing on** to Quentin's grandmother the one and only letter from her long-dead sweetheart, Charles Bon. Through this passage, then, the daughter of Thomas Sutpen and Ellen Coldfield weaves an exquisite metaphor for the individual and collective struggle of life through the loom imagery she describes at length. This description, once again, is a meta-narrative commentary on the evanscent attempt to leave a mark, a scratch, something to be remembered. In the end, though, it is the human **act** of passing on "from one hand to another," from "one mind to another" which matters and which endures. "And so," says Judith Sutpen,

> ...maybe if you could go to someone, the stranger the better, and give them something - a scrap of paper - something, anything, it not to mean anything in itself and them not even to read it or keep it, not even bother to throw it away or destroy it, at least it would be something just because it would have happened, be remembered even if only from passing from one hand to another, one mind to another, and it would be at least a scratch, something, something that might make a mark on something that *was* once for the reason that it can die someday, while the block of stone can't be *is* because it never can become *was* because it can't ever die or perish. (127-8)

Pages before in this same chapter (4) set in Jefferson, Mr. Compson had contemplated faded letters exhumed from old trunks and drawers but, as we recall, "nothing happens; you re-read tedious and intent, poring, making sure that you have forgotten nothing, made no miscalculation; you bring them together again and again nothing happens." (101) What will suffice, then, is not the reading and rereading, try as we might to decipher and understand those scratches left on stone/letters/texts; the essential, memorable act is that which connects and **joins** human beings as it **passes on** life by passing on the narrative.

As Quentin and Shreve "connect" and **join** to recreate the stories that are **passed on** to them in chapters seven and eight, the text expresses this "marriage" of young minds (299), their "marriage of speaking and hearing," (316) through a variety of characteristically meta-narrative images. In chapter seven, for example, Quentin Compson's psyche gives voice to his grandfather's description of the delicate and ephemeral joining of individual human solitude achieved by

> "language (that meager and fragile thread, Grandfather said, by which the little surface corners and edges of men's secret and solitary lives may be **joined** for an instant now and then before sinking back into the darkness where the spirit cried for the first time and was not heard and will cry for the last time and will not be heard then either). (251)

If, as Peter Brooks argues in discussing "the recovery of the past" which he takes to be "the aim of all narrative," the novel *Absalom, Absalom!* is an "unending dialogue informed by desire for a 'revelatory knowledge,'"[29] these climatic New England chapters could be described as an unending dialogue informed by desire for a "joining experience," a desire for human connection and collaboration. Finally joined by "some happy marriage of speaking and hearing," the youths' creative experience is described thus:

> It was not the talking alone which did it, performed and accomplished the overpassing, but some happy marriage of speaking and hearing wherein each before the demand, the requirement, forgave condoned and forgot the faulting of the other - faultings both in the creating of this shade whom they discussed (rather, existed in) and in the hearing and sifting and discarding the false and conserving what seemed true, or fit the preconceived." (316)

Connected by the "fluidity of youth's immemorial obsession" with love, experienced and recreated through the story of Sutpen's offspring Henry/Judith/Bon, Quentin/Shreve join together in order to create.

Perhaps the most ambitious image of connection proposed by the text is that of the "umbilical cord," an image that at one and the same time "connects" **passing on** and **joining** together, in both a literal and figurative sense. Echoing the birth imagery which engrossed Rosa's mind and voice earlier in the text, this image also reflects "the curves of life," as Theodore Cook titles his study of the spiral in nature, science and art. The human umbilical cord, in fact, combines both linearity - it is a cord - and circularity - it is a spiral formation.[30] The text lists common experiences that have joined the two roommates, in order to depict the collaborative connection achieved by two young men "who four months ago had never laid eyes on one another yet who since had slept in the **same room** and eaten side by side of the **same food** and used the **same books** from which to prepare to recite in the **same freshman** courses." In an ultimate attempt to erase geographical boundaries and individual distinctions, the text actually joins the young Canadian to the young Southerner by joining the whole North American continent through "that River which runs...through the physical land of which it is a geological umbilical." It is interesting to note, as a geographical aside, that the mighty Mississippi River, by connecting to the Missouri River, which very near the Canadian border connects with the Milk River, does run into the province of Alberta, Shreve's birthplace according to the text. The novel itself reflects this geological/geographical connection when it joins "Shreve, the Canadian the child of blizzards and of cold" and "Quentin, the Southerner, the morose and delicate offspring of rain and steamy heat" (346) and describes the process thus:

> ...both young, both born within the same year: the one in Alberta, the other in Mississippi; born half a continent apart yet **joined, connected** after a fashion in a sort of geographical transubstantiation by that Continental Trough, that **River** which runs not only through the physical land of which it is the geological umbilical, not only runs through the spiritual lives of the beings within its scope, but is very Environment itself which laughs at degrees of latitude and temperature. (258)

A few minutes later, the umbilical river becomes circular as it portrays the matrix of human imagination and consciousness, connecting the "spreading ripples" to "sounding like father." While the reverberations of this image mirror and echo the reverberations of the ripples "spreading" and "feeding" on each other, Quentin thinks: "Maybe we are both Father. Maybe nothing happens once...but like ripples...on water after the pebble sinks, the ripples...spreading...attached by a narrow umbilical water-cord to the next pool which the first pool feeds...Yes, we are both Father." (261)

Any reader of *Absalom, Absalom!* has, at this point, come a long way from the trickle of Rosa's haunted voice searching for an appropriate listener at the very beginning of the text. Indeed, by participating in the collaborative creation and recreation of the story, the reader of this novel has also been drawn into the dynamic process portrayed by the image of ripples spreading on water - an expanded and expansive image of narrative fluidity, a connected/collective image of narrative circularity. Such a dynamic textual process repeats circularity on multiple levels and reflects human attempts at perceptive and cognitive experiencing and understanding. As a consequence, such epistemological preoccupation and tendency force the reader to participate actively in the elaboration and recreation of the story of Sutpen and the novel *Absalom, Absalom!*. This text highlights and examines "the importance of learning to read," says David Krause, who explains: "Faulkner's technique generates some deliberate indeterminacy about who is speaking and who is not, about what is in the book and what is not, about presence and absence, seducing even the most disciplined of readers into an intimate, if illusive, engagement."[31] Enthusiastically taking on the challenge of what, in Warwick Wadlington's terms is "an outrageous narrative" made of "the thickened webs of language, the reader is drawn into making sense of "the syntactical and structural deferments of meaning and the novel's reticences."[32] David Minter takes this perspective: "One part of the unusual delights that informs *Absalom, Absalom!* derives from Faulkner's pleasure in playing his imaginative and rhetorical games. Another part derives from his pleasure in making us play them, too."[33] As if describing what John T. Matthews has called the "play of Faulkner's language," William Faulkner himself explains the epistemological dimensions of *Absalom, Absalom!* playfully as "14 ways of looking at a blackbird:"

I think that no one individual can look at truth. It blinds you. You look at it and you see one phase of it. Some one else looks at it and sees a slightly awry phase of it. But taken all together, the truth is in what they saw though nobody saw the truth in fact...Quentin's father saw what he believed was truth, that was all he saw. But the old man (Sutpen) was himself a little too big for people no greater in stature than Quentin and Miss Rosa and Mr. Compson to see all at once. It would have taken perhaps a wiser or more tolerant or more sensitive or more thoughtful person to see him as he was. It was...13 ways of looking at a blackbird. But the truth, I would like to think, comes out, that when the reader has read all these 13 different ways of looking at the blackbird, the reader has his won 14th image of that blackbird which I would like to think is the truth.[34]

Indeed, an extremely eloquent example of the Derridian play of "difference" and "decentering" in modern literary discourse, the dialogical ripple pattern of *Absalom, Absalom!* might be diagrammed in the following manner:

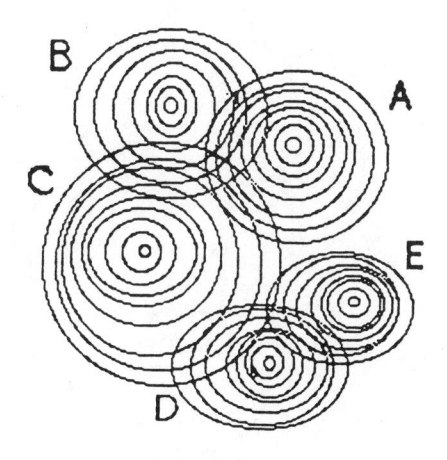

"ripples on water"
Absalom Absalom!

In my diagram, Rosa Coldfield's telling of the Sutpen story corresponds to ripples "A," Mr. Compson's to ripples "B," Quentin's to "C and Shreve's to "D," while the reader's recreation of the story reflects yet another mind, ripples "E," and so on, in an endlessly fluid process. So dynamic is this oral narrative and process, that, when joined together, the stories of Sutpen expand to paradigmatic proportions, becoming the story of the South dealing with slavery and familial demise.

CHAPTER IV

A "DESIGN"

Due to the rhetorical fluidity and ripple of dynamics of *Absalom, Absalom!*, the narrative "design" of this Faulknerian novel becomes a resounding collective and circular success. Not so for Thomas Sutpen's social design, which the novel portrays as a singular and linear failure. Instead of establishing and perpetuating his family line and social standing, Sutpen's design leads ultimately to personal and social destruction and demise. Combining a stylistic and thematic perspective when he discusses Faulkner's "major novels," James A. Snead contrasts "a style that mixes and connects entities as much as their social function tends to divide and distinguish them."[1] Indeed, the elaborate narrative "freeplay" that the overlapping ripples of this text portray is in constant tension with the linear genealogical "Design" created by the rigid patriarchal "masterplotter,"[2] Thomas Sutpen; the joining/connecting function that characterizes the narrative circularity of this novel, is in constant contension with the separation and division prescribed by social convention and pretension. While ripples spreading across the pages of *Absalom, Absalom!* portray collective collaboration and a potentially endless and expanding epistemological process which joins narrative voices and listeners/readers, Sutpen's design and Southern society follow a rigid course of division and separation and ultimate destruction.

Writing early in 1934 about what would develop into *Absalom, Absalom!*, William Faulkner describes the plot succinctly, as he explains the time frame in which he will tell his story of "a man who outraged the land:"

> The one I am writing now will be called *Dark House* or something of that nature. It is the more or less violent breakup of a household or family from 1860 to about 1910. It is not as heavy as it sounds. The story is an anecdote which occurred during and right after the civil war; the climax is another anecdote which happened about 1910 and which explains the story. Roughly, the theme is a man who outraged the land, and the land then turned and destroyed the man's family.

Later that same year, Faulkner had already titled the novel *Absalom, Absalom!* when he wrote that "the story is of a man who wanted a son through pride, and got too many of them and they destroyed him."[3] "Connecting events of the nineteenth century recovered and recounted in the early twentieth century,"[4] *Absalom, Absalom!* spans the turbulent years of a family and a nation torn by a racial and generational strife which actually pitted brother against brother in the bloodiest national conflict the United States has seen. Fought between 1861 and 1865, the great Civil War led the South to the tragic realization that, in the words of its twentieth-century beleaguered heir Quentin Compson, "it was paying...the price for having erected its economic edifice on the shifting sands of opportunism and moral brigandage." (260) Founded on the "shifting sands" of racial and social inequality, in a nation purportedly founded on the "solid rock of freedom and equality for all," the South was made to pay the price for an American dream that had not quite survived in reality. Lewis Simpson evaluates the "Great Experiment" of the United States and says: "The nation that, flaunting all the historical evidence certifying man's irresistible disposition to folly and evil, had based itself on the premise that man is a rational and beneficent being, had within seventy years of the establishment of the Great Experiment in human nature engaged in one of the bloodiest internecine conflicts in history."[5] The Civil War experience split such a nation geographically, but the psychic split that resulted was much more lasting and detrimental. Repeatedly admonished until the outbreak of the was in 1861 that "we are still in Eden," nineteenth-century America,[6] and especially the South, slowly realized its fall from paradise and evaluated its fulfillment of the Biblical jeremiad: "And I brought you into a plentiful country, to eat the fruit thereof and the goodness thereof, but when ye entered, ye defiled my land, and made mine heritage an abomination." (Jeremiah 2:7)

Especially since the North interpreted the outcome of the war as a victory for North American democratic ideals, it was the Southern psyche, of course, which was left most devastated by its experience of America. Haunted by her existence in what she calls "a land primed for fatality and already cursed with it, "for example, the twentieth-century survivor Rosa Coldfield examines and questions, repeatedly and obsessively asking "why and why and why" (170) of herself and of her Southern American reality. Also heir to such psychic self-examination, and split between loving/hating the South - "I don't hate it!" (378) are his final desperate words - Quentin Compson is young and ambivalent to the end, as he listens to his Canadian (as North American as possible) roommate Shreve describe Quentin's Southern heritage as living "among defeated grandfathers and freed slaves (or have I got it backward and was it your folks that are free and the niggers that lost?) and bullets in the dining room table and such, to be always reminding us to never forget." (361) Within the pages of *Absalom, Absalom!*, of course, no one is allowed to forget - neither Rosa, nor Quentin, nor the other characters, nor especially its readers.

On a grand scale, then, the Southern portion of the United States assumed and was forced to assume the guilt of an entire nation which, for the first time in its short history, had seriously doubted its ability to live up to its divine - later to be called "manifest"- destiny, and had questioned its role as a country set apart and chosen by both God and history to be an example for all the world. Quentin and Rosa's obsessive self/regional examination revolving around the crucial central question of "Why God let us lose the War" (11) is characteristic especially of the defeated South, but also of a nation such as the Untied States which, as a whole, is prone to periodic self-examination. Analyzing and describing the experience of what he terms an "almost chosen people," Russel B. Nye says:

> Americans...are no doubt the only people in the world who blame themselves for not having finally created the perfect society, and who submit themselves to persistent self-examination to determine why they have not... The nation spent nearly a century, for example, rationalizing its acceptance of slavery, fought a bloody war to eliminate it, and has since subjected itself to an agonizing self-appraisal because it has not completely rid itself of the consequences of having once tolerated the system. No other nation has quite the same feelings of guilt over its failures.[7]

So predominant has been this tendency toward self-examination in the face of a dream unfulfilled, of a Paradise potentially lost "west of Eden," that North American literature demonstrates a profound and recurrent preoccupation with innocence and guilt, i.e., the loss of innocence. True to his North American heritage, therefore, Thomas Sutpen begins as an innocent, untainted by the corruption and injustice which surrounded him, until the age of puberty and initiation into the ways of the world. Born in the mountains of what was then West Virginia before it was admitted into the Union, the young Sutpen knew only a communal and harmonious existence within a pre-division-of-labor-and-property society

> where the only colored people were indians...he had never even heard of, never imagined, a place, a land divided neatly up and actually owned by men who did nothing but ride over it on fine horses or sit in fine clothes on the galleries of big houses while other people worked for them... Because where he lived the land belonged to anybody and everybody and...the man who would go to the trouble...to fence off a piece of it and say "this is mine" was crazy. (221)

Coming from such a rugged yet idyllic, seemingly pre-lapsarian existence, the institution and practice of slavery was, of course, totally foreign to the young and innocent Thomas Sutpen, for, as Quentin recounts,

> he didn't even know there was a country all divided and fixed and neat with people living on it all divided and fixed and neat because of what color their skin happened to be and what they happened to own, and where a certain few men not only had the power of life and death and barter and sale over others, but they had living human men to perform the endless repetitive personal offices...which no man ever has or ever will like to do, but which no man that he knew had ever thought of evading anymore than he had thought of evading the effort of chewing

> and swallowing and breathing...because he just thought that some people were spawned in one place and some in another...because it had never once occurred to him that any man should take any such accident as that as authority or warrant to look down at others, any others. So he had hardly heard of such a world until he fell into it. (221-2)

Suspended in this timeless realm, the cart on which the young Sutpen journeys into Southern society comes upon horizontal, i.e. chronological, time only once it reaches the flat land of the South "all divided and fixed," as Quentin describes to Shreve:

> He didn't remember whether it was that winter and then spring and then summer that overtook and passed them on the road, or whether they overtook and passed in slow succession the seasons as they descended, or whether it was the descent itself that did it, and they not progressing parallel in time but descending perpendicularly through temperature and climate - a (you couldn't call it a period because...as he told Grandfather..., it didn't have either a definite beginning or a definite ending. Maybe attenuation is better) - an attenuation from a kind of furious inertness and patient immobility...during which they did not seem to progress at all but just to hang suspended while the earth itself altered, flattened and broadened out of the mountain cove where they had all been born...and the country flattened out now with good roads and fields and nigggers working in the fields while white men sat fine horses and watched them...with a different look in the face from mountain men. (224-5)

Dropped into this new and strange world, "he knew neither where he had come from nor where he was nor why." (227)

Such are the mythical roots of Sutpen's life and subsequent design, that his own story (retold through the male Compsons to Quentin who tells Shreve in chapter seven of the novel) begins with the brief but complex affirmation: "Sutpen's trouble was innocence." (220) In the pages that follow, the actual narrative discourse revolves around this word "innocence," as the image of a young boy waiting at the door of a big mansion evolves into the will of the man Sutpen, actually building his own mansion and plantation, and attempting to realize his very own personal design. So basic is innocence to Sutpen's being, that the experience of a boy rejected at the door becomes a sort of stepping-through-the-looking-glass experience, separating the before and after, the reflected other side of reality which he had not "known" before going up to the big house. The text describes Sutpen's innocence-shattering experience thus:

> He didn't even know he was innocent that day when his father sent him to the big house with the message... He was a boy either thirteen or fourteen, he didn't know which...following the road...up past where still more niggers with nothing to do all day but plant flowers and trim grass were working, and so to the house, the portico, the front door, thinking how at last he was going to see the inside of it...never for one moment thinking but what the man would be as pleased to show him the balance of his things as the mountain man would have been to show the powder horn and bullet mold that went with the rifle. Because he was still innocent. He...told Grandfather how, before the monkey nigger who came to the door had finished saying what he said, he seemed to kind of dissolve and a part of him turn and rush back through the two years they had lived there, like when you pass through a room fast and look at all the objects in it and you turn and go back through the room again and look at all the objects from the other side and you find out you had never seen them before, rushing back through those two years and seeing a dozen things that had happened and he hadn't even seen them before. (229-30)

Having gained consciousness of social mores and codes, the young Sutpen feels an overwhelming urge to think and straighten out the pieces:

> He was not crying, he said. He wasn't even mad. He just had to think, so he was going to where he could be quiet and think, and he knew where that place was. He went into the woods... He said he crawled back into the cave and sat with his back against the uptorn roots, and thought. Because he couldn't get it straight yet. He couldn't even realize yet that his trouble, his impediment, was innocence, because he would not be able to realize that until he got it straight. (232-3)

The process of "getting it straight," of drawing lines setting boundaries and delineating his design involves a psychic split within the young Sutpen, as "the two of them argued inside of him, speaking in orderly turn, both calm...*But I can kill him. - No. That wouldn't do no good - Then what shall we do about it? I don't know.*" (237) This coming of age forces upon him the adult world of slavery and segregation and inequality. Initially a victim of these Southern social norms, Sutpen formulates the vindictive process whereby he himself will become the victimizer. By playing according to the rules and codes set by his adopted world, he begins to erect from such innocence his own individual monument to Southern American society: Sutpen's Design. Recalling his experience and realizing his relative insignificance in the scheme of life, he thinks:

> *He never give me a change to say it and Pap never asked me if I told him or not and so he cant even know that Pap sent him any message and so whether he got it or not cant even matter, not even to Pap; I went up to that door for that nigger to tell me never to come to that front door again and I not only wasn't doing any good to him by telling it or any harm to him by not telling it, there aint any good or harm either in the living world that I can do to him.* It was like that, he said, like an explosion - a bright glare that vanished and left nothing, no ashes nor refuse; just a limitless flat plain with the severe shape of his intact innocence rising from it like a monument. (237-8)

Phallic from the start, Sutpen's design underlines and delineates the patriarchal perspective whereby, as David Krause says in reference to Quentin's search, "identity involves (inescapably) inheritance, genealogy and paternity."[8] Examining the play of Faulkner's language and the language of Sutpen's design, John T. Matthews observes:

> The language of Sutpen's design wants to make a simple statement; it tries to restore the aura of total coherence that mark's Sutpen's childhood. It depends on making one "right" marriage, having one firstborn son, and establishing a legitimate dynasty. Dictated by the "pillar" of Sutpen's innocence, erected in the middle of a limitless plain, the design honors a phallic, paternal model of meaning.[9]

After two failed attempts at constructing his design and with the Civil War behind him, Thomas Sutpen feels time running out, and actually calculates the shots left in "the old cannon," as the rifle alternative his divided self considered as a boy, merges with his untiring phallus, the alternative "weapon" he did take as a young boy for shaping his vindictive design. Returning from the war, then, Sutpen realizes "*that he was now past sixty and that possibly he could get but one more son, had at least one more son in his loins, as the old cannon might know when it has just one more shot in its corporeality.*" (279) Dependent "upon genealogical clarity and purity, on the ability to chart a clear authoritative relationship between origin and endpoint,"[10] Sutpen's design follows the linear paradigm of patriarchy as the source of individual identity, family lines and social codes of conduct. Heir to Old Testament Biblical tradition, which Nancy Blake calls "largely a treatise on genealogy,"[11] the title/lament "Absalom, Absalom" is that of the archetypal patriarchal figure David, searching for solace from his sons in his old age, but instead weeping over the dead body of his son Absalom. David's lament echoes through the novel: "O my son Absalom, my son, my son Absalom. Would God I had died for thee, O Absalom, my son, my son!" (II Samuel 18:33)

In his characteristically succinct manner, Thomas Sutpen describes his design by listing its basic ingredients very simply. "You see," he told Quentin's grandfather, "I had a design in my mind... To accomplish it I should require money, a house, a plantation, slaves, a family - incidentally of course, a wife. I set out to acquire these, asking no favor of any man." (263) Such simplistic catagorization of social requirements seems naive and, of course, cruel. But Sutpen is, after all, heir to a moral code which measured the amount and proportion of black blood that coursed in one's veins and actually labeled, for example, a third generation offspring of an interracial coupling an "octoroon," i.e., 1/8 black blood, and then went on to estimate this octoroon's offspring to have 1/16 black blood. Such is the case, for example, of Charles Bon's octoroon wife and their son Charles Etienne in this novel. (194) Well aware of the moral code which divides Southern society, Bon himself, Sutpen's first son born in the West Indies, acknowledges the patriarchal system which created the octoroon: "We - the thousand, the white men - made them, created and produced them; we even made the laws which declare that one eighth of a specified kind of blood shall outweigh seven eights (sic) of another kind." (115) True to his Southern heritage, then, Sutpen measures and divides and combines the "ingredients of his morality" in a naive attempt to produce the particular social design he desires. "It was that innocence again," says the text, "that innocence which believed that the ingredients of morality were like the ingredients of pie or cake and once you had measured them and balanced them and mixed them and put them into the oven it was all finished and nothing but pie or cake could come out." (263)

As Sutpen sets his plan into action, however, he learns a new fact after the birth of his first son Charles Bon which "rendered it impossible that this woman and child be incorporated into his design." (264) Pages later he reveals the reason to his all-white son Henry: "His mother's father told me that her mother had been a Spanish woman. I believed him; it was not until after he was born that I found out that his mother was part negro." (355) Accompanied still by "that innocence he had never lost because after it finally told him what to do that night he forgot it and didn't know that he still had it," Quentin says that Sutpen "told Grandfather how he had put his first wife aside like eleventh-and twelfth-century kings did: 'I found that she was not and could never be, through no fault of her own, adjunctive or incremental to the design which I had in mind, so I provided for her and put her aside.'" (240) Measured and discarded in this manner by the social codes he knew all too well, Charles Bon does not exist as a flesh and blood person, but is, as Mr. Compson puts it, "shadowy, a myth, a phantom: something which they engendered and created whole themselves; some effluvium of Sutpen blood and character, as though as a man he did not exist at all." (104) Finally, upon burial, Bon is acknowledged by Rosa to have been "*the abstraction which we had nailed into a box.*" (153)

At one point in his career, William Faulkner spoke of *Absalom, Absalom!* as a story of revenge, saying that Sutpen "wanted revenge as he saw it... He said, I'm going to be the one that lives in the big house. I'm going to establish a dynasty, I don't care how, and he violated all the rules of decency and honor and pity and compassion, and the fates took revenge on him"[12] Along with the revenge inherent in Sutpen's design and the final revenge of the Fates on this tragic masterplotter, *Absalom, Absalom!* is also the story of Charles Bon's revenge on Sutpen, the story of the rejected son's ultimate revenge on the rejecting father. As Bon's own son Charles Etienne substitutes his dead father and, through his idiot son Jim Bond, underlines the final destruction of Sutpen's patriarchal design, the revenge of sons versus unjust fathers takes on increasingly tragic, and at the same time parodic, dimensions. Such portrayal of and preoccupation with sons in relation to fathers is, of course, central to a novel such as *Absalom, Absalom!*, a text which explores various "relationships to inherited material"[13] within a patriarchal system. Demonstrating a male perspective passed on by paternal socio/cultural structures, John Matthews describes Bon's search for identity within the patriarchal paradigm: "Bon embodies the **search of every individual for paternity**, for an intelligible personal history that **fathers** one's independent identity. Bon's demand for his father's acknowledgement is a **search for self-comprehension.**"[14] (My emphasis.) Hopelessly waiting for a sign, any sign, Charles Bon thinks:

> *He would just have to write "I am your father. Burn this" and I would do it. Or if not that, a sheet, a scrap of paper with the one word "Charles" in his hand, and I would know what he meant and he would not even have to ask me to burn it. Or a lock of his hair or a paring from his finger nail and I would know them because I believe now that I have known what his hair and his finger nails would look like all my life, could choose that lock and that paring out of a thousand.* (326)

So fundamental to self-identity is the need for the father's recognition within such a paradigm, that all other relationships in life revolve around and evolve from this primary need, as Bon's relationships to the women in his life - his mother, the octoroon and Judith - readily exemplify. Judith, Bon's half-sister and Sutpen's all-white daughter by Ellen Coldfield, becomes merely the personification of Bon's attempts to wrest the words of paternal recognition he wants so desperately to hear from his father. So overwhelming and primal is the need for self-identity, that Bon offers his father the ultimate challenge by becoming engaged to Judith. As Peter Brooks describes it: "Bon's insistence on marriage to Judith becomes the choice of scandal in order to force the admission of paternity. What appears to be erotic desire reveals itself to be founded on the absolute demand for recognition by the father."[15] Such a course finally leads the "fatherless" son Bon to the war of brother versus brother, the Civil War.

Along with Thomas Sutpen, therefore, Charles Bon and Henry Sutpen, Judith's brother and Bon's half-brother, participate in the four years of civil war which pitted brother against brother. One part-black, the other white, these two brothers embody what Eric J. Sundquist has termed in his study *The House Divided*, "the several fratricidal dimensions of America's national sin" whereby "the sins of the fathers (have) led necessarily to the violence of the brothers."[16] Just as the national war nears its end, the civil war within Sutpen's family line comes to a climax when Colonel Thomas Sutpen calls Henry to his tent. Acknowledging this child with the words Bon has waited so long to hear - "Henry, my son." (353) - the nearly defeated patriarch passes on to this son the one piece of information he knows to be completely unacceptable within Southern codes of segregation and division: Bon has black blood. Henry, who had learned just before the war that Bon was his brother, had gradually accepted the incest Bon's marriage to Judith would imply; his Southern heritage, however, can never accept crossing color lines. Hearing of this meeting, Bon observes:

> -So it's the miscegenation, not the incest, which you cant bear. Henry doesn't answer.
> -And he sent me no word?... No word to me, no word at all? That was all he had to do, now, today; four years ago or at any time during the four years. That was all. He would not have needed to ask it, require it, of me. I would have offered it. I would have said, I will never see her again before he could have asked it of me. He did not have to do this, Henry. He didn't need to tell you I am a nigger to stop me. He could have stopped me without that, Henry. (356)

Torn between his own love for Bon and his inbred abhorrence of black blood, Henry utters the desperate words of fraternal recognition which, within a patriarchal system and society, can not measure up to the paternal recognition Bon has sought all his life: "You are my brother," (357) which Bon immediately translates into the language of social division and separation: "No, I'm not. I'm the nigger that's going to sleep with your sister. Unless you stop me, Henry." (358) Sutpen's white son, of course, does stop him once and for all, soon after, at the gate of Sutpen's Hundred.

Olga Vickery calls the image of "a boy seeking admittance and being turned away in the name of the social code"[17] the central image of *Absalom, Absalom!*. Just as Sutpen was turned from the big house when he was a child, so his son Charles Bon is repeatedly turned away by Sutpen himself. In fact, Bon's persistent attempts to gain recognition from his father revitalize this image repeatedly, especially as Sutpen's house and his design begin to lose their seemingly pure and straight lines. Faced with the dilemma of whether to tell Henry that Bon is part black or to remain silent and allow Judith to marry Bon, (a man no one realizes is black and only Henry knows is Sutpen's son), the struggling patriarch recalls the cornerstone of his design, "the boy-symbol at the door" (261):

> ...either I destroy my design with my own hand, which will happen if I am forced to play my last trump card, or do nothing, let matters take the course which I know they will take and see my design complete itself quite normally and naturally and successfully to the public eye, yet to my own in such fashion as to be a mockery and a betrayal of that little boy who approached the door fifty years ago and was turned away, for whose vindication the whole plan was conceived and carried forward to the moment of this choice. (274)

The final destruction of both Design and House begins when Charles Bon appears for the first time at Sutpen's Hundred, visiting with his university friend Henry Sutpen for the Christmas holidays. Fifty years after the first experience, Sutpen has now assumed the role of owner and master, while Bon is most certainly the "forlorn nameless and homeless lost child:"

> ...he stood there at his own door, just as he had imagined, planned, designed, and...after fifty years the forlorn nameless and homeless lost child came to knock at it...and Father said that...even though he knew that Bon and Judith had never laid eyes on one another, he must have felt and heard the design - house, position, posterity and all - come down like it had been built out of smoke. (267)

Springing from misguided innocence and Southern patriarchal society, Sutpen's Design does go up in smoke, literally, as the house is consumed in flames in the final pages of the novel and as Sutpen's family line is reduced to the black idiot great-grandson, James Bond.

While Sutpen's design is rooted in the divisive social codes and mores of the South, and especially in the traumatic experience of the Civil War, it is also a very North American design, stemming from a future-directed belief upholding equality of opportunity for the individual, and from the United States experience of linear social and individual renewal along the frontier. Blatantly speaking from within the male paradigm too, John T. Irwin evaluates Sutpen's design in terms of the "doctrine of equality" of a son struggling against the patriarchal powers that be. "Clearly," says Irwin, "the **doctrine of the equality of men** is at odds with the **patriarchal principle that fathers are inherently superior to sons,** for obviously the doctrine of equality is the **doctrine of a son.**" (My emphasis.) According to Irwin, patriarchal authority stems, very simply, from the fact that the father is born before the son.

> "for the essence of authority, the mastery, that a father has over his son is simply priority in time - the fact that in time the father always comes first. And against the patriarchal authority whose basis is priority in time, the son's will is impotent, for the will cannot move backwards in time, it cannot alter the past.

Except that "altering the past," starting fresh and anew without the restraints of the past and looking toward the future, is at the very core of Sutpen's design, and at the heart of the concept and dream of America. Comparing Fitzgerald's Great Gatsby with Faulkner's Thomas Sutpen, Irwin himself observes: "Clearly, what Gatsby and Sutpen both seek in their quests is to alter the past - to repeat the past and correct it... When Nick Carraway realizes the enormity of Gatsby's dream, he tells him, 'You can't repeat the past,' and Gatsby with his Sutpen-like innocence replies, 'Why of course you can.'"[18] Lewis P. Simpson affirms that the United States, as the "first nation deliberately to dispossess the past, became the first to be possessed by the concept of modern history as a progressive enchantment of the status of the person,"[19] a project and process based on a New World doctrine of equality and future progress, versus patriarchal principles of the Old World. Faithful to this North American heritage of dispossessing the past, therefore, Thomas Sutpen not only abandons his poor white family past forever, but also has a very hazy picture of his father and his past, for he "didn't know just where his father had come from, whether from the country to which they returned or not, or even if his father knew." (223) Like father, like son, Bon repeats his father's self-made existence without any past, for "he came into that isolated puritan country household almost like Sutpen himself came into Jefferson: apparently complete, without background or past or childhood." (93) Keeping the same pattern "in the family," Bon's son Charles Etienne is the boy who "had been produced complete and subject to no microbe...entering the actual world not at the age of one second but of twelve years." (196)

The progenitor of such a line of self-made-because-rejected offspring, Thomas Sutpen is the prototypical self-made man. His gaze rigidly fixed on the future, he resolves on the day of his traumatic childhood experience

> (to) take that boy in where he would never again need to stand on the outside of a white door and knock at it: and not at all for mere shelter but so that the boy...could shut that door himself forever behind him on all that he had ever known, and look ahead along the still undivulged light rays in which his descendants who might not even ever hear his (the boy's) name, waited to be born without even having to know that they had once been riven forever free from brutehood. (261)

Such is the scope of Sutpen's innocence, that he delineates his design by only "looking ahead" to the future and totally disregarding the past. So obsessed does the persistent patriarch become with the future, that the very basis of his design becomes a desperate attempt to write the story of his family line prospectively, a persistent effort to control and direct the future. Considering "the aim of narrative" to be "the recovery of the past" and arguing "that all narrative must, as a system of meaning, conceive itself as essentially retrospective," Peter Brooks relates the aim of narration to that of Sutpen's design when he writes: "Sutpen attempts to write the history of the House of Sutpen prospectively, whereas history is evidently always retrospective... Only the sons can tell the story of the fathers."[20] In the end, of course, Sutpen's sons do indeed "write" the story of Thomas Sutpen, and it is a story of demise and final destruction of the father's design, as the emblematic figure of Father Time - Wash Jones armed with the scythe - cuts down the failed patriarch's life. The past can never be abandoned completely, even in a society such as that of the United States which, like Sutpen's Design, is oriented toward and directed by the linear paradigm of future progress.

A New World plan for future-directed progress which is based on the son's doctrine of equality, Sutpen's Design is, therefore, destroyed by the very forces it seeks to direct and control. While indeed stemming from an overwhelming need for equality of opportunity - as symbolized in the boy at the door - Sutpen's design is, of course, not rooted in equality for all - as personified in the black son Bon before the *"expressionless and rocklike face"* (348) of the rejecting father. "Sutpen sets out to vindicate the right of every poor white boy to an equal opportunity to become the rich planter," says Irwin, "but...once he has vindicated that right by becoming the rich planter, he immediately denies that same right to black boys...to his black son Charles Bon."[21] Not only does he deny equality to his part-black son, but Thomas Sutpen, the poor white boy turned away from the home of the plantation owner, becomes himself the ultimate symbol of the patriarchal landowner ordering the world according to his genealogical design of inequality. Stemming from the New World doctrine of equality for all, the experience of America portrayed in *Absalom, Absalom!* ultimately leads back to Old World patriarchy and inequality in the name of a rigid white Western social code which rejects "difference," which, in the end, rejects the non-Occidental blood brought to America from the "dark" continent, Africa.

Along with being a future-oriented struggle for equality within a patriarchal system, the linearity of Sutpen's Design is rooted in North American soil and actually reenacts the frontier experience of starting over within a linear paradigm. Abandoning the traditional cyclical model of natural renewal, Sutpen's Design, then, follows the linear model of wave-like renewal which is characteristic of the North American frontier concept. As if transferring Turner's theory of North American social development along the frontier, to the pattern of narrative suspension in the novel *Absalom, Absalom!*, Michael Millgate uses terminology which seems to echo that of the noted American historian who spoke of fluid, wave-like movement and "rebirth" along the physical surface and within the social development of the United States.

> Again and again...Faulkner stops us short of elucidation, constantly reinforcing in this way a suspense which, throughout the book, is created not so much by the withholding of narrative facts - almost all of these, indeed are supplied in the opening chapter - as by the continual frustration of our desire to complete the pattern of motivation, of cause and effect. The movement of the book becomes almost wave-like - surging forward, falling back, and then surging forward again.

A few pages earlier, Millgate had called Sutpen "the archetype of the American settler" and described his reenactment of North American history with these words"

> After his "fall" into Tidewater decadence (the exhausted Europe of his career), Sutpen discovers the West Indies with the eye of an Adam ("set out into a world" which even in theory he knew nothing about [53]). Drawing on French colonial design (35) and Spanish coin (34), Sutpen re-enacts in miniature the entire history of America.[22]

As Sutpen re-enacts the history of North American frontier movement, he does utilize Spanish coin to buy the land for his plantation and draws on a French architect to design his mansion; he is, however, a post-lapsarian Adam originating from a region of childhood innocence, the naturally harmonious tidewater region of West Virginia before statehood. In addition, the wave-like pattern of suspense that characterizes the narrative "design" of this novel follows a circular, ripple "pattern of motivation," of waves and troughs as each individual consciousness tells and retells the story of Sutpen and of the South. In the end, this **circular narrative design** parodies and ultimately destroys **Sutpen's linear social design**.

A "representative 'new man' hacking an estate out of the Southwestern wilderness, a Yankee secularized Puritan, a nineteenth-century rugged individualist,"[23] as Albert Guerard puts it, Thomas Sutpen begins his North American design by emigrating to the West Indies, the site of New World discovery and subsequent slavery exportation. Still exhibiting colonial social structures, Haiti is described as "the halfway point between what we call the jungle and what we call civilization, halfway between the dark inscrutable continent from which the black blood, the black bones and flesh and thinking and remembering and hopes and desires, was ravished by violence, and the cold unknown land to which it was doomed." (250) Blown by the winds that took the doomed slave ships and fertilized by two hundred years of black blood, Haiti is the halfway point between two races/continents/worlds, "a little lost island" made up of

> a soil manured with black blood from two hundred years of oppression and exploitation until it sprang with an incredible paradox of peaceful greenery and crimson flowers and sugar

> cane sapling size and three times the height of a man and a little bulkier of course but valuable pound for pound almost with silver ore, as if nature held a balance and kept a book and offered a recompense for the torn limbs and outraged hearts even if man did not, the planting of nature and man too watered not only by the wasted blood but breathed over by the winds in which the doomed ships had fled in vain, out of which the last tatter of sail had sunk into the blue sea, along which the last vain despairing cry of woman or child had blown away - the planting of men too; the yet intact bones and brains in which the old unsleeping blood that had vanished into the earth they trod still cried out for vengeance. (250-1)

Charles Bon is, of course, the child born to the new man Sutpen in this land crying out for vengeance, the first-born son of his part-negro wife whom he believed to be Spanish; i.e., instead of originating in Europe, she was from Africa. Once he discovers the "new fact" which, as he put it, "rendered it impossible that this woman and child be incorporated in my design," Sutpen abandons the colonial island and moves northwest to Jefferson, Mississippi, a second frontier where he will try once again to establish his design. The second attempt will prove to be, of course, his most promising effort. In true frontier fashion, this stranger, first of all,

> rode into town out of nowhere with a horse and two pistols and a herd of wild beasts that he had hunted down singlehanded because he was stronger in fear than even they were in whatever heathen place he had fled from...a man who fled here and hid, concealed himself behind respectability, behind that hundred miles of land which he took from a tribe of ignorant Indians, nobody knows how. (16)

From land originally occupied by Indians, then, this rugged frontier man fashioned "a plantation; inside of two years he had dragged house and gardens out of virgin swamp, and plowed and planted his land with seed cotton which General Compson loaned him." (40) Years later, with his daughter Judith a young woman and his son Henry forty miles away at the University of Oxford, Thomas Sutpen was

> the biggest single landowner and cotton-planter in the county now, attained by the same tactics with which he had built his house - the same singleminded unflagging effort and utter disregard of how his actions which the town could see might look and how the ones which the town could not see must

> appear to it... He was not liked (which he evidently did not want, anyway) but feared, which seemed to amuse, if not actually please, him, but he was accepted; he obviously had too much money now to be rejected or even seriously annoyed any more. He accomplished this - got his plantation to running smoothly...within ten years of the wedding, and now he acted his role too - a role of arrogant ease and leisure which, as the leisure and ease put flesh on him, became a little pompous. (72)

It was at this time, of what appeared to be Sutpen's total success in achieving his design, that Henry met the older and urbane Charles Bon at university and brought him to his father's home for the Christmas break, as the sins of the first attempt at design catch up with the second attempt, as the past revindicates its place in the present and future, as the land begins to take revenge on such artificial growth. In Mr. Compson's dramatic mode, the doomed patriarch "was unaware that his flowering was forced blooming...and that while he was still playing the scene to the audience, behind him Fate, destiny, retribution, irony - the stage manager, call him what you will - was already striking the set and dragging on the synthetic and spurious shadows of the next one." (73) In the following image proposed by the text, the land itself trembles with the impending tragedy of Sutpen's Design, as it gives shape to the gorge which will empty out the water of life/the family of Sutpen that this very land has cradled and nurtured for twenty years:

> Because the time now approached (it was 1860, even Mr. Coldfield probably admitted that war was unavoidable) when the destiny of Sutpen's family which for twenty years now had been like a lake welling from quiet springs into a quiet valley and spreading, rising almost imperceptibly and in which the four members of it floated in sunny suspension, felt the first subterranean movement toward the outlet, the gorge which would be the land's catastrophe too, and the four peaceful swimmers turning suddenly to face one another, not yet with alarm or distrust but just alert, feeling the dark set, none of them yet at that point where man looks about at his companions in disaster and thinks When will I stop trying to save them and save only myself? and not even aware that that point was approaching. (74)

And the land does indeed tremble during the long years that it is made to absorb the blood of its divided sons split in civil war, as this land also begins to engulf the life of Sutpen's family line, the heart of Sutpen's divisive linear design.

The incorrigible designer, however, true to his North American heritage of trying again on a new frontier, does attempt to start over again. Instead of moving physically, now Sutpen worries only about time running out and about not having enough future in which to start all over again for yet a third time. Riding back into Jefferson after the Civil War, the failing patriarch "was not for one moment concerned about his ability to start the third time. All that he was concerned about was the possibility that he might not have time sufficient to do it in, regain his lost ground in. He did not waste any of what time he had either." (278) In a doomed last effort to "regain lost ground" during the dramatic phase of social Reconstruction, then, the drama of Sutpen loses all pretense at social convention and human civilization, as the aging patriarch assumes the tragic, yet parodic, role of an animal in heat searching for the female of the species who will take his seed and produce a male descendant. Delivering the ultimate affront to Miss Rosa - that they postpone marriage until she proves her capability of delivering him a son - Sutpen then actually impregnates Milly Jones, the fifteen-year-old granddaughter of his loyal companion Wash Jones. When she delivers a girl instead of a boy, however, she is less than an animal in the disparaging male's eyes. "Well, Milly," says Sutpen on the morning she gives birth, "too bad you're not a mare... Then I could give you a descent stall in the stable" (286) and walks out. Having finally reduced his linear family design to the mere reproductive function of an animal, Sutpen's own life of sixty-two years is cut down by the ultimate patriarchal figure, Wash Jones "with the scythe above his head," (292) Father Time come to take revenge on his wayward son. Ultimately, Thomas Sutpen, "who went to war to protect (his land) and lost the war and returned home to find that he had lost more than the war," (313) is once again reduced to the powerless role of the son, as he dies at the hand of the perennial figure of the old man.

Waiting at Sutpen's Hundred for the War to end, says Rosa, "that triumvirate mother-woman which we three, Judith, Clytie and I, made" (162) not only feel fearful as they watch the returning soldiers, but also harbor a desperate hope as they construct their own Reconstruction period by still looking to the absent patriarch. Beginning to understand the final devastation of the War, Miss Rosa Coldfield describes the existence of this female "triumvirate" on the demon's land, and the human drama that passed before their eyes as returning soldiers came upon "a ruined land:"

> We slept in the same room, the three of us (this for more than to conserve the firewood which we had to carry in ourselves. We did it for safety.) It was winter soon and already soldiers were beginning to come back...men who had risked and lost everything, suffered beyond endurance and had returned now to a ruined land, not the same men who had marched away but transformed - and this the worst, the ultimate degradation to which war brings the spirit, the soul - into the likeness of that man who abuses from very despair and pity the beloved wife or mistress who in his absence has been raped. We were afraid. We fed them; we gave them what and all we had and we would have assumed their wounds and left them whole again if we could. But we were afraid of them... We talked of him, Thomas Sutpen, of the end of the War (we could all see it now) and when he would return, of what he would do: how begin the Herculean task which we knew he would set himself, into which (oh yes, we knew this too) he would undoubtedly sweep us with the old ruthlessness whether we would or no. (157)

Speaking of Faulkner's portrayal of women as passive and accepting characters, David Williams writes that "Generally...women are regarded as being more capable of accepting evil and/or the limitations of life, while men strive in a kind of desperate innocence to assert the reality of an ideal, unlimited world."[24] Judith Wittenberg, in her study *American Novelists Revisited*, attempts to reinterpret and explain Faulkner's motivation in his portrayal of women within a patriarchal system, when she says that

> Faulkner was obviously aware of the effects of a rigidly patriarchal social structure upon its female members. Even though his own status as a product of that structure sometimes led him to imply that it was more admirable to accept than to rebel, his awareness of its oppressiveness was responsible for a number of memorable portraits of women...suggesting that at every level the patriarchy is a powerful force that inhibits their emotional and intellectual development.[25]

Whatever may have been Faulkner's personal perspective and artistic concern in portraying women, the world he creates in *Absalom, Absalom!* is certainly patriarchal, from its socio/cultural structure and foundation, to its narrative motivation and transmission. The obsession with the personal role and social function of the father which this text portrays is, in fact, not only pronounced but indeed overwhelming, as Quentin Compson's beleaguered consciousness exemplifies repeatedly. With his roommate Shreve up in Cambridge, for example, the young man thinks:

> *Am I going to have to have to hear it all again...I am going to have to hear it all over again I am already hearing it all over again I am listening to it all over again I shall have to never listen to anything else but this again forever so apparently not only a man never outlives his father but not even his friends and acquaintances do.* (277)

So overpowering does patriarchy prove to be within this text, that a consideration of the function of women can be all too easily dismissed and forgotten. Yet, the role of women as mothers and daughters, and sisters and aunts and wives and spinsters will lead to a better understanding of both the narrative discourse and thematic concerns of this text. Very briefly, and in an attempt at balance after so much consideration of fathers and sons, I would like to consider mothers and daughters.

In contrast to the textual and social prominence of fathers, mothers are extremely limited in terms of resources and recourse to action. Either they suffer and waste away under the system, as happens in Ellen Coldfield's case, "the butterfly, the moth caught in a gale and blown against a wall and clinging there beating feebly...in bewildered and uncomprehending amazement," (85) or they take action, but only if assisted, as in the case of Bon's mother who can only challenge the father who rejects her son through the sanctioned legal help of a lawyer. In the end, though, her "fury and fierce yearning and vindictiveness and jealous rage" (298) not only does not suffice within a patriarchal system but, in fact, leads her child to reject the role of parenting, for the young Bon "took it for granted that all kids didn't have fathers too" and that his mother's

> incomprehensible fury and fierce yearning and vindictiveness and jealous rage was part of childhood which all mothers of children had received in turn from their mothers and from their mothers in turn from that Porto Rico or Haiti or wherever it was we all came from but none of us ever lived in. So that when he grew up and had children he would have to

pass it on too and...deciding then and there that it was too much trouble and bother and that he would not have any children or at least hoped he would not. (299)

The matrix of Bon's self-made existence is the fact that he was "created between a lawyer and a woman" (306), "with for background the shadowy figure of a legal guardian rather than any parents." So evanescent is the heritage which the mother passes on to the child within such a social system, that Bon becomes "a personage who in the remote Mississippi of that time...appeared almost phoenix-like, full sprung from no childhood, born of no woman and impervious to time and vanished, leaving no bones or dust anywhere." (74) Daughters, in their turn, become stunted and live to bury the haunted legacy of their fathers, as happens to Miss Rosa Coldfield, feeding her self-imprisoned father, enclosed within his own attic and defeated mind. In terms of Sutpen's daughters, Judith lives to buy the headstones and bury the tragic offspring engendered by her father, as Clytie is left to literally wither away inside the haunted shell of her father's house, collecting the "tinder and trash" along with the kerosene (374) which will finally destroy the structure within seconds. While Judith makes the "scratches" on the headstones which mark the gravesites, Clytie strikes the match at the end that will "efface the demon's lineage from the earth," as Rosa put it at the beginning of the novel.

Able to say as Dilsey in *The Sound and the Fury*, "I have seen the first and the last," Miss Rosa Coldfield and Clytie watch the House of Sutpen go up in flames within the last pages of the novel. Because a few months earlier Rosa had summoned Quentin Compson to her Jefferson parlor and then taken him out to Sutpen's Hundred, however, she is not alone in watching the "dark house" go up in smoke, for the trickle of her voice has initiated the psychic and narrative process of *Absalom, Absalom!* that leads to Quentin and Shreve's recreation of that scene and of the complex story of Sutpen's rise and fall. In fact, it is only once her voice is joined to Quentin's patriarchal narrative line, that the ripple circularity of collective collaboration leads to the textual experience and literary creation of this Faulknerian novel. Throughout this process, as a result, circularity is in constant and mounting tension with linearity; as narration upon narration expands and increases the destructive linear shape and final outcome of Sutpen's social design, that same narrative dynamic expands and increases the constructive and deconstructive circular freeplay of *Absalom, Absalom!*. Very simply, as the patriarch's design divides and separates and begins to fall, the ripple narrative joins and connects all the more desperately, especially in chapters seven and eight; the more Sutpen's design falls apart, the more Quentin and Shreve become one in narrative creation and recreation.

In an article about "what Clytie knew," Loren F. Schmidtberger makes an interesting observation within a footnote when she writes: "Judith's use of the "loom" image, incidentally, parodies Sutpen's complaint to General Compson about the impending destruction of his own 'design.'"[26] I would take this critical observation made in passing, and weave Judith's "loom image" and her "scratches on headstones" and General Compson's "language as meager thread" and Miss Rosa's haunted, searching voice, to Quentin and Shreve's "happy marriage of speaking and hearing," in order to demonstrate the extremely pronounced concern with connection and joining which characterizes the textual dynamics and narrative desire of this North American novel. In the end, two voices from within the polyphonic collaboration which is *Absalom, Absalom!*, express this tension between linearity and circularity. As the bellow of the idiot great-grandson Jim Bond seals the tragic fate of Thomas Sutpen's linear genealogical design, Rosa Coldfield's haunted voice echoes the literary success of narrative ripples, asking to be heard/read, and warning North America not to forget its tainted past and its romance and innocence, warning America not to forget that it is both reality and dream.

CHAPTER V

A "GYRATING WHEEL"

Summarizing the role of the artist in a 1954 interview, William Faulkner describes the dynamics of aesthetic creation and recreation when he affirms: "The aim of every artist is to arrest motion, which is life, by artificial means and hold it fixed so that one hundred years later, when a stranger looks at it, it moves again, since it is life."[1] Interestingly enough, "arrest motion" within a "one-hundred year" span is what the Latin American writer and 1982 recipient of the Nobel Prize for literature, Gabriel García Márquez, succeeded in doing so admirably in his acknowledged masterpiece *Cien años de soledad*. Whereas *Absalom, Absalom!*, along with most of Faulkner's work, is set in the fictional but quotidian reality of Yoknapatawpha County, Mississippi and the Southern region of the United States, García Márquez sets his novel in the mythical and magical region of Macondo, the name of a banana plantation from his childhood in Columbia, and then proceeds to trace the development and destruction of this microcosm of Latin America. Combining fantastic elements with ordinary reality, *Cien años de soledad* tells the story of seven generations of the Buendía family, from the discovery and founding of Macondo to its final demise and obliteration from the face of the earth.

Grounded in the socio-historical reality of Latin America, therefore, *Cien años de soledad* projects itself beyond this diachronic frame to the synchronic level of archetypal myth and cosmological reality. Referring in general to the so-called "boom" generation of Latin American writers, the following observation by Katalin Kulin certainly holds true for this novel by Gabriel García Márquez: "The works of this generation, similar to their ideology, immerse their roots in their socio-historical experience, but project before the public a vision which, although inspired in these experiences, assumes an *a priori* totality of the world."[2] In the fancifully portentous mode of *Cien años de soledad*, this totality is simply rendered metaphorically when the patriarchal figure of the Buendía clan, José Arcadio Buendía, emerges from his imaginary voyage of discovery to affirm that "The world is round like an orange." (12) Speaking of *Cien años de soledad* specifically, Lucila Ines Mena contrasts the synchronic projection of this text with its diachronic framework when she observes: "That which on a diachronic level is presented as a succession of seven generations of a race and one hundred years of political repression within the life of a community, on a synchronic level becomes the vision of one of the infinite cosmic cycles within the history of the human race."[3] Vicenzo Bollettino, in his turn, speaks of the temporal dimensions of this novel as "historical, lucid and chronological time" in relation to "mythical, circular and achronological time."[4]

This tension between a chronological and linear conception of time and an achronological and circular conception is indeed basic to *Cien años de soledad* and the world it creates. At once a recreation of the socio-cultural trajectory of Latin American history and an expression of the existential solitude inherent to the human condition, this text weaves the history of the Buendía family into the magically real world of Macondo. So formed, this novel is a fancifully self-conscious recreation of the parameters which shape human experience and perception of time and history, a recreation molded by a New World perspective on the temporal and historical experience of the Western World. In this sense, therefore, *Cien años de soledad* helps to discover and uncover a whole "new world" of aesthetic and cultural expression which the rationalism and bourgeois tradition of Old World philosophy and history for centuries helped silence. While discussing the artistic expression of Hispanic America's "new novel" in relation to "our long history of lies, silences and empty speech," the Mexican author Carlos Fuentes speaks of the need to invent a new language in order to "say all that history has silenced"[5] in order to allow those peoples which the dominant mode of Western tradition and history has excluded, to tell their own story and write their own history. In *Cien años de soledad*, Gabriel García Márquez tells the story of Latin America and joins his hearty voice to the many that are writing and rewriting the history of this region and its people from a twentieth-century perspective.

Heir to Western tradition, nevertheless, *Cien años de soledad* patterns the story that it tells after the two historical paradigms which have traditionally formed and informed human experience: circular, cyclical motion and linear eschatological direction. While exploring the human search for and preoccupation with *Meaning in History*, Karl Löwith describes universal "approaches to the understanding of history" and explains just how fundamental these two geometric configurations are:

> it seems as if the two great conceptions of antiquity and Christianity, cyclical motion and eschatological direction, have exhausted the basic approaches to the understanding of history. Even the most recent approaches to an interpretation of history are nothing else but variations of these two principles or a mixture of both of these.[6]

The "new science" elaborated by Giambattista Vico during the first half of the eighteenth century, for example, combines these two historical paradigms, as it attempts to distinguish the analysis of socio/cultural phenomena within the social sciences, from the analysis of physical nature within the natural sciences. Considering the "efforts of human beings to endow their world with meaning," and analyzing how tropes function in the discourse of the human sciences in his study *Tropics of Discourse*, Hayden White discusses the "deep structure" of Vico's *New Science* and also summarizes the noteworthy work of this historian, in terms of these two historical paradigms, when he observes that Vico's "employment of human history is elaborated on two levels: the Hebrew-Christian, which describes a progressive evolution of consciousness in the light of revealed truth; and the pagan, which describes a pattern of cyclical recurrence."[7]

Playfully orchestrating these two historical configurations, the narrative development of *Cien años de soledad* not only erases linear conceptions of time, but actually reshapes its world according to the repetitive circularity of cyclical motion. Once again, the text is extremely forthright in expressing the temporal trajectory that forms and informs the world of Macondo; this time it is Ursula, the matriarchal figure of the Buendía family, who reshapes the linear cliché which says that "Time passes," into cyclical temporal patterning. Due to her many years of experience, the aging matriarch "knows" the true nature of time, while her great-grandson José Arcadio Segundo must continue studying the magical manuscripts left by the gypsy Melquíades, because he has not yet succeeded in deciphering their enigmatic tale:

> José Arcadio Segundo sequia releyendo los pergaminos...Al reconocer la voz de la bisabuela, movió la cabeza hacia la puerta, trató de sonreir, y sin saberlo repitió una antigua frase de Ursula:
> -Qué queria - murmuró -, el tiempo pasa.
> -Asi es - dijo Ursula -, pero no tanto.
> Al decirlo, tuvo consciencia de estar dando la misma réplica que recibió del coronel Aureliano Buendía en su celda de sentenciado, y una vez más se estremeció con la comprobación de que el tiempo no pasaba, como ella lo acababa de admitir, sino que daba vueltas en redondo. (291-2)
>
> (José Arcadio Segundo continued re-reading the manuscripts...Upon recognizing his great-grandmother's voice, he turned his head toward the door, tried to smile, and without knowing it, repeated an old phrase of Ursula's.
> "What can I say," he murmured. "Time passes."
> "Yes, it does" said Ursula, "but not so much."
> Upon saying this, she was conscious of having received the same answer from Colonel Aureliano Buendía in his cell, and she once again shuddered with the certainty that time did not pass, as she had just finished saying, but that it went around in circles).

Two other characters share this intuitive insight into the true nature of time: the elusive gypsy Melquíades and the concupiscent fortune teller Pilar Ternera. True to their natural tendency for overstepping temporal boundaries, Melquíades and Pilar, along with Ursula, seem to live on and on as they overcome the traditional conception of the passage of time. In keeping with the magical margins which he inhabits, Melquíades actually dies and returns to life still wearing his "chaleco anacrónico" (164) ("anachronic vest"), "porque no pudo soportar la soledad," (50) because he could not bear the solitude of death. The two matriarchal figures - Ursula the legitimate Buendía mother and Pilar, mistress and illegitimate mother to the clan - give birth to the first generation of the Buendía family, assist in periodic attempts at regeneration, and accompany the gradual degeneration of the Buendías and of Macondo. Coming full circle in the end, Ursula is reduced to the shape and size of a decrepit old woman who looked newly born, until she finally dies, after having lived much beyond one hundred years. Joining the beginning to the end of the family, she is buried in a box only slightly larger than the cradle which holds her great-great-great grandson, the very last Buendía who attends her funeral as a baby. Uniting past and present, the archetypal matriarch, the ageless Ursula Buendía, steps far beyond chronological time in appearance and attitude, in life and death:

> Liegó a revolver de tal modo el pasado con la actualidad, que en las dos o tres ráfagas de lucidez que tuvo antes de morir, nadie supo a ciencia cierta si hablaba de lo que sentía o de lo que recordaba. Poco a poco se fue reduciendo, fetizándose, momificándose en vida, hasta el punto de que en sus últimos meses era una ciruela pasa perdida dentro del camisón... Parecía una anciana recién nacida... Amaneció muerta el jueves santo. La última vez que la habían ayudado a sacar la cuenta de su edad...la había calculado entre los ciento quince y los ciento veintidós años. La enterraron en una cajita que era apenas más grande que la canastilla en que fue llevado Aureliano. (297 & 298)

> (She ended up confusing the past with the present to such an extent that, during the two or three lucid moments she had before dying, no one knew for sure if she was talking about what she felt or about what she remembered. Slowly she shrank, becoming like a fetus or a mummy, so that in her last months she looked like a raisin lost in her nightgown... She looked like an old woman recently born... She died on Holy Thursday morning. The last time that they had helped her calculate her age...they had figured it to be between one hundred fifteen and one hundred twenty two years. They buried her in a little box which was barely larger than the cradle which contained Aureliano).

Pilar Ternera also gives up on calculating her age. Realizing that the young man who has just entered her brothel is her great-great grandson Aureliano, Pilar joins the past, present and future, as she prepares the last

Buendía for his ultimate revelation and demise by telling him about the development, about the grandeur and misfortune of his family and of Macondo. The night Aureliano appears at her door.

> ...la espléndida y taciturna anciana que vigilaba el ingreso en un mecedor de bejuco, sintió que el tiempo regresaba a sus manantiales primarios, cuando entre los cinco que llegaban descubrió un hombre óseo, cetrino, de pómulos tártaros, marcado para siempre y desde el principio del mundo por la viruela de la soledad... Estaba viendo otra vaz el coronel Aureliano Buendía...Era Pilar Ternera. Años antes, cuando cumplió los ciento cuarenta y cinco, había renunciado a la costumbre de llevar las cuentas de su edad, y continuaba viviendo en el tiempo estático y marginal de los recuerdos, en un futuro perfectamente revelado y establecido, más allá de los futuros perturbados por las acechanzas y las suposiciones insidiosas de las barajas. (342)

> (...the splendid and taciturn old woman who watched the entrance in a wicker rocking chair, felt that time returned to its primordial origins, when among the five men who arrived she discovered a thin melancholy man with pale cheeks, marked forever and from the beginning of time by the virus of solitude... She was seeing Colonel Aureliano Buendía again... It was Pilar Ternera. Years before, when she reached one hundred forty five, she had renounced the pernicious habit of counting one's age, and continued living in the static and marginal time of memory, in a perfectly revealed and stable future, far beyond the bothersome future of waiting and of insidiously reading the cards).

Throughout the novel and her long life, the ageless matriarch Ursula Buendía repeatedly alerts the reader to the cyclical temporality which patterns and shapes *Cien años de soledad*. As Macondo "naufragaba en una prosperidad de milagro" ("floated lost in a sea of miraculous prosperity"), Ursula accompanies this precarious progress by comparing it to previous phases and observing that "Ya esto me lo sé de memoria... Es como si el tiempo diera vueltas en redondo y hubiéramos vuelto al pricipio." (173) ("I already know all this from memory... It's as if time were revolving in circles and we had returned to the beginning.") Furthermore, as the strike and subsequent massacre of the banana plantation workers draw near, the intuitive matriarch feels tormented by "algo que ella misma no lograba definir pero que concebía confusamente como un progressivo desgaste del tiempo." (215) ("something which she herself could not define but which she perplexedly perceived as a progressive wearing down of time"). So attuned is Ursula to the cyclical repetition which shapes the life of her family and house, that blindness only makes her more acutely aware of the physical "geography" of her house and of the static existence of her family:

> Nadie supo a ciencia cierta cuándo empezó a perder la vista... Conoció con tanta seguridad el lugar en que se encontraba cada cosa, que ella misma se olvidaba a veces de que estaba ciega. En cierta ocasión, Fernanda alborotó la casa porque había perdido su anillo matrimonial, y Ursula lo encontró en una repisa del dormitorio de los niños. Sencillamente, mientras los otros andaban descuidadamente por todos lados, ella los vigilaba con sus cuatro sentidos para que nunca la tomaran por sorpresa, y al cabo de algún tiempo descubrió que cada miembro de la familia repetía todos los dias, sin darse cuenta, los mismos recorridos, los mismos actos, y que casi repetía las mismas palabras a la misma hora. (216)

> (No one knew for certain when she began to lose her sight... She was so sure of where everything was, that she herself forgot sometimes that she was blind. Once, when Fernanda upset the whole house because she had lost her wedding ring, Ursula found it on a shelf in the children's bedroom. While the others went carelessly from place to place, she simply watched them with her four senses so that they would never take her by surprise, and after some time she discovered that each family member unconsciously traversed the same distance, and repeated the same gestures and almost the same words at the same time each day).

While repeated psychic obsession with Thomas Sutpen shapes the telling and retelling of his story in *Absalom, Absalom!*, recurrent cyclical repetition permeates every thread of *Cien años de soledad* as it weaves the story of the founding, development and final destruction of Macondo and the Buendía family. So fundamental is recurrent cyclicity, that the narrative fabric of this fanciful text actually thrives on excessive repetition, taking it to exaggerated proportions. The most obvious examples of this tendency are: the recurrent use of the same names and combinations thereof, especially "Aureliano" and "José Arcadio;" the inherited tendency toward existential solitude which *all* members of the family exhibit; as well as the overwhelming attraction toward physical incest which many experience. So basic is repetition to this novel, that many critics have discussed this characteristic. In his classic study of Gabriel García Márquez's work, *Historia de un deicidio*, the Peruvian writer Mario Vargas Llosa, for example, observes:

> In *Cien años de soledad*, many things apparently happen, a profusion of beings, objects and especially events, seems to be a characteristic of this fictional world: something is always happening. An objective reading shows us, however, that fewer things happen than would seem, for *the same things happen various times.*[8]

Josefina Ludemar, in her turn, finds *Cien años de soledad* to be a continuous play of variations, substitutions and transformations of certain signifiers and signifieds.[9] Perhaps one of the most blatant examples of fancifully exaggerated repetition is the case of Ursula's 17 Aureliano grandsons, all fathered by her famous and solitary son Colonel Aureliano Buendía, during his twenty-year career in the civil wars which only served to leave him feeling "disperso, repetido, y más solitario que nunca" (149) ("scattered, repeated and more solitary than ever"). These seventeen sons, then, certainly do "scatter and repeat" the Colonel's solitude as García Márquez, true to his vocation of "providing a magnifying glass" in order to better reveal and see reality[10] through the use of the fantastic, transforms metaphorical and figurative images and situations into actual physical beings and circumstances. As news spreads of festivities honoring the Colonel's premature retirement, ordered by the government in power and contrary to the military leader's wishes, these sons arrive one by one, forming a living chronicle of the twenty years of civil war which have made Colonel Buendía retire more and more into his solitude and defeat.

> Entonces el coronel Aureliano Buendía quitó la tranca, y vio en la puerta diecisiete hombres de los más variados aspectos, de todos los tipos y colores, pero todos con un aire solitario que habría bastado para identificarlos en cualquier lugar de la tierra. Eran sus hijos. Sin ponerse de acuerdo, sin conocerse entre si, habían llegado desde los más apartados rincones del litoral cautivados por el ruido del jubileo. Todos llevaban con orgullo el nombre de Aureliano, y el apellido de su madre. Durante los tres dias que permanecieron en la casa, para satisfacción de Ursula...Amaranta buscó entre antiguos papeles la libreta de cuentas donde Ursula habia apuntado los nombres y las fechas de nacimiento y bautismo de todos, y

agregó frente al espacio correspondiente a cada uno el domicilio actual. Aquella lista habría permitido hacer una recapitulación de veinte años de guerra. (190-1)

(Colonel Aureliano Buendía then unlocked the door and came face to face with seventeen males of all aspects, types and coloring, but all with a solitary manner which would have been enough to identify them anywhere on earth. They were his sons. Without planning it, without knowing each other, they had come from the furthest regions of that coast, captivated by the festive plans. All were proud to be called by the name Aureliano and by their respective mother's surnames. During the three days they stayed in the house, in order to satisfy Ursula...Amaranta found the account booklets where Ursula had written down their names and dates of birth and baptism, and added the present address of each one in the corresponding space. That list would have permitted a recapitulation of twenty years of war).

Having tired of the "circulo visioso de aquella guerra eterna" (149) ("the vicious circularity of that never-ending war"), Colonel Buendía retires to his workshop to make and melt and remake little goldfish, a "circulo visioso exasperante de pescaditos de oro." (177) As evidenced by the solitary military figure, the Buendía "vicio de hacer para deshacer," (274) a "vice" of making and unmaking, of doing and undoing, marks other members of the family in what Raymond L. Williams calls "activity without substance...which indicates a rejection of linear movement."[11] Caught in her incestuous circle of solitude, Ursula's only daughter and the Colonel's sister, Amaranta, weaves and unravels and reweaves her own burial shroud. Two generations later and after years of rain, Fernanda del Carpio, wife of Ursula's great-grandson, Aureliano Segundo, watches her husband trying to avoid boredom by fixing various defects in the house. Observing him "montar picaportes y desconectar relojes, Fernanda se preguntó si no estaría incurriendo también en el vicio de hacer para deshacer, como el Coronel Buendía con los pescaditos de oro, Amaranta con... la mortaja ... y Ursula con los recuerdos." (274-5) ("installing latches and disconnecting clocks, Fernanda asked herself if he hadn't also caught the vice of doing in order to undo, like Colonel Buendía with his little gold fish, Amaranta with her shroud...and Ursula with her memories").

Although Aureliano Segundo exhibits a spurious interest in restoring the Buendía house after the rains which lasted "4 yeas, 11 months and 2 days," (274) it is Ursula who repeatedly preoccupies herself with the periodic renovation and restoration of the Buendía house. While in *Absalom, Absalom!* the fragile Ellen Coldfield is completely overcome by her husband's will and design, and the haunted Rosa Coldfield is caught in the narrative ripple pattern she initiates, in *Cien años de soledad* Ursula Buendía is vigorous and enterprising and characteristically undaunted in her attempts at maintaining the physical structure and spiritual existence of the Buendía "house." Robert Lewis Sims speaks of this matriarch as "the Great Mother who nourishes her race" and observes that Ursula "demonstrates an overpowering effort to encompass all the members of her clan ... and is extremely active in keeping the family intact."[12] Ursula's physical and spiritual space, the Buendía house, expresses and encompasses what Gaston Bachelard, in his analysis of *The Poetics of Space*, calls the "maternal features of the house." Referring to the space of our birth, Bachelard goes on to say:

> in short, the house we were born in has engraved within us the hierarchy of the various functions of inhabiting. We are the diagram of the functions of inhabiting that particular house, and all the other houses are but variations on a fundamental theme.[13]

As if confirming the importance of this space, Gabriel García Márquez had originally entitled his masterpiece "La Casa," just as William Faulkner had originally called *Absalom, Absalom!*, "The Dark House."

From the very beginning of Macondo and of *Cien años de soledad*, the house is Ursula's, for she refused to leave it and Macondo behind because, as she tells her husband José Arcadio Buendía, "Aqui nos quedamos porque aqui hemos tenido un hijo." ("Here is where we will stay because it's where we have had a son.") When the introspective young patriarch replies that "Uno no es de ninguna parte mientras no tenga un muerto bajo la tierra," ("We are from nowhere until we have a dead one under the ground"), she simply retorts, "Si es necesario que yo me muera para que se queden aqui, me muero." (19) ("If it's necessary that I die so that we will stay here, then I'll die.") So central is Ursula to the mythical founding and cyclical development of Macondo, that her activities, according to Sims, reach beyond "the matriarchal realm" as "the men abandon their patriarchal duties and she fulfills them in their absence."[14] Ironically, it is Ursula who hinders her husband's exploratory projects to leave Macondo since, he laments, "nos hemos de pudrir en vida sin recibir los beneficios de la ciencia," (19) ("we will rot here without receiving the benefits of science"); yet, a few pages later, after a five-month search for her young son José Arcadio who had run away from Macondo with a band of gypsies, it is the hearty young matriarch who returns "excited and rejuvenated" and accompanied by a group of new faces, with the news that she had found "la ruta que su marido no pudo descubrir en su frustrada búsqueda de los grandes inventos." (38 & 39) ("the route which her husband had never been able to find in his frustrated search for great inventions"). At the moment that José Arcadio Buendía gives in to his wife's decision to stay, and begins to resettle into his own particular space within Macondo - his alchemy laboratory,- "the center of power in the Buendía family," according to Michael Palencia-Roth, "passes invisibly and forever...from the husband to the wife, from the men to the women, from the alchemy laboratory to the maternal home."[15]

True to her maternal role, Ursula occupies and preoccupies herself with the physical and existential space of the Buendía "house." Unlike the linear design of Thomas Sutpen's obsessive design, the pattern and shape of Ursula's house is unequivocally cyclical and founded on the prolific reproductive and repetitive tendencies of the various Buendía generations. While her husband, José Acardio Buendía, remains in his lab occupied with his discoveries and inventions - the most recent of which, at this point in the text, is an attempt to scientifically prove the existence of God through the use of daguerreotype,- Ursula watches her children grow older and ready to have children of their own. In order to keep them near her, she pools her resources and decides to expand the house. Extremely sensitive to the function of space and to the place of her family, Ursula maintains "common sense" and acts as the cohesive force within an "extravagant house." As she is followed, during the reconstruction, by "docenas de albaniles y carpinteros...Ursula ordenaba la posición de la luz y la conducta del calor, y repartía el espacio sin el menor sentido de sus limites." (55) ("dozens of masons and carpenters...Ursula ordered the position of light and the channeling of heat, and divided space without any sense of its limits.")

Periodically, then, as if following the natural cyclical renewal of the physical world, this perennial matriarch restores and rejuvenates the Buendía house in order to maintain and revitalize the Buendía family. When Colonel Aureliano actually escapes the firing squad after the civil wars, for example, Ursula dedicates herself once again to the renewal of the house.

> Con una vitalidad que parecía imposible a sus años, Ursula habia vuelto a rejuvenecer la casa. "Ahora van a ver quién soy yo," dijo cuando supo que su hijo viviría. "No habrá una casa mejor, ni más abierta a todo el mundo, que esta casa de locos."... Decretó el término de los numerosos lutos superpuestos, y ella misma cambió los viejos trajes rigurosos por ropas juveniles. La música de la pianola volvió a alegrar la casa. (161)

> (With a vitality which seemed impossible at her age, Ursula was rejuvenating the house once again. "Now they're going to see who I am," she said when she heard that her son would be allowed to live. "There will be no greater or more open house in all the world, than this crazy house."... She ordered the end to mourning and herself exchanged the old stuffy outfits for young clothing. The music of the pianola once again brightened the house.)

The last time that she attempts to renew the family house, the aging matriarch is already blind and the house is suffering the ravages of 4 years, 11 months and 4 days of rain. Strong as Ursula's invincible heart may be, the forces of nature which have thrived in the deluge are threatening and menacing, and will ultimately prove more vital and powerful. While the actual structure is eaten away by termites and the contents are destroyed by moths, the giant red ants which signal the beginning of the end, congregate. While Ursula is physically blind,

> el ánimo de su corazón invencible la orientaba en las tinieblas...Ella no necesitaba ver para darse cuenta de que los canteros de flores, cultivados con tanto esmero desde la primera reconstrucción, habían side destruidos por la lluvia...y que las paredes y el cemento de los pisos estaban cuarteados, los muebles flojos y descoloridos, las puertas desquiciadas, y la familia amenazada por un espíritu de resignación y pesadumbre que no hubiera sido concebible en sus tiempos.

> Moviéndose a tientas por las dormitorios vacios percibía el trueno continuo del comején taladrando las maderas, y el tijereteo de la polilla en los roperos, y el estrépito devastador de las enormes hormigas coloradas que habian prosperado en el diluvio y estaban socabando los cimientos de la casa... "No es posible vivir en esta negligencia," decia. "A este paso terminaremos devorados por las bestias." (290 & 291)
>
> (The life in her invincible heart oriented her in her darkness... She didn't need to see in order to know that the flower beds, planted so carefully during the first reconstruction...had been destroyed by the rains...that the walls and cement floors were cracked, the furniture worn and discolored, the doors unhinged, and the family threatened by a resignation and gloom which would have been unthinkable in her day. Feeling her way through the empty rooms, she could hear the continuous din of termites eating away at the wood, the clipping sound of moths in the closets, and the devastating clamor of enormous colored ants which had prospered in the deluge and which were digging into the cracked cement of the house... "It's impossible to live in this neglect," she would say. "At this rate, we will end up devoured by the beasts).

Just like her great-great-great grandmother, Amaranta Ursula, the last Buendía female, will once again restore and rejuvenate the house thirty pages later (327). All of this will prove futile, of course, for, as Ursula's words quoted above predict, at this rate of negligence and resignation, the Buendía house and family do indeed end up devoured by nature.

The theme of civilization versus "barbarie," of human beings versus the forces of nature, is a recurrent theme in Hispanic-American literature. The short stories of Horacio Quiroga, Sarmiento's *Facundo: civilización y barbarie*, and Ribera's *La vorágine*, for instance, come to mind right away. Summarizing this perspective, Michael Wood writes that geographically, Latin America "is a beautiful but hostile landscape which earlier fiction always represented as a killer."[16] Whereas North American literature is ambivalent in its treatment of nature, caught between the great drive to conquer and control nature versus guilt for having violated the purity and innocence of the natural state, Hispanic-American literature presents nature as an overwhelming force that ultimately envelops and swallows human attempts at civilization, attempts which, in this region, have all too often resulted, not in civilization, but in cruelty, injustice, oppression and destruction. Extending his analysis of nature in *La nueva novela hispanoamericana* to include sociological implications, Carlos Fuentes calls nature "an enigma which devours, destroying will and purpose, diminishing dignity and leading to annihilation." Ultimately, this writer and critic affirms, nature is the protagonist of a literature and of a social condition in which "it is better to be devoured by the jungle than to suffer a slow death in a society which is enslaved and cruel and bloodthirsty."[17]

Caught in a vicious cycle of social injustice and oppression, Macondo is overwhelmed by the cycle of a voracious nature which acts as metaphor for the social condition of Latin America. At once the center of the family and of the town, Ursula's house is finally destroyed by the apocalyptic winds which close the great cycle recreated by *Cien años de soledad*, a great cycle comprised of the original founding, the illusory development and the final destruction of Macondo and of the Buendías. "Like any human victim," says Palencia-Roth, "the house only waits for the 'biblical wind' which will wipe Macondo from the face of the earth, thereby completing the great circle of jungle-civilization-jungle." D. P. Gallagher says very simply, "Only nature is permanent. Ultimately, it is the cyclical rhythm of nature that predominates," while Robert Sims concentrates on the temporal element when he observes that "Nature assaults Macondo and separates it from time."[18] Perhaps the image that most graphically captures Ursula's role within the cyclical pattern of nature and of the Buendía house, is the thread of blood which runs from the body of her dead son José Arcadio. (121) Like an umbilical cord searching for its source, the trickle of José Arcadio's blood threads its way from his recently shot body, through streets and corridors and rooms, until it finds the mother Ursula, in the kitchen ready to break thirty-six eggs to make bread. Having found the body which gave it birth, José Arcadio's blood goes "in search of its origin" and returns to the dead body from which it flowed, thereby uniting the beginning and the end, and closing the cycle of life and death.

Although Ursula Buendía is the character who is most aware of the cyclical patterning which shapes the story of her family and the life of Macando, it is the fortune teller Pilar Ternera, the "other" mother figure, who provides the image of circularity and cyclical repetition which best illustrates the narrative movement and thematic development of *Cien años de soledad*. Making her as aware of this non-linearity as Ursula is only toward the end of the story, Pilar's powers of divination finally give her the necessary insight to propose the image of a gyrating wheel which would have spun eternally were it not for the irreparable breakdown of its central axis. Having just recognized the great-great grandson Aureliano coming into her brothel, and feeling that "time returned to its primordial sources," (342) Pilar realizes her full potential as fortune teller to Macondo and unsanctioned matriarch of the Buendía clan, when she thinks:

> No había ningún misterio en el corazón de un Buendía, que fuera impenetrable para ella, porque un siglo de naipes y de experiencias le había enseñado que la historia de la familia era un engranaje de repticiones irreparables, una rueda giratoria que hubiera seguido dando vueltas hasta la eternidad, de no haber sido por el desgaste progresivo e irremediable del eje. (343)

> (There was no mystery in the heart of a Buendía which was beyond her insight, because a century of cards and of experience had taught her that the history of the family was a gear of irreparable repetitions, a gyrating wheel which would have spun eternally, were it not for the progressive but irreparable breakdown of its central axle.)

Pilar's sense of primordial time as the final moments of Macondo's existence approach, joins the end to the beginning, joins "la última madrugada de Macondo" (357) ("the last dawn of Macondo") to its primordial founding, when

> Macondo era entonces una aldea de veinte casas de barra y cañabrava construidas a la orilla de un rio de aguas diáfanas que se precipitaban por un lecho de piedras pulidas, blancas y enormes como huevos prehistóricos. El mundo era tan reciente, que muchas cosas carecian de nombre, y para mencionarias había que señalarlas con el dedo. (9)

> (Macondo was then a village of twenty houses constructed of clay and wild cane on the edge of a river whose diaphanous waters rushed through a bed of polished rocks, enormous and white as prehistoric eggs. The world was so new, that many things lacked names and had to be indicated by pointing a finger.)

At once a fanciful parody of the Bible and of the Exploration of the New World, *Cien años de soledad* takes its characters to "la tierra que nadie les habia prometido." (27) ("the land no one had promised them"). Relating the founding of Macondo to the discovery of America, Robert Sims calls Macondo "a variant of the myth of the golden age," and says that its "story is written in the context of timelessness where the myth of Macondo as a golden age acquires a greater scope." Indeed, drawing on the ancient myth of a golden age and on the belief that this El Dorado lay in the Americas, García Márquez creates the myth of El Dorado unfulfilled or, as Laurence Porter terms it, "a lost paradise embodied in the family name Arcadio."[19] Tracing the trajectory of a human civilization according to the archetypal myth of creation-development-destruction, then, *Cien años de soledad*, follows the cyclical pattern of Pilar's "gyrating wheel." Encompassing this mythical cycle, the gyrating wheel contains within its perimeter the vicious, repetitive circularity which characterizes the seven generations of the fantastic and fanciful Buendía family. Its de-centered axle, irreparably worn by continuous vicious revolution, becomes the point that unites these cycles into one all-encompassing and eternal instant, conducting the human experience of one hundred years of solitude and constructing the literary creation of *Cien años de soledad*.

William Faulkner, as described previously, struggled against the sequential nature of language by employing complex and convoluted syntactical structures as well as a narrative ripple pattern in *Absalom, Absalom!*. Gabriel García Márquez, in his turn, neutralizes the linearity inherent in his simple, straightforward syntax, by employing fancifully exaggerated cyclical repetition and vicious circularity. Along with this cyclical patterning, which René Cuadra calls "the most existential and immediate way of living a-chronicity."[20] *Cien años de soledad* recasts linear chronology and conceptions of time and history into a synchronic patterning characterized by perfect, atemporal coincidence of all "times." Describing both of these patterns, Emir Rodríguez Monegal affirms that this novel is "heir to a narrative tradition in which time is alive and capricious, sometimes turning on itself, biting its own tail furiously, and other times lying dormant and totally immobile." Gregorio Salvador, in his turn, describes a time which "goes around in circles, that bites its own tail, that shatters and fragments itself, stationary, curved and circular."[21] Just as Ursula shapes the cyclical trajectory of the Buendía house and Pilar Ternera foretells the breakdown of the gyrating wheel, the third and most markedly "timeless" figure of the novel, Melquíades patterns the manuscripts of one hundred years of solitude according to the synchronicity of total and final existential revelation. While the two matriarchal figures embody cyclical time, the enigmatic gypsy Melquíades incorporates simultaneity and atemporality into his magical existence and his mysterious manuscripts. Written and contained within the room Ursula had constructed especially for him when she originally expanded the house (69), the manuscripts of the magical gypsy partake of the eternal fraction of time which characterizes this room, where "it is always March and always Monday." (303)

During his many alchemical experiments and parodic discoveries, the patriarch of the family, José Acadio Buendía, regretfully surmises that "la máquina del tiempo se ha descompuesto" ("the machine of time had broken down"), since, as far as he can surmise, in Macondo every day is Monday. (75) Fulfilling this patriarchal observation, Melquíades' room becomes the archetypal atemporal space within Ursula's cyclical house. Consequently, when the young Aureliano and his uncle José Arcadio Segundo look in, they "see" the figure of the gypsy and an eternal fraction of time:

> En el cuartito apartado, adonde nunca llegó el viento árido, ni el polvo ni el calor, ambos recordaban la visión atávica de un anciano con sombrero de alas de cuervo que hablaba del mundo...muchos años antes de que ellos nacieran. Ambos descubrieron al mismo tiempo que allí siempre era marzo y siempre el lunes, y entonces comprendieron que José Arcadio Buendía no estaba tan loco como contaba la familia, sino que era el único que habia dispuesto de bastante lucidez para vislumbrar la verdad de que también el tiempo sufria tropiezos y accidentes, y podía por tanto astillarse y dejar en un cuarto una fracción eternizada. (303)

> (In the remote room, where neither dry wind, nor dust, nor heat ever reached, both remembered the ancient vision of an old man wearing a hat adorned with crows wings, who spoke of the world... many years before they had been born. At the same time, both discovered that in that room it was always March and always Monday. Then they understood that José

Arcadio Buendía was not as crazy as the family said, but was the only one lucid enough to discern the truth, that time also stumbled and tripped, and that it could shatter and leave an eternal fraction within a room)

This fanciful but profound negation of the most basic notion of temporal chronology, obliterates traditional Western conceptions of cause-effect relationships. Moreover, the broken time machine, which turns out to be the irreparably worn axle of Pilar's gyrating wheel, expresses the redundant reality of a people living on the forgotten edge of a world dominated by Occidental thought and existence. Simultaneously, this broken and negated time recreates the synchronic dimensions of total human perception and revelation, the eternal instant in which, as Jorge Luis Borges might say, a person truly "knows" totality of being. Traditionally depicted as the moment of death, this eternal moment of totality occurs at the end of *Cien años de soledad*, as the last Buendía finally achieves a total vision of the eternal manuscripts and dies, at the same moment that Macondo is wiped from the face of the earth.

While in *Absalom, Absalom!* each re-telling of the Sutpen story both differs from the previous telling and also defers interpretation and meaning, the trajectory of García Márquez's novel moves inexorably toward synchronicity, toward the totality of human perception and self-knowledge which occurs with the prophetic revelation of the final paragraph. As the Apocalyptic winds begin to blow at the very end of the narrative, Aureliano discovers his destiny by finally succeeding in deciphering the prophetic manuscripts left by the enigmatic Melquíades:

> ...entonces sabía que en los pergaminos de Melquíades estaba escrito su destino...empezó a decifrarlos en voz alta. Era la historia de la familia, escrita por Melquíades hasta en sus detalles más triviales, con cien años de anticipación... Melquíades no había ordenado los hechos en el tiempo convencional de los hombres, sino que concentró un siglo de episodios cotidianos, de modo que todos coexistieran en un instante...saltó once páginas...y empezó a descifrar el instante que estaba viviendo, descifrándolo a medida que lo vivía, profetizándose a si mismo en el acto de descifrar la última página de los pergaminos. (358-60)

> (...he then knew that his destiny was written in the manuscripts of Melquíades...he began to decipher them out loud. It was the history of the family, written by Melquíades even in its most trivial details, one hundred years before...Melquíades had not ordered the events within conventional human time, but had instead concentrated a century of daily episodes so that they coexisted within one instant...he skipped eleven pages...and began to decipher the very instant he was living, deciphering it as he lived it, prophesying his own existence as he deciphered the last page of the manuscripts.)

Given the temporal simultaneity which characterizes the narrative discourse of *Cien años de soledad*, it is not surprising that this end (*present* time) of Macondo should be contained within the prophetic (*future*) writings of Melquíades, which simultaneously contain the origins (*past*) of Aureliano, the last Buendía, finally deciphering the last page of the enigmatic manuscripts within the last paragraph of the novel.

This macrocosmic simultaneity, which encompasses the total experience of a people, of a "race condemned to one hundred years of solitude," is recreated on a microcosmic and individual level through the very first sentence of the novel. In fact, the very first sentence of *Cien años de soledad* sets this precedent of temporal simultaneity by recreating a-historical synchronicity, as Colonel Aureliano Buendía re-lives a key *past* experience (his father taking him to see ice for the first time), which he will remember in the *future* whenever he recalls this moment in the *present*. Thus begins the story of "one hundred years of solitude": "Muchos años después, frente al pelotón de fusilamiento, el coronel Aureliano Buendía habia de recordar aquella tarde remota en que su padre lo llevó a conocer el hielo." (9) ("Many years later, facing the firing squad, Colonel Aureliano Buendía would remember that distant afternoon when his father took him to see ice for the first time.") This syntactical and temporal patterning recurs throughout the text, as the narrator refers to *key moments* in the various characters' lives, moments which live on in memory and consciousness, moments which unite past, present and future, moments of perfect existential coincidence.

In addition, this very first sentence sets the precedent followed throughout *Cien años de soledad* of rendering in a literal manner a metaphorical image, a technique mentioned earlier in this study with respect to the seventeen Aurelianos. In this first sentence, the image of ice is especially significant and noteworthy, for it congeals memory, i.e. human time, forever. The symbolic meaning of this element has been described by J. E. Cirlot as follows:

> Given that water is the symbol of communication between the formal and informal, the element of transition between different cycles, it follows that ice represents principally two things: first, the change induced by the cold, that is, the "congelation" of its symbolic significance; and secondly, the stultification of the potentialities of water. Hence ice has been defined as the rigid dividing-line between consciousness and unconsciousness.[22]

Couched within a syntagm which, as has been discussed, depicts-temporal simultaneity on a syntactical level, ice represents the mediating element between the conscious and the unconscious, between diachronic and synchronic perception, i.e. perceptive simultaneity on a symbolic level. Phenomenologically, it is the frozen moment of remembered experience which divides unconscious reality from conscious reality, which divides the a-historical origins of human existence from the historical past of the race. And thirdly, on a semantic level, the first sentence of this novel joins history - in a figure taken from the military ranks of Latin America's civil wars between liberals and conservatives, the liberal Colonel Aureliano - with the a-historical and archetypal - "that afternoon" of experiencing ice when "the world was so new" and Aureliano was an innocent child.

Numerous critics have pointed out the significance of this first sentence to the novel as a whole. René Cuadra, for example, observes that "the entire novel is structured according to the sentence which begins the story."[23] Mario Vargas Llosa speaks of this syntactical structure in circular terms, and finds that its circularity is characteristic of the principal episodes and of the entire narrative structure of the novel:

> Almost all the units (episodes in their own right) correspond to this circular temporal construction: movement to the future, movement back to a remote past and, from there, a linear trajectory until reaching the moment which opened the unit; the episode bites its own tail, begins and ends in the same place, suggests the notion of totality, of something finished and sufficient unto itself which inspires the circle.[24]

Zunilda Gertel finds, in her turn, that "the syntagmatic components of the initial paragraph function as crystalized, correlated paradigms throughout the novel, thereby closing the fundamental cycles of the novel." Viewing the novel in terms of the Colonel, she goes on to explain that three parallel paradigms occur exactly a) at the beginning of the book; b) at a crucial instant in the life of Colonel Aureliano (p. 115); and c) at his death, as nostalgic memory when he sees the gypsies for the last time (p. 229). According to Gertel, then, the novel would be divided into three paradigmatic cycles: a world of myth (pp. 9-115); an historical world (pp. 116-229); and the return to a world of myth (pp. 230-251), cycles which correspond to "three parallel and key moments in the life of Colonel Aureliano."[25] By utilizing a semiotic perspective and focusing on syntagmatic and paradigmatic parallelism, Gertel follows the cyclical trajectory of nature-culture-nature. The Cuban writer Alejo Carpentier seems to unite the cyclical and synchronic patterning I have been discussing, as he describes the world of Latin America by superimposing the natural cyclical patterning of the physical world onto a synchronic layering of different epochs. While describing the magically real, he affirms that in

> Latin America everything is outsized and disproportionate; towering mountains and waterfalls, endless plains, impenetrable jungles. An anarchic urban sprawl overlies breathless virgin expanses. The ancient rubs elbows with the new, the archaic with the futuristic, the technological with the feudal, the prehistoric with the utopic. In our cities skyscrapers stand side by side with Indian markets that sell totemic amulets.[26]

In addition, the cyclical motion and simultaneous patterning which characterize this text, lead to final revelation and point to a recurrent theme within *Cien años de soledad* specifically, and within Latin American literature in general. While North American literature, as already discussed, is centrally concerned with innocence and loss of innocence, Latin American literature is predominantly concerned with the search for identity, on both an individual and collective level. Speaking of both *Pedro Párma* by the Mexican Juan Rulfo and *Cien años de soledad*, Suzanne Jill Levine observes that "the search for identity that both novels, present is not just a search for personal and family identity, but also for national and cultural identity."[27] The apparent obsession with history, with the retelling of the past in ways and modes that differ from traditional and officially sanctioned accounts is, indeed, an attempt to discover the personal and national identity of a people too long silenced by dominant Western rationalist culture, of a people too long resigned and passive and unable to find their own voice. Called "the great Latin American novel" by many, and "a metaphor for Latin America" by García Márquez himself,[28] *Cien años de soledad* is a search for identity which, within the magical space of Macondo and the mythical hundred-years' time, encompasses a continent and the lifespan of a civilization. Focused, of course, on the enigmatic manuscripts written by Melquíades in Sanskrit, one of the first languages within the Indo-European family of languages, this search becomes a search for "the origin of Spanish linguistic genealogy."[29] Throughout the novel, various of the Buendía male descendants occupy the gypsy's timeless room in order to attempt to decipher his elusive manuscripts. A mystery on both a linguistic and temporal level, the manuscripts prove indecipherable because they are written in the ancient language of Sanskrit and according to temporal simultaneity. Ultimately unlocking the origins of human expression and the totality of human experience, the last Buendía finally deciphers the prophetic manuscripts and discovers his personal and collective identity. Contained within a prophecy, moreover, this identity and history is transformed into a warning, a vision of a dark *future* contained within an ignoble *past* and *present*.

This fundamentally cyclical and synchronic patterning of narrative discourse is, nevertheless, in constant play with the diachronic dimensions of a novel which recounts the chronological trajectory of Macondo and of the Buendía family. In fact, the narrative development of this novel is apparently sequential, as it takes the reader through the various developmental phases of Macondo, phases which mirror the history of Columbia and, by analogy, the history of all Latin America. Contrary to the fragmented and unsequential piecing together of the past which creates the narrative ripples of *Absalom, Absalom!*, *Cien años de soledad* follows a sequential pattern that traces Macondo's history, from its primordial founding to its eventual apocalyptic destruction. Arriving in a "tierra que nadie les habia prometido" (27) ("land no one had promised them"), the Buendía patriarch and matriarch found a race whose history at once imitates biblical eschatological direction and parodies the story of Genesis to Apocalypse. In the end, the prophecy of *Cien años de soledad* reveals that, for Latin America, the discovery and founding of the Americas have not led, by any means, to a "new Jerusalem."

Briefly, the phases of Latin American history recounted within this novel can be listed and summarized as: the establishment of a patriarchal regime, led by José Arcadio Buendía; the instillation of civil and religious authorities; the breaking out of civil wars between liberals and conservatives; and the neo-colonial period of banana fever, based on the period from the establishment of the United Fruit Company in Colombia in 1899 to the violent repression of its worker's strikes in the region of Magdalena in 1928. Numerous critics have delineated and analyzed the diachronic dimensions of this novel, which is now "required reading in many Latin American history and political science courses."[30] Among them, Lucila Inés Mena presents a lengthy and informative analysis in her book *La función de la historia en Cien años de soledad* and Roberto González Echevarria, focusing on the Latin American novel's "obsession with history and myth," describes the historical trajectory of García Márquez's famous work in the following manner:

> ...there is lurking in the background of the story the overall pattern of Latin American history, both as a general design made up of various key events and eras, and in the presence of specific characters and incidents that seem to refer to real people and happenings. Thus we have a period of discovery and conquest, when José Arcadio Buendía and the original families settle Macondo. There is in this part of the book little sense that Macondo belongs to a larger political unit, but such isolation was in fact typical of Latin America's towns in the colonial period. Even the viceroyalites lived in virtual isolation from the metropolitan government. The appearance of Apolinar Moscoso and his barefoot soldiers is the beginning of the republican era, which is immediately followed by the outbreak of the civil wars in which Colonel Aureliano Buendía distinguishes himself. Though Colombia is the most obvious model for this period, nearly the entire continent suffered from civil strife during the nineteenth century, a process that led to the emergence of dictators and *caudillos*. This period is

followed by the era of neocolonial domination by the United States and the struggle against it in most Latin American countries. These culminate in the novel with the general strike and the massacre of the workers. There are, unfortunately, countless models for this last, clearly defined period in the novel. After the flood, there is a time of decay before the apocalyptic wind that razes the town at the end.[31]

While Ursula's house and Pilar's gyrating wheel express cyclical patterning, and Melquíades' manuscripts embody synchronic patterning, the image of the Buendía patriarch, José Arcadio Buendía, tied to the chestnut tree in the family yard depicts the fate of genealogy and linearity within *Cien años de soledad*, a novel which at once chronicles the founding of America and traces the family tree of its founders.[32] Called a "genealogical and a philological emblem" by Anibal González, the tree to which the founder of the Buendía line is tied, symbolizes the axis of the world and the presence of a center, along with representing the phallus as well as the virility and creative action of the male, according to Graciela Maturo.[33] Significantly, José Arcadio Buendía is forcibly tied to the tree when the discovery that in Macondo every day is Monday since the "máquina del tiempo" is broken, leads him into a destructive rampage, indicative of the frustration which results from the lack of scientific development and technological progress which characterizes some regions of the Americas.

> Entonces agarró la tranca de una puerta y con la violencia salvaje de su fuerza descomunal destrozó hasta conventirlos en polvo los aparatos de alquimía, el gabinete de daguerrotipía, el taller de orfebrería, gritando como un endemoniado en un idioma altisonante y fluido pero completament incomprensible. Se disponia a terminar con el resto de la casa cuando Aureliano pidió ayuda a los vecinos. Se necesitaron diez hombres para tumbarlo, catorce para amarrarlo, veinte para arrastrarlo hasta el castaño del patio, donde lo dejaron atado, ladrando en lengua extraña y echando espumarajos verdes por la boca. (76-7)

(He then grabbed the lock on one of the doors and, with a savage violence proportionate to his unusual strength, destroyed his alchemy utensils, the daguerreotype closet and the gold shop, crying insanely in a resonant and fluid but totally incomprehensible language. He was about to destroy the rest of the house when Aureliano asked the neighbors for help. It took ten men to stop him, fourteen to tie him and twenty to drag him to the chestnut tree in the yard, where they left him tied, barking in a strange language and foaming at the mouth.)

While, as we have seen, genealogy and a "clean," i.e. "white," linearity define Sutpen's design and reason for being in *Absalom, Absalom!*, family lines and genealogy are put "outside" and out of the way early in *Cien años de soledad*, only to be followed by prolific and promiscuous procreation. Himself a searcher and researcher, José Arcadio's tirade can be interpreted as the frustrated scientist's reaction to "a whole continent which resists assimilation into the Western race to progress," as Patricia Tobin puts it, and into Western conceptions of time and history. Speaking of a genealogical enterprise which is emptied of authority by the language and style of *Cien años de soledad*, Tobin goes on to say that "fatherhood is denied any metaphorical significance in this text." As traditional historical and patriarchal systems break down, including the "vicious circularity of civil wars" (124) which traps Colonel Aureliano Buendía and the military, the ultimate patriarchal system, the novel, says Tobin, "is fused once more to organic life, as lived beyond and before paternal deliberation." By rejecting "the paternal guarantee of knowledge and by embracing the whole immediacy of everything," concludes Tobin, García Márquez "has severed the novel from its hidden alliance with knowledge and fused it once more to organic life, as it is lived beyond and before paternal deliberation." Affirming "circular rhythms of the cosmos over linear history,"[34] then *Cien años de soledad* by Gabriel García Márquez expresses the reality and consciousness of Latin Americans for whom, according to Jaime Mejia Duque, "history is not linear."[35] In the end, the apparent chronology of this text proves, of course, to be illusory. Just as the Aureliano of the last paragraph re-lives the redundant and enlightening experience of totality that Colonel Aureliano experiences in the first sentence of the novel, the various generations of the Buendía family re-live varying experiences of redundancy and degrees of enlightenment. Tied to and devoured by nature, the Buendía family fulfill the prophecy of Melquíades' manuscripts in which, for a "prodigious instant," the beginning and the end is revealed to the last Aureliano, as he deciphers the magical phrase pronouncing the fate of the Buendía genealogical enterprise: "*El primero de la estripe está amarrado en un árbol y el último se lo están comiendo las hormigas."* (358) (*"The first of the line is tied to a tree and the last is being eaten by ants."*) This revelatory phrase refers, of course, to Aureliano's great-great-great grandfather and to his and Amaranta Ursula's infant son, born only to be eaten by the enormous colored ants.

Comparative analyses of the work of William Faulkner and Gabriel García Márquez have often devoted attention to *La hojarasca* (*Leaf Storm*) the Columbian writer's first novel published in 1955. In this work, García Márquez first creates Macondo, a region whose narrative import will come to stand next to that of Yoknapatawpha County, and experiments with multiple narrators trapped in the circularity of their psychological labryinths. Recalling *As I Lay Dying* as they revolve around the dead body of the town doctor lying in his casket awaiting burial, the interior monologues of the Colonel, Isabel and Isabel's young son represent three generations which together give narrative expression to their individual realities and to the history of Macondo. Having **discovered** the world of Macondo, Gabriel García Márquez's writing seems to **uncover** a "world of circularity, as it **recovers** a range of significance traditionally attributed to the circle.

The circle as a closed and static, stagnant space which traps and retards expresses the reality of Macondo from its creation within García Márquez's work. Macondo, of course, proves to be a world within which its citizens feel as if they are "flotando en circulos concéntricos dentro de un estanque de gelatina," ("floating in concentric circles within a pond of gelatin"), words which describe the condition of the Colonel and his wife desperately "rotting alive"[36] and waiting fifty years for his military pension which never arrives in *El colonel no tiene quiene le escriba* (*No One Writes to the Colonel*) published in 1957. In *Cien años de soledad* ten years later, the feeling of being trapped within the vicious circularity of repetitive stasis and static repetition is expanded to express the redundant human experience of all "estirpes condenadas a cien años de soledad" (306) ("races condemned to one hundred years of solitude"). In García Márquez's famous novel, moreover, this vicious circularity is as much a result of oppressive socio-political regimes and foreign neo-colonial exploitation, as it is a result of the passive forgetfulness and resigned acceptance of its people, as can be seen by

Macondo's ready acceptance of the "official" proclamation denying the massacre of 3,000 banana plantation workers and by the insomnia plague during which everyone has to be reminded of the most elementary details of every day life, like the fact that cows give milk which, when mixed with coffee, makes "café con leche." Macondo is certainly guilty of forgetfulness, the most unpardonable sin according to traditional belief and myth.[37]

The short story "Los funerales de la Mama Grande" is the first work by this Columbian writer into which magical and fantastic elements are interwoven. Within this narrative, published in 1962, circularity becomes "una intrincada maraña de consanguinidad que convertió la procreación en un círculo vicioso" ("an intricate tangle of consanguinity which transformed procreation into a vicious circle"). The death and funeral of the long-lived and powerful matriarch around whom all creation revolved, prompts "algunos de los alli presentes...(a) comprender que estaban asistiendo al nacimiento de una nueva época"[38] ("some of those present to understand that they were present at the birth of a new era"), thereby reflecting the potential for renewal inherent to the cyclical motion of the circle. Five years later, the cyclical patterning of *Cien años de soledad* springs from the traditional paradigm of periodic renewal attributed to the cycle of nature and the physical world. Because "cyclical time is periodic," the final destruction and disappearance of Macondo "implies a new beginning,"[39] as Julio Ortega puts it. Although implied but not contained in the novel, renewal is so basic to cyclical motion that García Márquez himself quoted Faulkner's own Nobel acceptance phrase, "I decline to accept the end of men," as he himself accepted the Nobel prize in 1982; he then ended by envisioning "a new and sweeping utopia of life, where no one will be able to decide for others how they die, where love will prove true and happiness be possible, and where the races condemned to one hundred years of solitude will have, at last and forever, a second opportunity on earth."[40]

Simultaneous to circularity as entrapment within vicious repetition and as potential for cyclical renewal, *Cien años de soledad*, the innovative and audacious novel which García Márquez published in 1967, presents circularity as the moment of total vision and perception, as the instant of complete self-knowledge and identity. Reflecting the existential preoccupation of other twentieth-century writers, this instant could be called "the ultimate epiphany" in James Joyce's terms, "the ultimate moment of being" for Virginia Woolf, the ultimate "momento privilegiado" for the Brazilian writer Clarice Lispector, or the perfect "Aleph of time"[41] for Jorge Luís Borges, the influential Argentinian writer whom many critics relate to García Márquez's writing and to twentieth-century Hispanic American writing in general. In his own work, Borges himself returns constantly to a traditional image of circularity, ⊙, the point within a circle. A symbol which first appears, according to Georges Poulet, in "a pseudo-hermetic manuscript of the twelfth century," the circle with the point in the middle represents God, "a sphere whose center is everywhere and whose circumference is nowhere."[42] In discussing *Cien años de soledad*, critics have readily acknowledged its basic circularity and many have spoken in terms which recall the circle with the point in the middle. Ricardo Gullon, for example, says that "the novel has the circular and dynamic structure of a 'gyrating wheel;'" Robert Sims emphasizes this wheel's "immobile center" and "revolving perimeter," while Vargas Llosa describes "a great circle composed of numerous concentric circles, contained one within the others."[43]

However, the gyrating wheel of *Cian años de soledad* is characterized by a broken axle which ultimately causes it to spin itself into oblivion, i.e., causes the cyclical stasis of Macondo to spin off-center and disappear from the face of the earth. Whereas Faulkner's ripples de-center narrative circularity by multiplying and expanding circularity to infinite proportions, García Márquez's gyrating wheel spins off-center due to its vicious repetitive oscillations. Contained within a prophecy, this gyrating wheel obliterates human forgetfulness and unconsciousness of social injustice and evil, as it simultaneously becomes a warning to races which neglect and forget, races which accept official manipulation and political oppression. So constructed, it becomes "la márquina de memoria" (49) which José Arcadio had tried but failed to invent for his family and for Macondo; so shaped, it reflects the historical frustration and a-historical reality of human experience in Latin America. Uniting the beginning and the end, Genesis and Apocalypse, the dark point at the top of the diagram I propose, represents the worn axle of an elliptical trajectory which ultimately obliterates time and space, in the guise of the Buendía family and the region of Macondo. At the same time, this point represents the all-encompassing *present* moment of temporal simulaneity and total self-knowledge, containing within itself all *past* and *future*. In its turn, the parameters of the larger outer circle expand to paradigmatic proportions through the magically archetypal evocation of "100 years," while the solitude of Latin American existence goes in circles endlessly, simultaneously following the trajectory of the seven generations of the Buendía family and tracing the various cycles of collective history which characterize this region. So dominant, however, is projection into the future, the narrative mode of a novel which is in the end a prophecy, a warning to be deciphered, that the circularity of *Cien años de soledad* "ends up" pointing to the possibility of natural cyclical renewal, the dotted line leading out of the a-temporal point in my diagram.

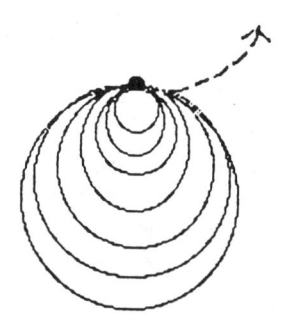

"una rueda giratoria"

Cien años de soledad

As with *Absalom, Absalom!*, the circularity of *Cien años de soledad* implicates the reader for, as the last Buendía succeeds in deciphering the prophetic manuscripts, the reader of this novel also participates in an "instant" of total vision, i.e. the completion of the novel. Contrary to the partial nature of the interpretative process in *Absalom, Absalom!*, then, the reader of *Cien años de soledad*, along with Aureliano, assumes the vantage point of paradigmatic synchronicity reflected in the circular totality of the eternal instant of revelation. From this vantage point, the reader also has a total vision and experience of the fundamental tension between the historical and a-historical dimensions of the text, as the novel unabashedly challenges its reader to participate in the pleasantly playful yet philosophically profound erasure of clear distinctions between "reality" and "fiction." Indicating just how central this ontological game is to his work, García Márquez himself, as noted in chapter 2, describes his greatest problem as that of "destroying the line separating what seems real from what seems fantastic."[44] Examples of the novel as game appear both in the title, where the word "SOLƎDAD," written with a backward E, is "an invitation to play"[45] according to José Antonio Bravo; and within the text itself. As the last Aureliano becomes more and more enlightened, he realizes that literature is "el mejor juguete que se había inventado para burlarse de la gente." (337) ("the best game ever invented to make fun of people.") Ironically enough, it is the playful and fanciful aspects of this novel which have made it a literary phenomenon, "one of those very rare cases of a major contemporary work which everyone can read, understand and enjoy,"[46] as Vargas Llosa puts it.

Indeed, as circularity and simultaneity break down the barriers between history and synchronicity, and between "reality" and "fiction," the narrative discourse of *Cien años de soledad* plays with the reader by mixing historical figures, both human and numerical, with imaginary recreations. Exemplifying the former, García Márquez himself (336-49), his "real-life" wife Mercedes (394) and actual situations from his "real life" appear and participate in the novel, as do fictional characters from novels by the Latin American writers Alejo Carpentier, Carlos Fuentes and Julio Cortázar. An example of numerical play would be the very significant number of massacred strikers taken away after Macondo's banana strike, a number which is slowly forgotten by Macondo's survivors, as they passively accept the false but official story which "los historiadores habian admitido y consagrado en los textos escolares," (303) ("historians had admitted and made official within school textbooks"). In the end, the event is totally erased from the characters' minds, a case of fiction being erased from fictional characters' minds if we take into account the historically "real" sources of this important episode. In an interview, García Márquez explains how reality became fiction for this episode, and how, in true Marquezian circular fashion, fiction became reality once again:

> That episode didn't come from any story telling. It is, more or less based on historical reality. The reasons, the motives and the manner in which the events around the strike occurred were exactly as in the novel - though there were not 3000 dead, of course. There were very few deaths. If 100 people had been killed in 1928, it would have been catastrophic. I made the death toll 3000 because I was using certain proportions in my book. One hundred wouldn't have been noticed. I was also interested in achieving a certain imagery; I wanted the bodies to be taken away in a train, a train such as the ones that were loaded with clusters of bananas. I did research and found that to fill such a train, you'd need at least 3000 bodies... Let me tell you something very curious about that incident. Nobody has studied the events around the real banana strike - and now when they talk about it in the newspapers, even once in the congress, they speak about the *3000* who died! And I wonder if, with time, it will become true that 3000 were killed.[47]

Affirming the precedence and predominance of the imaginary in yet another interview, and asserting its importance for the Latin American narrative, García Márquez declares: "Yo creo que este sistema de explotación de la realidad, sin prejuicios racionalistas, le abren a nuestra novela una perspectiva espléndida. Y no se crea que es un método escapista: tarde o temprano, la realidad termina por darle la razón a la imaginación." ("I believe that this system of exploiting reality, by forgetting rationalist biases, offers our novel a splendid perspective. And I don't believe this to be an escapist method: sooner or later, reality has to admit that the imagination is right [translated literally, 'that imagination has reason']"). Very simply, this writer says: "Lo único que sé sin ninguna duda es que la realidad no termina en el precio de los tomates."[48] ("All I know for sure is that reality doesn't begin and end with the price of tomatoes.")

As the reader participates in this real/fantastic game, the novel partakes of total circularity and shapes Latin American history according to the circular paradigm, retelling the history of *this* America in a different mode from that which has traditionally dominated the Western world, including North America, with its linear paradigm focused on progress and the future. Gerald Martin offers this appraisal of Latin American experience in relation to Occidental tradition and development which is symbolized by the various objects mentioned:

> Conceived by Spain in the sixteenth century (the stranded galleon, the buried suit of armour), the characters awaken in the late eighteenth century Enlightment (magnet and telescope as symbols of the two pillars of Newtonian physics), but are entirely unable to bring themselves into focus in a world they have not made.[49]

In his Nobel prize acceptance speech, Gabriel García Márquez himself devotes special attention to this issue, which he calls "the lack of conventional means for expressing Latin American reality" as he relates it to the all-encompassing theme of *Cien años de soledad*, the theme of human solitude. Describing the "outsized reality" of Latin America, at the same time that he focuses the central concern and "quest for our own identity," he says that

> our crucial problem has been a lack of conventional means to render our lives believable. This, my friends, is the crux of our solitude. And if these difficulties, whose essence we share, hinder us, it is understandable that the rational talents on this side of the world, exalted in the contemplation of their own cultures, should have found themselves without a valid means to interpret us. It is only natural that they insist on measuring us with the yardstick that they use for themselves, forgetting that the ravages of life are not the same for all, and that the quest for our own identity is just as arduous and bloody for us as it was for them. The interpretation of our reality through patterns not our own serves only to make us ever more unknown, ever less free, ever more solitary.[50]

Isolated, then, within their individual and collective circle of solitude, Latin Americans live to the ultimate degree the universal human experience of solitude, of knowing that it is impossible to ever know a person completely.[51] Within a novel which makes its characters "bite into the bitter fruit of shared solitude," as Emir Rodríguez Monegal puts it, the "humorous and playful style" of this novel is paradoxically constructed from "the saddest, most solitary and most lucid gaze."[52] Trapping his unforgettable characters within the circle of human solitude, Gabriel García Márquez presents "a vision of humans abandoned to total earthly solitude,"[53] in the words o Zunilda Gertel. In so doing, he creates the "labyrinth of solitude" which the

Mexican writer and thinker, Octavio Paz, had described in his classic study published in 1950, a labyrinth within which García Márquez's characters suffer the "sleep of one hundred years" of solitude, as Paz had put it seventeen years before *Cien años de soledad* was published. While describing the universal experience of solitude in our modern de-centered world, Paz joins Latin American experience to that of the Western World when he affirms that today "we are all at the edge, because the center has disappeared."[54] As the gyrating wheel of *Cien años de soledad* describes its vicious circular trajectory, its central axle wears down and becomes de-centered, simultaneously spinning Macondo right off the face of the earth and creating an unforgettable circular experience of solitude in America and in the modern world.

CHAPTER VI

A "SPIRAL ON A SQUARE"

In a 1974 interview, the Brazilian writer Osman Lins describes his most ambitious work, the novel *Avalovara* published in 1973. While rejecting the *nouveau roman* as too "intellectual and civilized," yet acknowledging "something of the intellectual" in his own work, Lins strongly affirms his "primitiveness" and attraction to the "instinctual" and "incomprehensible in life," as he explains his view of the modern novel thus:

> ...if we are more or less familiar with the great novelists, if we know Sterne along with some texts by Diderot (who was a faithful reader of Sterne's), if we know Joyce, Virginia Woolf, William Faulkner, there is nothing to be surprised about: the current revolution in the novel didn't start with the *nouveau roman*. Not only that. The *nouveau roman* is an intellectual and civilized current. While something of an intellectual, I am a primitive, in the sense that instincts, the basic elements of life, the incomprehensible are what count in my view. This is more or less what happened with Faulkner and with Joyce. Their work is, at one and the same time, very innovative and very archaic.

As interest in his work increased among French critics and readers, Lins was interviewed in Paris during the following year. At this time, he described the difference between Joyce's work and his own by explaining that "Joyce, above all, explored language and words. My work is primarily directed toward the structure of the novel and toward the construction of characters." Earlier, Osman Lins had already emphasized his great preoccupation with narrative structure when he compared his work to that of another famous twentieth-century Brazilian writer, João Guimarães Rosa, in the following manner: "The focus of Guimarães Rosa's work is on syntax and on lexicology, while mine is on structure." Once again considering Faulkner in a 1976 interview, Lins states categorically that "with respect to *Avalovra*...the structure of the text has nothing to do with the novels of Joyce or of Faulkner."[1]

While such a point-blank denial can be understood in terms of this writer's desire to affirm his technical and literary independence, the declaration that the structure of *Avalovara* has "nothing" to do with the novels of two acknowledged "giants" of twentieth-century narrative seems exaggerated at first. Ultimately, such a statement stems from the great emphasis Lins has placed on narrative structure and construction, an emphasis which has led him to view his fictional trajectory as distinct from other twentieth-century narrators. In fact, though, an analysis of Faulkner's work reveals that his experimentation with multiple narrative perspectives and viewpoints led ultimately to marked re-elaboration and innovation in terms of narrative structure. A mere mention of the time references and narrative voices which structure *The Sound and the Fury* readily exemplifies the strides this North American author took in terms of shaping the development of twentieth-century narrative structure and construction. With respect to *Absalom, Absalom!*, considered by many to be Faulkner's most significant single work, the ripple pattern I have described is the basis from which the entire novel evolves and develops. Contrary to what the Brazilian author Osman Lins affirms, furthermore, I would argue that both Faulkner's *Absalom, Absalom!* and his own *Avalovara*, like García Márquez's *Cien años de soledad*, are shaped and formed according to circularity, presented in tension and contention with linearity. As already discussed, in *Absalom, Absalom!* the ripple pattern of the multiple narrative voices and an overwhelming desire for joining and connecting, are in constant tension with the linearity of Sutpen's design and with the search for the authority of genealogical and narrative lineage. *Cien años de soledad*, in its turn, parodies the linear paradigm which has dominated Western conceptions of time, as it gives voice to those that had previously been silenced and retells Latin

American history according to the circular paradigm of natural cyclical motion.

The work of Osman Lins is also profoundly affected by the cyclical repetition of nature. This writer, however, takes a step further and expands the rhythms of nature to the entire cosmos. So pronounced has been Lins' preoccupation with cosmology, that his work has prompted one critic, Anatal Rosenfeld to speak of "cosmocentrism." Exhibiting a post-humanist perspective, Lins' writing moves beyond anthropocentrism and depicts human experience as part of the universe and cosmos:

> Undoubtedly a privileged being, the *homo sapiens* is, nevertheless, a being among others, frail and precarious, removed from his central position in the universe. Since the Renaissance, he had been accustomed to conceive the universe after his own image, placing himself before it, building systems after his own. The universe was part of man, not man part of the universe. To describe Osman Lin's world, we may, perhaps employ the term "cosmocentrism" instead of anthropocentrism.[2]

Osman Lins' own words corroborate such an observation. Different from Faulkner's preoccupation with human psychic processes and obsessions, this writer says of his own work: "Little attention is given to psychology: I want to expand my focus to the world and not limit it to the enclosed space of psychic problems."[3] Defining "artistic activity" as "the triumph of the cosmos over chaos"[4] and fiction as "a personal vision of the world, often absurd and almost always strange, which becomes confused with the universe which we all inhabit,"[5] Osman Lins affirms writing to be for him a cosmology, and then goes on to describe the process whereby a literary **work** becomes a **literary world**, i.e. primordial chaos is transformed into cosmic order, in the following manner:

> The cosmos is ordered. Narrative form is a cosmology. As I see it: the world exists, words exist, as does our experience of the world and our experience of words. And all of this has order, is a cosmos. At the moment a writer sits before the blank page to write his book, his narrative, words explode and he is once again before the chaos of the world and the chaos of words, to which he will give order. Once again, chaos will be transformed into a cosmos.[6]

Whereas the circularity of Faulkner's *Absalom, Absalom!* focuses on the world of the human psyche and that of García Márquez's *Cien años de soledad* portrays a fancifully portentous cycle of human civilization, circularity in Lins' *Avalovara* projects human artistic creation onto the universe and cosmos. Signaling this conjunction of cosmological order and aesthetic creation, the narrator of *Avalovara* observes that "Enquanto o sol avança nos degraus estelares do zodíaco...rege o nosso romance uma mecânica que se pretende tão rígida quanto a que move os astros." (71) ("While the sun advances along the stellar houses of the zodiac..our novel follows a mechanical order which attempts to be as rigid as that which governs the heavenly bodies.") From the tragic House of Sutpen, to the mythic cycle of the Buendia House, we come to the cosmic cycle of the Houses of the Zodiac, as these novels of the Americas interweave the symbol and function of the dwelling place of humans - the house - with the variable form and dynamics of circularity. From a spreading ripple pattern in Yoknapatawpha, to the elliptical spinning motion of Macondo, we come to a spiral labyrinth animating the cosmos and guiding the narrative trajectory of this Brazilian novel, a trajectory which creates what Julia Cuervo Hewitt calls a "Dantean voyage to the transcendental depths of the cosmos."[7]

The reference to Dante is not gratuitous, for Lins himself relates the structure of this novel, where the number of lines per chapter follows pre-established patterns of 12's and 20's, to the rigor of *The Divine Comedy* and to the inspiration of its author. As an epigraph to *Avalovara*, Lins unites cosmology and Dantean rigor; from Mircea Fliade's *The Sacred and the Profane* we read that "every construction or creation has as its model cosmogony," and from E. R. Curtius' analysis of *The Divine Comedy* we learn that "Units of three's and ten's weave themselves into the whole Numbers, in this case,...are symbolic of cosmic order."[8] Notwithstanding what he himself calls a "rational and rigorous composition," Lins affirms that the inspiration and general idea of the novel preceded its structure and stemmed from his desire to write "a novel which would evoke cosmological myths and, at the same time, be related to the act of writing...to both artistic fulfillment and to human fulfillment through love."[9]

In conjunction with these cosmological, aesthetic and human concerns, it is the dynamics of the spiral that impels this novelist to his fictional creation and acts as the "força motriz" (19) ("motivating force") of *Avalovara*, a narrative which is, as defined by the text itself, a "simulacro de uma ordem que intuimos e da qual somos nostálgicos." (48) ("simulacrum of an order which we intuit and of which we are nostalgic"). Upon publication of his collection of essays entitled *Guerra Sem Testemunhas* (*War Without Witnesses*) in 1969, Lins refers to his next project - which will become *Avalovara* - as a "novel about which I have thought for a few years and whose structure will be related to that of a spiral. Some geometric figures," he goes on to say, "really fascinate me."[10] When *Avalovara* was finally published in 1973, Lins elaborated on the meaning and function of the spiral formation by affirming that:

> I've always been preoccupied by the spiral. Then I found out that the periwinkle, upon which this form is etched, was a symbol of the human being to the ancients - the mollusc which is removed from the shells would be the soul which leaves the body. The shell which some peoples placed with the bodies of their dead, represented - due to their spiral shapes - the human aspiration for the infinite.[11]

Avalovara vibrates with varied circular objects and symbols, examples of which might be: "uma carrossel que range em torno do eixo" (15) ("a carrousel which grinds around an axle"); "o eixo do pião japonês ...com...a mola enroscada pronta a disparar" (57) ("the axle of the Japanese top...with...its spring wound and ready to spin"); and "uma grande roda cor de prata...girando na praia" (212) ("a huge silver-colored wheel revolving on the beach"). Similar to the gyrating wheel of *Cien años de soledad*, in fact, the spinning movement of these and other circular objects both traces and echoes the spiral pattern which shapes and orders *Avalovara*. As the text itself concedes, moreover, this spiral pattern is basic to nature and forms countless natural phenomenon: "Outras ilações pressentimos ainda entre as figidias naturazas da espiral...nas conchas dos moluscos, nos ciclones, bem como em chifres de caprídeos, de ovídeos e de antílopes." (73) ("We discern other conclusions from the evanescent nature of the spiral...in the shells of molluscs, in cyclones as well as in the horns of caprids [goats], ovinæ [sheep] and antelopes.")[12]

The spiral formation discussed earlier with respect to the image of the umbilical cord in *Absalom, Absalom*, takes on its full force as the vital pattern of nature and the universe in *Avalovara*. Realizing spirals to be, as the title to his 1914 study indicates, *The Curves of Life*, Theodore Andrea Coo, presents "an account of spiral formations and their application to growth in nature, to science and to art," in the words of his subtitle. Re-edited in 1979, Cook's study affirms the spiral formation to be, as he puts it, "intimately connected with the phenomenon of life and growth." This scholar then proceeds to illustrate and analyze the myriad manifestations of this configuration in nature, science and art. Beginning with and especially focused on spiral formations in nature, Cook's analysis moves from spiral nebulae, to shells and horns, and plant pods and leaves. In terms of the human body, spiral formations seem ubiquitous: from bone and muscle and tendon formation, to the shape of the inner ear and of the heart and of the umbilical cord; from the trajectory of valves and ducts and veins and arteries, to the very pattern of sweat glands on our fingertips, seen most readily when digital imprints are taken. Cook's in-depth study of a natural circular pattern, implying "strength" and "energy and growth under resistance,"[13] was further corroborated by the discovery of the double helix of DNA, proving that the very "building blocks" of life follow the "curve of life" - the trajectory of the spiral.

Whereas Quentin Compson in *Absalom, Absalom!* and Pilar Ternera in *Cien años de soledad* propose the images of circularity which shape the respective texts in which they participate, it is Osman Lins himself, ever conscious of narrative order, that offers the following diagram of the cosmic form and design which structures and animates his *Avalovara* at the very beginning of his text:

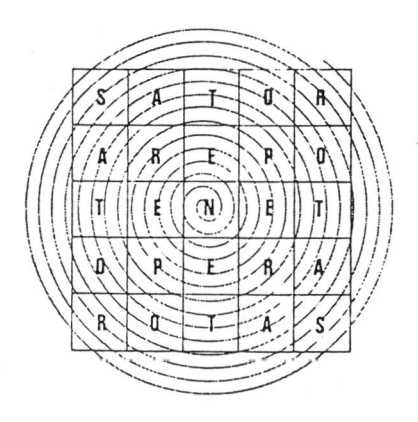

"a espiral e o quadrado"
Avalovara

The "espiral e o quadrado" ("spiral on a square") is, therefore, a diagram of a spiral labyrinth superimposed on a square which is divided into 25 smaller lettered squares. The text itself describes the conjunction of the spiral with the square in terms that parallel the movement of the earth through the signs of the zodiac; i.e., the rotation of the earth would correspond to the trajectory of the spiral, while the Houses of the Zodiac would mirror the lettered square:

> Concebei, pois, uma espiral que vem de distâncias impossíveis, convergindo para um determinado lugar (ou para um momento determinado). Sobre ela, delimitando-a em parte, assentai um quadrado. Sua existência...é que regerá com o seu vertiginoso giro a successão dos temas constantes do romance. Pois o quadrado será dividido em outros tantos, idealmente iguais entre si. E a passagem da espiral, sucessivamente, sobre cada um, determinará o retorno cíclico dos temas neles esparsos, do mesmo modo que a entrada da Terra nos signos zodiacais pode gerar, segundo algus, mundanças na influência dos astros sobre as criaturas. (19)
>
> (Imagine, then, a spiral from an impossible distance, converging on a specific place (or a specific moment). Over it, limiting it in part, set a square. Its existence...with its

vertiginous spiraling movement, will conduct the succession of the novel's specified themes. The square will be divided into as many other squares, each ideally like the others. And the passage of the spiral over each one, in succession, will determine the cyclical return of the themes spread over the square, in the same manner that the entry of the Earth into the signs of the zodiac can generate, according to some, varying influence of the stars over living creatures).

Through the pages of this novel, therefore, the spiral gives order and form to narrative discourse and to the world of *Avalovara* by animating the square and giving direction to the text. In effect, the eight major sections of the novel, corresponding to the eight letters which make up the square, recur in a cyclical manner each time the spiral/narrative moves into and out of a lettered square.

This lettered square is, in its turn, based on the so-called "SATOR square," various examples of which have been found by archeologists. The first, thought to be from the third century AD, was discovered in 1868 "on Roman wall-plaster in Cerincester," while the last, thought to be from the first century AD, was uncovered in 1963 among the ruins of Pompeii "on the plaster of a column of the palaestra (or campus)."[14] Interestingly enough, according to the *Encyclopedia Britannica* "it was still employed during the nineteenth century in Europe and the United States for fancied protection against fire, sickness and other disasters." Including the "SATOR square" as the first and foremost example in its entry on "Magic Squares," this encyclopedia reflects the reigning uncertainty as to the origin and meaning of this square by first calling it "the most familiar lettered square in the Western world," and then simply dismissing the phrase contained within it as "meaningless."[15] Written in Latin, this enigmatic square continues to elude scholars today, especially since the discovery at Pompeii which indicated that the magic square, until then attributed to Christian tradition, had been created before 79 AD, the date of the destruction of the ancient city of Pompeii. In an article from 1951 entitled "The Origin and Date of 'SATOR' Word-Square," Donald Atkinson analyzes the various examples as either of Christian or Jewish origin, and explains the difficulties thus: "The discovery at Pompeii caused something like consternation among scholars concerned with these studies," especially due to "the improbability (though not the impossibility) of the presence of Christians in Pompeii" and "the implication that Latin was familiarly used by Christians at so early a date, since all evidence asserts the exclusive use of Greek for teaching and liturgy (except in Palestine)."[16] In discussing the problematic word "AREPO," which does not translate from Latin as the other four words do, J. Gwyn Griffiths, in a 1971 article entitled" "'AREPO' in the Magic 'SATOR' Square," submits "with confidence that 'Arepo' is a personal name" which "originated in Alexandria, deriving from the Egyptian *Hr-Hp*," and ends by affirming, still with confidence: "That the 'SATOR' square is Egyptian rather than Semitic in ultimate origin is suggested by the more precise parallels which I have cited from hieroglyphic sources as well as by the derivation here suggested for the name 'Arepo'"[17] Two years later, Walter O. Moeller would publish *The Mithraic Origin and Meanings of the ROTAS - SATOR Square* in which he describes his interest, as well as that of others, in the enigmatic square and affirms its Mithraic origins:

> The ROTAS-SATOR/SATOR-ROTAS square has a history of at least two millennia and has appeared on all five continents. The attraction that men feel for it borders on the instinctual, and even in our supposedly rational age the magic formula still entices with its mysteries. Hardly a year passes that at least one investigator does not have a try at unravelling its meaning and determining its origin. Consequently the bibliography on the subject is enormous and constantly growing. Despite this considerable effort, however, the matter remains *sub iudice*.
>
> My interest in the word-square began in late 1969 when I sensed that the SATOR was Saturn and that the square transmitted a direct message concerned with sowing and reaping. In the spring of 1971 I began to speculate on it as a number-square. Since then many significant numbers have turned up and further word meanings have been deduced, all of which point to the Mithraic character of the formula. I now present these findings in the firm conviction that I have come upon the correct solution.

Notwithstanding this "correct solution," Moeller goes on to admit that:

> The most frustrating aspect of the ROTAS-SATOR square is that it has defied attempts at a direct translation of its five words into a meaningful sentence. This results from the fact that one of them, AREPO, has no firmly established meaning, and probably never will. From the outset all constructions of

the square that aim at a direct rendering of all five words are open to question.[18]

Accentuating the agricultural aspects of the magic square, Moeller describes one theory which would translate the phrase according to "boustrophedon," the ancient method of writing in which lines were written and read alternately from right to left and from left to right imitating the turning motion of oxen in plowing, from which the term originated. "As was noted in a French magazine over a hundred years ago," writes Moeller, "the square can be read boustrophedon starting with the S to give a complete sentence: SATOR OPERA TENET. Many have proposed this approach since and have construed it as meaning either 'as you sow, so shall you reap' or 'the creator maintains his works.'"[19] Lins himself unites the process and precision of agriculture, to the rigor of aesthetic and cosmic order, as he translates and describes the square which serves as "o recinto, o âmbito do ramance" (19) ("the space, the breadth of the novel"), thereby providing a metaliterary commentary on the very process he is elaborating. Writing out the phrase contained within the magic square, "SATOR AREPO TENET OPERA ROTAS," Lins then bifurcates its meaning into two possibilities: "*O lavrador mantém cuidadosamente a charrua nos sulcos. Ou, como também pode entender-se: O Lavrador sustém cuidadosamente o mundo em sua órbita.*" (72) (*The tiller carefully maintains the plow within the furrows. Or, as it can also be understood: The Creator carefully maintains the world in its orbit.*") Ana Luíza Andrade relates this double meaning to "cosmic fertility," as she observes in her study *Osman Lins: Crítica e Criação*: "The double meaning of the palindrome...symbolizes the agricultural fertility of cosmic nature transferred to literary creation."[20] Having presented the bifurcated meaning, the creator of *Avalovara* then proceeds to interweave the two meanings, thereby making the 5-word palindrome reverberate with luxuriant cultural, literary and cosmic signification:

> Difícil encontrar alegoria mais precisa e nítida do Criador e da Criação. Eis o lavrador, o campo, a charrua e as leiras; eis o Criador, Sua vontade, o espaço e as coisas criadas. Surge-nos o universo, evocado pela irresistível força dessa frase, como uma imensa planura cultivável, sobre a qual um vulto, com soberano cuidado, guia a charrua e faz surgirem, brilhantes,

para em seguida serem incendiadas, ceifadas ou esmagadas sob patas sanguíneas de cavalos, as suas lavouras: plantas, heróis, bichos, deuses, cidades, reinos, povos, idades, luzeiros celestes. Idêntica é a imagem do escritor, entregue à obrigação de provocar, com zelo, nos sulcos das linhas, o nascimento de um livro, durável ou de vida breve, de qualquer modo exposto - como a relva e os reinos - aos mesmos cavalos galopantes. Apesar desta certeza, desta ameaça, nenhum descuido é aceito. Sustém-se, com zelo e constância, a Charrua no seu rumo. (72)

(It would be difficult to find a more precise and clear allegory of the Creator and Creation. Here is the tiller, the field, the plow and the ridges; here is the Creator, the Creator's will, space and what has been created. The universe appears to our view, evoked by the irresistible force of that phrase, like an immense arable plain, over which a figure, with supreme attention, guides the plow and makes appear, brilliant only to be burned, harvested or crushed under the hooves of sanguine horses: plants, heroes, animals, gods, cities, kingdoms, peoples, ages, celestial lights. This image is identical to that of the writer, committed to the task of provoking, with zeal, within the furrows of the lines, the birth of a book, whether long-lasting or short-lived, exposed - like the grass or the kingdoms - to the same galloping horses. Despite this certainty, this threat, no carelessness is permitted. With zeal and perseverance, the Plow keeps to its course).

As the narrative spiral passes ten times in all through the "S" squares which are entitled "A Espiral e o Quadrado," *Avalovara* elaborates its own version of the creation of the SATOR square by the slave Loreius, subject to the merchant Publius Ubonius in Pompeii. "Extremely curious" about "Egyptian mathematics, Babylonian astronomy and Pythagorean teachings" and tending to "speculate about the incomprehensible," Ubonius promises Loreius his freedom should the slave discover "uma frase significativa e que possa, indiferentemente, ser lida da esquerda para a direita - e ao revés...deverá esta permanecer idêntica a si mesma." (23 & 24) ("a significant phrase which can, without changing, be read from left to right - and vice versa...it must remain identical to itself.") Having decided that the phrase must be composed of five words each containing five letters, in order to mirror the emblem of life, "o pentágono estrelado" (24) ("the star pentagon"), Loreius chooses the central word of the square - TENET - "por ser um verbo indicativo de posse, de dominio, factor de alta importância para ele, um escravo." (31) ("for being a verb indicative of possession, of authority, highly important matters to him, a slave"). Symbolic of the human drive for aesthetic and socio/cultural freedom, Loreius' search focuses first on the central cross formed by the horizontal and vertical disposition of the word TENET, which has for him special meaning, as the text explains:

> No dialeto dos seus pais originários de Lâmpasco, na Frígia, *net*, particula que resta da palavra *tenet* uma vez eliminada a sílaba inicial, significa "não mais," com o que entrevê o imaginoso servo de Ubonius, nesse jogo com o TENET, uma espécie de logrifo, acessível apenas à sua compreensão de escravo. Assim se traduz o seu entendimento da charada: "Loreius, caso descubra o que ambiciona o senhor, conduzirá livremente a sua existência e não mais será crucificado se tentar fugir." (31)

> (In his parents' dialect from Lampsac in Friesland, *net*, the particle remaining from the word *tenet* once the initial syllable is eliminated, means "never more," which leads Ubonius' ingenious servant to glimpse a kind of logograph in the TENET word play, accessible only to his slave mentality. His understanding would translate the riddle thus: "Loreius, if he succeeds in discovering what his master desires, will freely conduct his existence and never more be crucified should he try to escape").

Serving as anchor to the slave Loreius' search, this central cross also anchors and guides the creation of the novel *Avalovara*, leading to the passage from the primary chaos of words before creation, to the order of aesthetic and cosmic form which the completed novel signifies. Reaching to the four cardinal points of the universe, the central cross created by the clever slave also serves as compass, orienting the author/Loreius in the obscure ocean of language and words: "Com esta cruz central, formada pelo verbo TENET e que tão claramente lembra os pontos cardiais, já não está perdido nos oceanos turvos, sem margens, das palavras." (31) ("With this central cross, formed by the verb TENET which clearly evokes the cardinal points, he is no longer lost in the dark limitless oceans of words.")

The creation of the entire square, in addition, transcends temporal boundaries, as it unites the master Ubonius and the slave Loreius to the present twentieth-century narrator of *Avalovara*. While becoming the plan of the novel, the square unites past and present creators thus: "Preparam os dois homens, sem o saberem, o plano deste romance onde ressurgem e do qual são colaboradores. Contempla-os, com gratidão, o narrador, por sobre os dois mil anos que a eles o unem." (24) ("Without knowing it, the two men prepare the plan of this novel, in which they will appear and for which they are collaborators. Thankful, the narrator observes them through the two thousand years that unite him to them.") The words of the phrase thus created through time, when placed together in the prescribed order, make of the total square a 5-word palindrome converging on the central letter "N."[21] Truly magical in its weaving together of linguistic and geometric signification, this square palindrome yields the same phrase when read horizontally from left to right and right to left, as well as when read vertically from top to bottom and viceversa. Anchored by the central "N" and by the word "TENET," the phrase - SATOR AREPO TENET OPERA ROTAS - is itself, as can be readily discerned, a sentence palindrome. Considered in relation to the lettered square, the direction the spiral labyrinth takes also mirrors the potential movement of a palindrome itself. That is, since a palindrome can be read in a linear fashion, from left to right and vice versa, or up and down and vice versa, the central letter becomes the focal point, the central matrix, the ultimate center. This potential for linear, two-dimensional convergence inherent in the palindrome, becomes circular, three-dimensional convergence as the unicursal movement of the spiral funnels the narrative into the central letter of the square, the letter which maintains the order of both the word and the cosmos created by this text: the "N" of the word "TENET," of the five words that make up the square, the one which is itself also a palindrome. While characterizing Sutpen's design in *Absalom, Absalom!* and sketching the temporal chronology *Cien años de soledad* obliterates, linearity in *Avalovara* is, then, itself sucked into the dominant spiral movement of the novel, becoming itself circular and three-dimensional. As the text puts it, while referring to the eight themes represented by the eight letters of the palindrome: "A espiral sobrevoa os vários temas; e estes não voltam por acaso, nem por força do arbítrio ou da intuição do autor, mas governados por um ritmo inflexível, uma pulsação rígida, imemorial, indiferente a qualquer espécie de manejos." (54) ("The spiral flies over the various themes; and these do not return haphazardly, nor due to the author's choice or intuition, but are governed by an inflexible rhythm, a rigid, immemorial, pulsation, indifferent to any manoeuvering.")

Considered in relation to Lins' aesthetic beliefs, then, the square becomes the blank page before which the writer confronts the chaos of words prior to meaning, ultimately to be translated and made significant. Called a "closed geometric figure" within the novel, the square evokes "janelas...salas...folhas de papel, espaços com limites precisos, nos quais transita o mundo exterior ou dos quals o espreitamos." (19) ("windows...rooms...sheets of paper, precisely delimited spaces within which the outside world exists and from which we watch it"). Linked to time (73) - "nem a eternidade bastaria para chegarmos ao término da espiral, ou sequer ao seu princípio. A espiral não tem começo nem fim." (17) ("not even an eternity would allow us to reach the end of the spiral, or even its beginning. The spiral is without beginning or end") as it orders and transforms original chaos into a world, a cosmos. While time is fragmented and unsequential in *Absalom, Absalom!*, and repetitive and cyclical in *Cien años de soledad*, in *Avalovara* the magical spiral reaches toward a cosmic all-encompassing present, a "mundo presentificado" ("presentified world") which recalls the simultaneity of the Melquiadean instant. Relating this perspective to modern physics, Lins observes: "A few days ago I was overjoyed to realize that this is how the followers of Einstein view time."[22] Given the utopian thrust of this author's vision and literary production, in which human life is reintegrated in its totality into the rhythm of the cosmos, what Candace Slater observes about one of his most successful short stories, "Retábulo de Santa Joana Carolina," applies to Lins' work as a whole. Referring to the story, Slater says: "The language of the narrative is that of prophecy, a present which is at once past and future and in which all is known, if not revealed."[23] While prophecy in Gabriel García Márquez's novel is a warning to "races condemned to one hundred years of solitude," Lin's *Avalovara* is a "prophetic" vision of both human cosmological potential as well as universal cosmological creation.

As the circularity of *Absalom, Absalom!* radiates from multiple centers of consciousness, circularity in both Latin American texts moves toward the simultaneous totality and cosmological synchronicity implied by the center of the circle. Nevertheless, while the cyclical redundancy and breakdown of *Cien años de soledad* de-center the Malquiadean instant, as implied by the "progressive and irreparable wear and tear of the gyrating wheel's axis," the "spiral on a square" moves inexorably toward the central instant of *Avalovara*, contained, as in *Cien años de soledad*, within the final pages of the novel. "O Paraíso" ("Paradise"), the title given to this ultimate center, reflects the primordial simultaneity and cosmological totality of this focal point/section/letter: the letter is, of course, the "N;" the section is that which joins Abel and ♉, the central male character and the central female character, in "Paradise;" and the point is that within which Abel and ♉ achieve total unity and ecstasy, while the reader also succeeds in completing the novel and finally achieves, as in *Cien años de soledad*, a total vision of the text.

For, along with being a very self-conscious narrative, deliberately structured and ordered, *Avalovara* is a love story. Osman Lins himself affirms that it is "a novel about love, one of the few Brazilian attempts at a love story."[24] Expressing, says Lins, "my uneasiness with respect to life and to words," *Avalovara* is both "an allegory of the art of the novel,"[25] as well as, in the words of Regina Igel, "an allegory of love, a communicative expression of the gradual process of reaching understanding through the physical and spiritual union between a man and a woman."[26] This author goes on to explain that, in addition to being "related to the art of narrating...and to the ambiguity of words," *Avalovara* also springs from "human love," from the "suggestive symbolism of the body and the cosmic significance of carnal union." According to an ancient Hindu text that Lins cites, "There is no perfection or beatitude without the body." In an earlier interview, this writer of the Americas had explained that *Avalovara*:

> ...is a novel about love. Love, for me, has always been very important, because it exalts and involves the problem of unity, and depends on the very mysterious coming together of one human being with another. My book deals with all that. The main character, Abel, through three intense experiences of love which take place at different times and in different places (Europe, Recife, Sâo Paulo) succeeds simultaneously in experiencing both love and the creation of literature.[27]

Avalovara is, therefore, the story of Abel, an aspiring young writer, in relationship with three women, each of whom is presented in relationship to a city. While Thomas Sutpen comes from undefined regions to Yoknapatawpha County, and "Gabito," the "fictional" García Márquez in *Cien años de soledad*, goes off to Paris before the final destruction of Macondo, the 21 letter "A" section of *Avalovara* actually set this narrative of the Americas in Europe. Entitled "Roos e as Cidades" ("Roos and the Cities"), these sections recur each time the narrative spiral passes through the letter "A" (21 time in all) and recount Abel's wanderings through European cities - especially Paris - in the company of and also in pursuit of Annaliese Roos, a Dutch woman whose husband is in a Swiss sanitarium in Lausanne. Symbolic of Europe and Old World culture and history, Roos, in whom "subsistem tantas cidades" (31) ("so many cities exist"), is made up of "innumerable cities." (128) Abel, young, lured by the charm of Europe and impelled by the desire to write, "searches for a city and in the end, for the name of that city,"[28] the former emblematic of collective human existence and the latter symbolic of human collective creation.

Divided, as Lins says of the sixteenth-century missionary and writer Padre José de Ancieta, between his European cultural heritage and the cultural reality of Brazil and South America,[29] the young Abel, searching, discovering the cultural wealth of Europe and observing that he should have already written something worthwhile (76), feels attracted by Roos but thinks more and more of the city and region in which he grew up, the Brazilian city of Recife in the state of Pernambuco. Discovering "rare examples of civil architecture from the Middle Ages to the age of maritime discoveries" in the Loire Valley during an Easter trip, Abel muses that "No Recife, o dia está nascendo e o céu vermelho se reflete na areia das praias." (40) ("In Recife it is dawn and the red sky is reflected on the beach.") Finally, after a few years, Abel evaluates his relationship with Roos, realizes that their solitude cannot overcome the worlds that separate them and begins to think of accepting a job in Recife:

> Posso assumir o emprego no Recife até 15 de Julho; ...Os meus dias aqui, portanto, terminam em breve. Sabe Roos que regressarei, que estou de passagem e não lhe ocorreria

abandonar o homem que morre em Lausanne; cruzar o
Oceano; confiar a vida a mim, filho pouco hábil de uma região
a seus olhos sáfara e inculta, embora fascinante: o fascínio de
um animal subterrâneo. (216)

(I can take over the job in Recife until July 15; ... My days here,
therefore, will soon come to an end. Roos knows that I will
return and that I am passing through. It wouldn't occur to her
to leave the man who is dying in Lausanne; to cross the Ocean;
to trust her life to me, an inept son of a region she sees as an
uncultured wasteland, although fascinating like a subterranean
animal).

In the final "A" section, therefore, Roos has become for Abel "uma visão, um impossível...a ofuscante, a clara, a quase, a que intrevejo...a intangível, a vinda inconclusa, o perene ir" (297) ("a vision, an impossibility...the obscure, the clear, the almost, a glimpse...the intangible, the incomplete return, the eternal departure"). As the section ends, he is left, once again, "with nothing" repeated but his solitude: "Acena-me, dou ainda alguns passos, dou alguns passos ainda, e me vejo sem nada, mais uma vez sem nada, sem nada, mais uma vez, e cego, e cego, ante a minha ofuscante solidão, ante a minha ofuscante solidão." (300) ("She gestures to me. I take a few steps, I take a few steps, and find myself with nothing, once more with nothing, with nothing once more, and blind, and blind, before my obscure solitude, before my obscure solitude.") Just as he is a mystery to her, so Roos is an enigma that Abel can never truly understand,[30] according to Lins. Commenting on his incorporation of Europe into this novel, he explains and describes Abel's relationship with Roos in the following manner:

>...some people found it strange that part of this book should take place in Europe... It seems that no one has yet understood that the impossible love of my Abel for Annelise Roos expresses a clash of cultures, our fascination for European culture, which we observe but can never truly penetrate. Attracted to one another, Abel and Roos can never completely understand one another.[31]

Such is not the case with Cecília, the woman from Recife with whom Abel becomes involved in the 17 letter "T" sections entitled "Cecília entre os Leões" ("Cecilia among the Lions"). These sections, in which Abel is seen in relationship to his family and past, as well as to Cecilia, take the narrative to

Recife, an important coastal city in Brazil's tormented Northeast region, and to Olinda, the coastal city just north of Recife where Abel was born. Back in Brazil and in relationship to this woman who is a nurse to the poor, the aspiring writer begins to discover his own cultural roots: "Será que a gente encontra, morto, os nossos ancestrais?" he wonders.

> Não os parentes, mas os que povoaram a terra onde se nasce. Gostaria de encontrar o velho povo de Olinda. Os pioneiros que sairam de lá e povoaram toda a planicie costeira por ai. Arquitetos. Religiosos Guerreiros. (159)

> (I wonder if, once dead, we encounter our ancestors. Not our parents, but those that settled our native land. I would like to meet the people of Olinda's past; the pioneers who left here to settle these coastal plains. Architects. Religious. Warriors).

Inhabited by "the great masses of the Northeast and all of their problems,"[32] Cecilia incorporates into herself the existence and peoples of Recife and, by extension, of Brazil, be they living or dead or yet unborn. Becoming more and more aware of this collective reality, Abel says:

> ...vejo a espessura da carne de Cecília, povoada de seres tão reais quanto nós. Na substância da sua carne mortal, conduz Cecília o integro e absoluto ser de cada figura que atravessa a Praça, e não só dos homens e mulheres que agora povoam a Praça e os arredores, mas também dos que ontem a povoaram, dos que em maio ou junho a povoaram, dos que no ano findo a povoaram, dos que hão de a povoar ainda amanhã, destes e dos que em outras partes existem ou existiram, sim, nenhum está ausente em definitivo do corpo de Cecília. Cecília, deste modo, é ela e outros. (158)

> (...I see the thickness of Cecilia's flesh, inhabited by beings as real as we are. Within the substance of her mortal flesh, Cecilia leads the integral and absolute being of each figure crossing the central square, not only the men and women who now inhabit the square and its environs, but also those who inhabited it yesterday, those who inhabited it in May or June, those who inhabited it last year, those who will inhabit it tomorrow, these and those who exist or existed in other places, yes, none are definitely absent from Cecilia's flesh. In this way, Cecilia is herself and others).

On another occasion, Abel perceives "na sua carne, simulacro da memória, a presença de seres que haverei de amar, amando-a." (196) ("in her flesh, simulacrum of memory, the presence of beings whom I shall love, by loving her"), a collective experience reflected in the silver wheel mentioned earlier. Shiny and magical, this wheel collects singers and dancers and wanderers into a harmonious and melodious community, as it spins on Praia dos Milagros (the Beach of Miracles) in Recife and leaves its trace on the sand. (212-3)

Emblematic of the young writer's growing socio-political awareness, Cecilia is herself, as a nurse and active member of workers' groups (e.g., "Ligas Camponesas"), involved in easing the plight of her fellow citizens, tormented by their existence in a region plagued by periodic drought and in a country tormented by perpetual instability. Combatting, for instance, "meaningless government proposals" (175), Cecilia, "portadora de corpos, romã de populações, não é - ao contrário de mim - um ser à margem" (210) ("holds bodies within herself like a pomegranate, and is not - unlike me - a being on the fringes"), observes Abel. Her struggle against cruel and savage forces is symbolized by the photograph Abel finds showing Cecilia among lions, whence the title of her "T" sections. Describing the development of his own political consciousness in relation to the short story "Retábulo de Santa Joana Carolina" and to *Avalovara*, Lins counteracts his aesthetic concerns by emphasizing his social concerns, as he explains the character and function of Joana Carolina and Cecilia in a 1976 interview:

> (In) *Retábulo* ...the struggle of the central character, Joana Carolina, is not against a specific individual but against the world, against the land where she lives, against her country. And you will see that especially in the final section, which is that of her funeral, she is followed by the poor of the city, by workers, artisans, small businessmen, by men with rough hands, while the entire funeral follows a rigid, extremely violent rhythm. Characterized by aesthetic preoccupation, this narrative is perhaps, of all that I have written, the most politically involved. *Retábulo* is, in my view...a violent protest against the way the poor are treated in my country. Due to the complexity of *Avalovara*, certain characteristics haven't been understood...the main character is an unpublished writer, who is getting started like I did at the beginning of my career. He meets that woman in Europe, they experience cultural conflict but then he is indifferent to our political reality. Through...Cecilia, the second female character he meets, he learns Cecilia is interested even in the problems of the Ligas Camponesas...and when he meets the third woman in São Paulo, he tries, at one point, to deny love saying that since he

came to know suffering and injustice, love had come to signify something minor to him. And she asks, if we deny love because of that, what is left?... It is necessary to love our neighbor and be conscious of the reality that surrounds us, fighting to modify that reality but not diminishing our capacity to love...Abel loves Cecilia, a figure that is a woman and at the same time, many human beings...to which we are all linked and to which I, as a writer, am linked. All of this I tried to express through that parable.[33]

Actually incorporating another life into her being, Cecilia ends up pregnant with Abel's baby and commits suicide on the beach at Recife. As "the ocean devours the place where Cecilia died," Abel once again "sees himself alone," contemplating the waves and the sand in solitude (314). Linked to Cecilia, Recife itself is, as Lins sees it, a symbol of the precarious nature of human existence: "I attempted to capture what is terrifying in its existence as a coastal city, a city always threatened by water. Recife appears as a symbol of the precarious nature of human existence, surrounded - if you'll permit the image - by the waters of the unexpected." Within one of his stories, he goes on to say, "...there is what I call a 'chorus of Recifenses' which speaks of our precarious condition, continually exposed to the threat of the ocean."[34]

The story with a "chorus of people from Recife" is from the collection of nine stories entitled *Nove, Novena* (1966), a text which Lins sees as "a work exploring the ground"[35] for *Avalovara*. "Perdidos e Achados" ("Lost and Found"), is a story which recreates the search of a father for his son who has drowned by the sea. Bowing to the primordial power of the ocean - the origin of life - the father admits that the ocean called to itself the son which had been his for a short time on this earth: "Dizem que a vida começou no mar. Voltemos à origem." ("They say that life began in the ocean. Let us return to the beginning.")[36] Reaching back to prehistoric aquatic conditions, when "the earth was deserted and there were no vertebreates" (209) and when "the earth returned to cover the land it had lost" (219), "Lost and Found" is shaped by the cyclical geological formation of this planet, formed by "the cyclical covering of land by the ocean and its subsequent reappearance, according to the convulsions which modify the earth."[37] Designated by the cyclical wave pattern of the sign for infinity - ∞ - the "chorus of Recifenses" expresses the precarious condition of their existence, as they offer their lament:

> We, who have lost so much, surround this child. We, who search for so much, find this dead body, victim of the ocean in a city conquered by the ocean... Let us cry holding hands around the dead body - in whom we see ourselves - our salty lament... How many times were we invaded, covered, devastated, by oceans we cannot name?... For us from Recife, there is no safety, no matter how much we extend our arms. (233 & 237)

Expressing the precarious condition of life in the Northeast and in Brazil and, by extension, the precarious nature of human existence itself, another chorus of "Recifenses" raises its collective voice in the story previously mentioned, "Retábulo de Santa Joana Carolina." Also from the collection *Nova, Novena*, "Retábulo" is, in the words of its author, "a protest against the life and death of the poor in the Northeast."[38] As this narrative recreation of the life of Joana Carolina comes to an end with her funeral, this chorus, once again designated by the ∞ sign, offers its collective suffering as a eulogistic lament for her death:

> We, taking Joana to the cemetery...we, the nobodies of the city, always ignored by the others with money and power... How many times the world was sterile and blinding to her, a city of salt, with salt houses, salty fountains and avenues of salt?... She lived her years with meekness and justice, humility and firmness, love and commiseration. She died at the end of winter. Will another like her be born next season?... Humbly and silently, Joana Carolina takes her place, joining hands with Prados, Pumas and Figueiras...between Rosas, Leões and Margaridas...between Salgueiros...and Campos wearing the dress that was for Sunday afternoons and penetrated by the silence of her solitude. (134, 135, 137 & 138)

Ending in solitude and death, Joana Carolina takes an active part in the collective experience of life which the words of her story evoke. Candace Slater describes Joana's place in the community of humans and in the creation of words thus:

> The power of the word permeates the narrative. The chorus which appears at Joana's death to greet her affirms her membership in a more ample community through the use of a

language at once both concrete and symbolic. Thus in the very last paragraph where Joana takes her place among "Prados, Pumas e Figueiras...entre Rosas, Leões, e Margaridas," Lins summons up the flora and fauna comprising the physical universe - meadows, mountain lions, fig trees, roses, lions, daisies - thus suggesting Joana's place in an elemental creative order. However, because every one of these thirty nouns is also a common proper name - one can find a Margarida on every city block, a Cordeiro family in every little town dotting the interior - he also suggests Joana's role within a decidedly human community. This powerful ambiguity stems from Lins' belief that it is the word and not the individual speaker which "distinguishes, pinpoints, organizes, recreates."[39]

Relating his preoccupation with words to his interest in cosmology and creation, Lins affirms in "Retábulo" that "the world was created twice: when it passed from nothingness to existence; and when, projected onto a more subtle plan, it was made Word." (117) True to his fascination with language and communication, he recalls pictograms and ideographs, "the first attempts at human expression,"[40] by utilizing graphic signs to "name" his narrative voices and characters. It is in *Nove, Novena* that, for the first time, the linguistic sign becomes word, as this innovative author designates a child, for example, by ⸕ , while an adult becomes ⸖ in the story "Pentágono de Hahn," and the people of Recife are ∞, as mentioned, a man becomes O , a woman △ and both in unison ⊘ , in "Retábulo." As a writer, Lins feels that these narrative sign offer "great mobility" to his fiction,[41] by graphically and visually alerting the reader to narrative voice and point of view. This technique, moreover, reflects Lins' interest in drama (he is a recognized dramatist) and in textile weaving (his father was a tailor by profession), for it makes of the written page a woven pattern of individual and collective voices "speaking" on cue. With respect to this writer's work, Anatol Rosenfeld observes:

> The use of these signs allows the reader to *see* the voice change immediately, even before reading it on a page. When parallel, crisscrossed interior monologues occur or a sudden dialogue interchange, the process facilitates the rhythmical feel of the text.[42]

The use of these signs, I would add, highlights the semantic and syntactical *texture* of the woven literary pattern created by the narrative. Lins is a writer, after all, who insists that the modern novel is, in his words, a "narrative *text* which proposes itself as *text* and not as a simulacrum of life." He is, in the end, a twentieth-century writer who participates very deliberately in the creation and elaboration of the self-conscious, and self-reflective novel we have come to call modern, a novel no longer conceived as an imitation but as a conscious interpretation of life. Considering both the risk the writer takes and the effect on the reader, Lins elaborates his view of this narrative "play" in words that evoke the legerdemain of magicians:

> ...The present, contemporary novel...does not attempt to elude the reader, but follows a course which approximates that of Brecht, by offering the reader, not a simulacrum of life, but a...narrative text which proposes itself as text, and proposes characters as characters and not as flesh and blood figures... The novels of Stendhal and Balzac presented characters constructed with such precision that they seemed to be living figures. The contemporary novel does not try to trick the reader in this way, which is a risky move... It says: look, I am proposing a fictional creation, characters made of words. Nevertheless, as with that magical movement which shows the other side of the magician's cloak, it tries to involve and...bring the reader to its side. I find this a more fascinating and true (in the sense of faithful) effort.[43]

Given his perspective and preoccupation as a writer, Lins is concerned with presenting, in his own words, "a new conception of fictional characters." Speaking of *Nove, Novena*, in which, as already mentioned, he utilizes graphic signs for the first time, Lins observes that in this collection his characters "begin to run away from being pure flesh" and "begin to be made up of new material"[44] Such is the case with Joana Carolina, a character whose "life is inscribed in the mythical circular time of the celestial bodies,"[45] within a narrative which integrates its author's cosmological aspirations, literary experimentation and social involvement into the circular pattern of the signs of the zodiac. The very title of the story, "Retábulo de Santa Joana Carolina," indicates a "new" perspective on fictional characterization which reaches back to "old" aesthetic techniques. From an author fascinated, as he admits, by the stained glass windows and romanesque style of medieval artwork that he observed while visiting Europe in 1960,[46] we receive a narrative collage inspired by and modeled after the "retable," a religious art piece from the Middle Ages made up of various panels usually depicting saints and placed on a shelf around and behind the altar. "The term," according to Webster's *Third International Dictionary*, "refers to a more or less elaborate framework about the altar and enclosing a panel or panels decorated with painting, sculpture, mosaic or the like." Given the order and form Lins imparts to the narrative, Joana's life becomes a "retable," as the story becomes a meditation on suffering and consecration to sainthood.

The aesthetic, social and spiritual dimensions of this story are all integrated and interwoven into its circular structure, as the narrative follows the order of the cosmos, mirrored in the signs of the zodiac and in the twelve months of the year. While "Lost and Found" evokes prehistoric geological cycles, "Retábulo de Santa Joana Carolina" is actually divided into twelve sections patterned after the astrological and terrestrial cycle of a year. Called "mysteries" by the narrator, these sections, as Anatol Rosenfeld observes,

> suggest the "legend" of a saint - a modern counterpart of the "lives of the saints" of medieval times. The story treats the life of a poor, meek, unsophisticated elementary school teacher in the far-distant, rural Brazilian Northeast. The panel's twelve sections (the mysteries) portray, luminously and in vivid colors, her rich and poor existence and the anonymous insignificance of her Passion... It is one of the most beautiful hymns ever composed by a Northeastern writer on behalf of his people constantly assailed by pitiless nature and human forces.[47]

Beginning with the house of Libra - the beginning of spring in the southern hemisphere - and ending in Virgo - the end of winter, the multiple narrative voices, designated by as many varied graphic symbols, recreate Joana Carolina's passage from childhood, through marriage and childbearing, to old age and death.

While in *Absalom, Absalom!* Rosa Coldfield is incidental to Sutpen's linear design as her voice initiates the novel's circular ripple pattern, and in *Cien años de soledad* Ursula Buendía and Pilar Ternera are most aware of the vicious circularity of the cycle of Macando which they generate and nurture, the main female characters in "Retábulo" and *Avalovara* are both individual participants in the stories they inhabit and also collective montages inhabited by communities. Osman Lins' preoccupation with the construction of fictional characters has led him, therefore, from a more traditionally conceived collective voice or polyphonic discourse, to the actual composition of a "collective, polyphonic character," if I may be permitted the term. So guided and impelled, this writer creates Roos, a woman containing cities within her being, European cities which together recreate the collective heritage of Western culture, a vast world which the young Abel feels compelled to explore before he can deal with the reality of Brazil. Once on his own "new world" soil, finally, Abel is aided in the discovery of his personal and national identity by Cecilia, a woman inhabited by the great masses of Recife and the Northeast. Following the search-for-identity motif which dominates Latin American literature, and which I discussed earlier in relation to *Cien años de soledad* and in contrast to the loss-of-innocence motif which characterizes *Absalom, Absalom!* and the literature of the United States, Abel searches for his identity in relationship to these female collective characters. Each shaped by images of cities, these characters evoke the coming together of scattered families and tribes in order to form the collective conglomerations which became the first cities of ancient times. It is interesting to note that, according to Fustel de Coulanges in his work *The Ancient City: A Study on the Religion, Laws and Institutions of Greece and Rome*, the founding of these first cities unites the figure of a circle and the action of a plow, just as Lins' translation of the SATOR square discussed earlier, unites his narrative spiral to the creator's plow. Describing the founding of Rome by Romulus, the archetypal city and its mythical founder, de Coulanges explains the initial rite of the purifying sacred flame and then says:

> When this preliminary ceremony had prepared the people for the grand act of the foundation, Romulus dug a small trench, of a circular form, which he had brought from the city of Alba. Then each of his companions, approaching by turns, following his example, threw in a little earth, which he had brought from the country from which he had come.
>
> The trench into which each one had thrown a little earth was called *mundus*... When placing in the trench a clod of earth from their former country, they believed they had enclosed there the souls of their ancestors. These souls,

reunited there, required a perpetual worship, and kept guard over their descendants. At this same place Romulus set up an altar, and a lighted fire upon it. This was the holy fire of the city.

Around the hearth arose the city, as the house rises around the domestic hearth; Romulus traced a furrow which marked the enclosure. Here, too, the smallest details were fixed by a ritual. The founder made use of a copper ploughshare... Romulus, with his head veiled, and in the priestly robes, himself held the handle of the plough and directed it, while chanting prayers. His companions followed him, observing a religious silence. As the plough turned up clods of earth, they carefully threw them within the enclosure, that no particle of this sacred earth should be on the side of the stranger. This enclosure, traced by religion, was inviolable.[48]

Evoking the sacred plow and its circular trench, the cosmic narrative spiral of *Avalovara* creates character/cities which are prefigured in the woman/community Joana Carolina, at once a struggling individual and an oppressed people, within a narrative which is both a personal lament and a universal outcry projected onto the metaphysical aspirations of human beings. Very simply, Joana is one and is everyone. Lins describes the relationship between the mystical and cosmological dimensions of this text, and the personal and social reality it recreates, when he explains that "Retábulo" is:

the biography of my paternal grandmother. If not constructed as it is, it would be simply the story of a woman from the state of Pernambuco. But this narrative is constructed from twelve panels or mysteries, each one related to a symbol of the Zodiac. In this way, it is no longer the story of a woman living in Pernambuco, but the story of a woman who lived in Pernambuco projected onto the constellations, projected onto the world. Due to this she becomes, at one and the same time, much, much larger and much, much smaller.[49]

The third and final female character with whom Abel develops a relationship in the novel *Avalovara* interweaves the many aspects of Lins' writing into her very being and existence. So essential is she to the narrative, that she is the only character in *Avalovara* "named" by a graphic sign. Indicating her crucial role in Abel's search and realization, ☿ is composed from the circle, "the form of the perfection of the being," according to

Georges Poulet.[50] Her being, consequently, unites the smallest depiction of a circle - a point - with the limitless potential for enlargement that characterizes the circumference of a circle. At once smaller and larger like Joana Carolina, then, ☥ is a circular symbol of totality and convergence with two wings stretched out to eternity. Composed from the traditional mystical symbol which so occupied Jorge Luís Borges, ☥ evokes the twelfth-century definition of God, "a sphere whose center is everywhere and whose circumference is nowhere." Through this symbol/name the vastest possible circle of duration, the circumference, converges with the simultaneity of the fixed point. Osman Lin's aesthetic sensibility then accents the potential for infinite expansion of the circumference and stresses the spiritual significance of the traditional symbol, by adding two little "wings" stretched out toward infinity. These two graphic markings, moreover, also evoke the wings of the "avalovara," the magical bird which "guides" the relationship between and Abel along the spiral movement of its free flight. Its name derived from "**Avalo**kitsh**vara**," a Bodhissatva, an enlightened one within Buddhist tradition, the avalovara lends its name to a novel which, as Mary Daniel puts it, "has as its key concept the progressive gaining of knowledge and perception."[51]

It is with and through ☥, in fact, that Abel ultimately achieves total enlightenment and pleasure. Preparing for this final moment and mirroring her fundamental importance in the novel, the character of ☥ is central to four sections/letters. As the narrative spiral begins its trajectory with the letter "R" of "ROTAS," Abel and ☥ find themselves "no espaço ainda obscuro da sala" (13) ("in the still dark space of a room") on the very first page of the novel. These "R" sections are narrated from Abel's perspective and recount his experience of ☥ and their relationship. Entitled "☥e Abel: Encontros, Percursos, Revelaçãos" (" ☥ and Abel: Encounters, Trajectories, Revelations"), these sections actually reflect the fundamental spiral movement of *Avalovara*, as it weaves the discourse of the letter section into that of another, and then another, until the discourse of each of the eight letters ultimately creates a cosmic narrative spiral of *encounters* and *trajectories* leading to final *revelation* and enlightenment. Expressing the aspirations and fears of the writer, these "R" sections, in short, map out the narrative trajectory of *Avalovara*, as Ana Luisa Andrade has argued in her work.[52] Given that this letter recurs twice within the outer squares formed by "SATOR" and twice within the intermediate squares formed by the "REP" of "AREPO" and the "PER" of "OPERA," the "R" sections occur and recur as the narrative spiral moves from the outer circumference, to just before it reaches the central focus, the "N" which ultimately unites Abel and ☿ in "Paradise" and which completes his novel.

While Roos contains cities and lures Abel to explore the Old World culture of Europe, and Cecilia is inhabited by suffering masses as she guides him to social consciousness and the discovery of Brazilian reality, ☿ is both "palavra e corpo" (14) ("word and flesh") leading the young Abel to his full potential as a writer and as a human being. Since this is the fundamental allegorical and metaliterary premise of *Avalovara*, it is not surprising, then, that these "R" sections should, as just mentioned, occur within the outer orbit of the spiral and the intermediate "REP/PER" trajectory leading to the middle "N." Interweaving his experiences with all three female/collective characters, Abel deliberates and ponders his stance and situation as a writer in his "R" sections, as he experiences the process whereby a writer, having confronted the blank page, finally succeeds in ordering the initial chaos of words into a narrative cosmos. The eclipse which brings together Abel from the Northeast, ☿ from São Paulo and thousands of other people from Brazil on Cassino Beach later in the novel, prefigures the eventual textual and celestial "conjunçâo da simetria e das trevas" ("conjunction of symmetry and darkness") which will occur with the creation of his novel, as the words of the text come together to create order and enlightenment. While the narrative markers in *Absalom, Absalom!* constantly alert the listener/reader to the oral creation of the text, and the parchments of the enigmatic Melquíades whimsically prophesy and become *Cien años de soledad*, the contemporary tendency toward self-conscious metafiction becomes most pronounced and deliberate in *Avalovara*. True to the metaliterary aspirations of a writer who, in his own words, desires to "conquer a unique and intense vision of the universe," a vision which "will be at the same time the story of that very conquest,"[53] Lins' alter-ego Abel ponders the phenomenon of the eclipse with the perspective of a writer. As Abel *encounters* ☿, and is at once puzzled by and attracted to the duality and ambiguity of the texts that he "reads" in ♉, he contemplates the cosmic *trajectory* which will lead to final *revelation*-the creation of his text:

> Atraídos pelo eclipse, vindos eu do Nordeste e ela do Centro-Oeste, confluem as nossas trajetórias na Terra de um modo não de todo estranho ao fenômeno celeste... Seu rosto, animado por uma fugidia luz interior...oculta outro ser, velado...obstinado,....enigmático e que me contempla de outra clave do tempo, açulando minha inclinação por tudo que gravita, como os textos, entre a dualidade e o ambíguo. Presidem este encontro o signo da escuridão - símile de insciência e do caos - e o signo da confluência: germe do cosmos e evocador da ordenção, mental. Terra, espaço, Lua, movimento, Sol e tempo preparam a conjunção da simetria e das trevas. (36)

> (Attracted by the eclipse, I come from the Northeast and she from the Central Westcoast, as our trajectories on the Earth come together in a manner not at all unlike the celestial phenomenon... Her face, animated by a fleeting interior light...hides another being concealed...obstinate,...enigmatic, looking at me from another key in time, inciting my inclination toward all that gravitates, as do texts, between duality and ambiguity. Presiding over this encounter is the sign of darkness - a simile for non-knowledge and chaos - and the sign of confluence: germ of the cosmos and evocative of mental order. Earth, space, Moon, movement, Sun and time prepare the conjunction of symmetry and darkness).

Feeling persecuted by the "machinery of oppression" (260) and "dividido entre um obstinado projeto criador e a cólera ante um mundo armado de garras" ("divided between an obstinate creative project and anger at a world armed with claws"), Abel unites the personal and collective power of love to the shaping force of aesthetic creation, by immediately asking himself at this point whether he has the "power to love in relation to such a world." (319) It is in relationship to ♉ and his writing that Abel will ultimately find this power to love and confront the world that surrounds him. As this writer approaches fulfillment, and the aesthetic and amorous instant of cosmic creation contained within the letter "N," he resolves in his final "R" sections "not to be indifferent" since, as he puts it, "indifference is a mask of complicity." (354) It is finally ♉ and all she represents that lead Abel to this crucial moment of discovery and self-affirmation which "will furnish the bonds necessary to yank man out of the alienation in which he finds himself."[54] In the following passage, ♉ is at once physical body and metaphysical consciousness, incorporating into her existence the solace of the natural world and the promise of the instant of total being and love, which she here describes in relation to death, thereby foreshadowing the final outcome of their secret, furtive relationship. As Abel faces ♉, he thinks:

> Quero manter-me de pé e meus joelhos dobram-se e tudo na Terra, tudo, parece ao mesmo tempo grande e lastimável. Nu,...tenho o rosto sobre o sexo de ♉ , cheiro de mar e de capim sob a chuva...vejo o que sou, o que somos, dois entes escondidos, destinado a solver o insolúvel, sós na madrugada e no mundo, extraviados, batidos, habitados por visões, e clamo "O que será de nós?"...pois não vejo saída e uma tem de haver, e ela dobra os joelhos e abraça-me com força e eu clamo outra vez o que será de nós e ela responde "Morreremos, Abel!" o que significa "Aqui estamos, havemos de morrer mas ainda estamos vivos e afinal a vida, longa ou breve, dura apenas um dia, ninguém vive dois dias, ninguém, importa que haja nesse dia uma hora, um minuto, um instante que ilumine o resto...eu te amo, com garras e com dentes, ama-me.(321)

> (I want to remain standing and my knees fold and all on Earth, all, seems at the same time grand and lamentable. Naked,...my face on ♉'s sex, I smell the ocean and wild grass under rain... I see who I am, who we are, two hidden beings, destined to solve the unsolvable, alone in the dawn and the world, lost, beaten, inhabited by visions, and I clamor "What will become of us?" ...for I don't see a way out and there must be one, and her knees fold and she embraces me forcefully, and I clamor once again what will become of us and she responds "We will die, Abel!" which signifies "Here we are, we must die but we are still alive and, in the end, whether long or brief, life lasts but a day, no one lives two days, no one. What matters is that during that day there be an hour, a minute, an instant which illuminates the rest...I love you, with all my might, love me).

Ultimately symbolic to Abel of the idealistic power of romantic and selfless love versus the adversity and selfishness of the outside world, ♉ is in fact married. Her husband is the shadowy and sinister Olavo Hayano, a crazed military figure and emotionally impotent husband, who represents the political and aesthetic forces of oppression which Abel must learn to combat in order to become the socially and emotionally committed writer and human being to which he aspires. In short, the illicit nature of his relationship to ㊀ forces Abel to self-knowledge.

Designated as the "Historia de ㊀ , Nascida e Nascida" ("Story of ㊀, Born and Born"), the letter "O" sections give ㊀'s perspective of herself and of her relationship with Abel. The urban geography inhabited by Abel and this most central of *Avalovara*'s female characters, is São Paulo, a city whose population has multiplied alarmingly in this century, as thousands from all over Brazil have converged on this point seeking refuge and the opportunity denied them elsewhere. Such a migration *en masse* has, of course, created a particularly adverse urban environment especially emblematic of the problematic state in which Abel and ㊀ find themselves. In his writing, Osman Lins calls São Paulo the "El Dorado of laborers,"[55] thereby evoking the promise of a better life so many have sought there, and recalling that his fellow Nordestinos have fled in droves to this city, seeking respite from the harsh, devastating droughts which recurrently plague their region.

Himself plagued by the harsh blank page of the unproductive writer, the Nordestino Abel searches in São Paulo too for fulfillment and success, as he becomes more and more aware of the social and political problems which plague this huge metropolis and the huge country to which he belongs. Himself a dweller in São Paulo during his adult life, Lins, the "real-life" Abel, lived these problems daily. An indication of how concerned and aware this writer was of the present and future plight of the modern city, is his criticism of the "fictional country schools" to which urban parents with money send their children, and his elaborate proposal for "apartment schools" where children would learn how to live in harmony with their fellow apartment and city dwellers. Transferring the traditional quest for harmony with the natural world, to the modern need for harmony within the urban world so many inhabit, this very twentieth-century writer asks: "And what is the real relationship between their flowery school years in distant educational institutions surrounded by alfalfa fields, and their future life as city dwellers inhabiting skyscrapers?" only to conclude that: "With my apartment schools, students would not breath as freely as they would in country schools, but they would be, later on, better neighbors and better citizens."[56]

It is ♉ who makes Abel aware of his condition as urban dweller within one of the largest cities of the modern world, a city projected to be the most populous on earth by the year 2000. As ♉ describes herself in the following passage occurring early in the novel, she unites her existence as the Word and the power of verbal communication, to her existence as the central square, the meeting place in the city which symbolizes the power of collective urban collaboration. Incorporating into her very being the collective human expression and existence of the city, she begins by challenging her lover Abel and asking him:

> Serás capaz de ver as letras, as palavras que, em certas horas, vejo ainda ratejarem sob a minha pele e que, decerto, nunca silenciam? Ouço-as, dentro do meu corpo, ouço-as, vozerio distante, multidão agrupada numa praça, o murmurio das palavras ecoa em minhas coxas, nos meus peitos, no ventre, flui e reflui, continuado, não sei se alegre, nâo sei se feroz, flui, como se os limites do meu corpo fossem os limites da praça e meus ombros e axilas fossem abóbadas onde chegassem os últimos ecos das vozes, e os meus braços - que estendo - fossem extensões da praça avenidas também cheias de vozes. (34)

> (Will you be able to see the letter, the words which, at certain times, I see creeping over my skin and which, certainly, will never be silenced? I hear them inside my body, I hear them, a distant clamor, a multitude collected in a city square, the murmur of the words echoes in my thighs, in my breasts, in my womb, it flows again and again, continuous, whether happy or ferocious I can't make out, it flows, as if the limits of my body were the limits of the square, and my shoulders and armpits were the vaults where the last echoes reach, and my arms - which I extend - were the extensions of the square, of avenues also filled with voices).

As this passage so clearly and vociferously illustrates, ♉ is perhaps the ultimate Linsean "collective, polyphonic character," to use my term. She is, of course, the text and the city, "the name of the city" which Abel, the searching Northeastern writer living in São Paulo, realizes he must find early in *Avalovara* when he observes that "O texto que devo encontrar... assemelha-se ao nome de uma cidade." (64)

Along with being *the city* which Abel finally discovers, ♉ is the embodiment of love, the human affective experience which unites the most disparate beings in harmony and order, the creative ontological act which implies totality of being and communion. As might be expected in a novel by Osman Lins, in her capacity as lover, Ȍ is not one woman, but a synthesis of opposites living the duality of her existence, of her "two births" and of her "two bodies." (25) Speaking of this duality, Mary Daniel explains: " Ȍ has apparently narrowly escaped death in a fall experienced at the age of nine, and the 'new' or 'reborn' self she possesses from that moment on is seen in continual juxtaposition with her 'original' self." This fall prefigures, of course, the Garden of Eden motif which the "E" and central "N" sections elaborate toward the climax of the novel. Giving her interpretation, Daniel says that the fall of Ȍ and the text into which she is incorporated allow Lins, "to postulate a synthetic person incorporating ying-yang, male-female, young-old, past-present-future characteristics." Within a novel which asks the "nuclear question: What will the man/woman of the future be like?", Osman Lins, says Daniel, questions "the nature of human beings and their relationships as individuals with each other across or outside of time and space, and as a species with the potential for development beyond the present normal characteristics of *homo sapiens*."[57] Ultimately, Abel and Ȍ, are the new children of Adam and Eve, aspiring toward *creative unity* and *love* within an urban and modern post-lapsarian world, west of Eden. Frustrated and persecuted children of Western tradition and belief, they are inspired by Oriental mysticism. First explaining its divine, creative role and then alluding to its potential for unbounded love, Osman Lins describes the androgynous qualities of the Oriental deity Avalokiteçvara, the Buddhist Bodhisattva that lent its name to his novel, a divine figure that *unites creation* and *love* into its very being:

> There is an Oriental deity, a cosmic being, from whose eyes the Sun and Moon were born; from its mouth came the winds and from its feet, the Earth.
>
> This Avalokiteçvara is a deity filled with love. So much so that in India it is masculine, while in China it assumes feminine, maternal characteristics. And *Avalovara*...is a novel about love.[58]

As the creative force motivating Abel's cosmic, narrative spiral, then, ☿ is simultaneously a hermaphrodite who aspires to the cosmic duality of Avalokiteçvara, and an embodiment of love, the creative power which motivates this Oriental deity.

In addition to being an allegory about the creative and unifying power of love in a modern world, *Avalovara* is ultimately, of course, a novel about the creation of the novel, a meta-novel if ever there was one. Within such a novel, ☿ is, as she and Abel become aware, the spiral created by the fantastic and magical bird avalovara; i.e., ☿ is the cosmic motivating force of *Avalovara*. The character which, as Antonio Candido observes, "joins the ends of the spiral" in order to "realize the fulfillment for which the novel aspires,"[59] ☿ conjectures early in the text that the spiral flight of the avalovara is perhaps her name. While Abel explores and traces the contours of her face, ☿ contemplates the magical bird tracing its circular trajectory high in the sky. Her perspective at this point traces the avalovara's spiral flight in terms that echo the potential for expansion and concentration inherent in the symbol which names her, as I discussed earlier. Observing the aerial evolutions of the fantastic bird avalovara, as it moves in closer to the point where they are lying, ☿ thinks:

> Uma ave, bem no alto, faz evoluções. Voa tão longe que por vezes torna-se invisível, perdida entre as nuvens e o azul fulgurante. Com os lábios, de leve, Abel aflora meu rosto...contorna a linha das fontes, desliza pela face, busca-me a curva do queixo, sua respiração dobra-me os ossos, movo rápido a cabeça, mordo a sua boca. A ave solitária cresce e cada vez perco-a menos de vista. Custo a perceber que as suas evoluções são rigorosas. Voa com disciplina, traça uma espiral descendente, que se reduz em direção a um vértice. Esse vértice funde-se com o ponto em que estou deitada, vejo isto com clareza... Ao mesmo tempo, contenho um sobressalto: aquele vôo talvez seja o meu nome. (37-8)

> (A bird, way up high, traces evolutions. Its flight is so far off that sometimes it becomes invisible, lost amidst the clouds and the brilliant blue. With his lips, lightly, Abel reaches my face...follows the outline of my temples, glides over my checks, searches for the curve of my jaw, his breathing follows my bones. I move my head quickly and bite his mouth. The solitary bird grows and becomes easier to see. I find it difficult to understand its rigorous evolutions. Its flight is controlled

and traces a descending spiral which grows smaller as it approaches a vertex. This vertex fuses into the point where I am lying. I see this clearly... At the same time, I am taken by surprise: that bird might be my name).

Later in the novel, it is ☿ who discovers that the name of the magical bird is "avalovara" (239) and who describes it as "a being made up of birds small as bees. A Bird and a cloud of birds." (282) At once one and many, the fantastic avalovara reflects the individual/collective characters which populate Lins' fiction, as it represents *the* novel *Avalovara* and *all* novels simultaneously. In a 1974 interview, the author describes the allegorical significance of his narrative in relation to the art of narration in general by explaining that:

> When Abel [sic - it is ☿, as mentioned above] says that the Avalovara is a bird made up of many birds small like bees, he is describing the bird Avalovara and not the novel *Avalovara*. But really, that bird, along with other things, is a symbol of the novel. Not of this novel only, but of the novel in general. The novel agglutinates other narratives, shorter thematic units, smaller birds. It's not just my novel, but any novel, that does this. And I've already said earlier that *Avalovara* is, in a certain way, an allegory of the novel.[60]

The narrative spiral created by this magical bird and the themes of *Avalovara* which it joins together into a dynamic circular narrative, converge on ☿, as she observes: "Sou o ponto ou o ser para onde converge, com suas múltiplas faces, o que o homen conhece, o que julga conhecer, o de que suspeita, o que imagina e o que nem sequer lhe ocurre que exista." (135) ("I am the point or the being onto which converege, in their many forms, what man knows, what he thinks he knows, what he suspects, what he imagines and what exists but doesn't even occur to him.") Ultimately, all converge on ☿ and Abel, joined together making love. Offering a definition of her name and a description of the novel *Avalovara*, ☿ thinks: "Vasto é o *circulo* traçado entre as nuvens pelo Avalovara, e nós somos o *centro do seu vôo*." (285 - Emphasis is mine.) ("Vast is the *circle* traced among the clouds of Avalovara, and we are the *center of its flight*.") Circle, center, flight; ☿ is the narrative spiral movement of the avalovara, the cosmic force of the novel.

As the circumference of the narrative spiral moves closer to the cosmic center, ☿ and Abel move closer to the final moment of total convergence. This occurs when the narrative discourse passes through the letter "E" of the "TENET" cross and reaches the threshold of Paradise in the seventeen "E" sections entitled " ☿ e Abel: ante o Paraíso" (" ☿ and Abel: before Paradise"). Experiencing "pleasure" and aspiring to "unity," "enlightenment" (377) and knowledge, Abel makes love to ☿, as together they reach closer and closer to the climactic moment of amorous and aesthetic convergence. The closer they are, the more the actual discourse of the text reflects the spiral movement of the novel as, in the words of Alexandrino Severino, "sentences spin on themselves and go round and round"[61] forming a spiral-like, screw-live syntax. While Gabriel García Márquez counteracts the linearity of his simple syntax through the repetitive, vicious circularity of his novel's action, Osman Lins, as William Faulkner, also struggles against the sequential nature of language in order to create his spiral narrative. As *Absalom, Absalom!*, therefore, *Avalovara* also accumulates adjectives and nouns and verbs, producing a dizzying, vertiginous discourse which increases in intensity as the textual lovemaking comes closer and closer to climactic unity. While the spiraling tendencies of the syntax increase, so the amorous excitement of Abel and ☿ , and the erotically graphic description of their lovemaking also increase in tension and intensity. In the eighth "E" section, ☿ 's body with its "green uterus" (45) begins to meld into the primordial scene which makes up the carpet on which they are performing their lovemaking, as her body and breasts become the abundant and luxuriant world of nature within Abel's reach:

> Mordo os seios, zona de textura indefinível...sugo as aréolas, ela ergue uma perna e joga-se sobre as minhas, soam guizos em torno do tapete, vara a janela um vento súbito e morno,...sobre nós range uma fronde, o vento agita-a e eu tenho nas mãos, na boca, os grandes frutos da fronde, seus frutos gêmeos, redondos, únicos, maduros, impossível colher esses pomos encantados e cuja pele não os fecha ao mundo, antes encerra na sua polpa o mundo, e, no mundo, outra árvore com novos frutos gêmeos, fruíveis mas inseparáveis da árvore e nos quais o mundo mais uma vez - e sempre - se repete. Ouço passos, pés descalços sobre folhas? (350)

(I bite her breasts, a zone of undefined texture...I suck the areolas, she lifts her leg and throws herself on mine, small bells around the carpet ring, a warm, brisk wind comes through the window,...a frond rustles above us, the wind shakes it and I have in my hands, in my mouth, the great fruits of the frond, its twin fruits, round, unique, ripe, it is impossible to pick those enchanted apples whose skin does not separate them from the world, but instead they enclose within their pulp the world and, in the world, another tree with new twin fruit, which is fruitful but inseparable from the tree and through which the world once more - and forever - repeats itself. Do I hear footsteps, bare feet on leaves?)

Clearly reflecting his role as the creator of "the new story of Adam and Eve," Lins/Abel begin to discern the synthesis of opposites proposed by the body of ♉, "the new twin fruit" which is one with the tree of life.

Plunging into this "new world" of aesthetic and amorous revelation contained in the luxuriant ambiguity and synthetic duality of ♉'s being, Abel is impelled in his lovemaking and novel-making by the spiral discourse of the narrative. In this amorous, creative act, as Julia Cuervo Hewitt puts it: "Mother earth is penetrated by the masculine God who organizes the primordial chaos."[62] Within what could be called "A Portrait of the Artist as a Male Novelist," Abel is the archetypal masculine Creator giving order and form to his world by impregnating Mother Earth/the text with his phallus/pen. The novel expresses clearly the action of the male phallus "perforating" and "screwing" the word/text of ♉'s body: "o confronto do meu corpo com o seu atende a um esforçe de perfuração ou rompimento" (323) ("the confrontation of my body with hers attends to an effort of perforation and tearing") and "Aqui o texto, em caracteres totalmente desconhecidos e resistentes á decifração, entra pelas bordas, vindo do mundo exterior, vindo do princípio - e enrosca-se em espiral, griando para o centro." (326) ("Here the text, through characters totally unknown and resistent to deciphering, comes into the borders [of the carpet] from the outside world, from the beginning - and screws like a spiral, revolving toward the center." As Abel and his novel reach closer to fulfillment and completion, the writer discerns in ♉'s body the passage to the center he desires so viscerally: "abrem-se as coxas e revela-se o acesso, a entrada, a via, o esconderijo, o N, o centro."

(399) ("her thighs open to reveal the access, the entrance, the way, the hiding place, the N, the center.")

With and through ⊗ , therefore, Abel finally reaches the two central "N" sections entitled " ⊗ e Abel: o Paraíso" (" ⊗ and Abel: Paradise"). As together they are woven into the carpet's garden motif, the novel ends and the ultimate center assumes the first person plural voice of unity:

> ...nos integramos no tapete somos tecidos no tapete eu e eu margens de um rio claro murmurante povoado de peixes e de vozes nôs e as mariposas nós e o pássaro benévolo mais e mais distantes latidos dos cachorros vem um silêncio novo e luminoso vem a paz e nada nos atinge, nada, passeamos, ditosos, enlaçados, entre os animais e plantas do Jardim. (413)

> (...we are integrated into the carpet we are woven into the carpet I and I margins of a clear murmuring river populated with fish and voices we and the moths we and the sunflowers we and the kind bird ever more distant is the barking of dogs a new and luminous silence comes peace comes and nothing reaches us, nothing, we walk, blessed, intertwined, among the animals and plants of the Garden.)

Both *end* and *center*, this point is the ultimate instant of total being, the moment when, as does the last Aureliano Buendia ín *Cien años de soledad*, Abel *knows* once and for all who he is. In *Avalovara*, as in García Márquez's famous novel, the instant of complete self-revelation is the *end*, because it is the moment of *death*. In fact, while Abel and ⊗ continue their socially illicit relationship and make love on the woven carpet, ⊗'s frenzied husband finds them and fires the two decisive shots from his avenging army pistol. Simultaneously, this point in the novel is the *center*, because it is the *beginning*, the instant of cosmic creativity inherent in love/life/art.

Just as their orgasmic moment of sexual and verbal fulfillment is "written" into the text of the woven carpet, so ⊗ and Abel are together incorporated into its edenic scene. Emblematic of the unifying power of love, this unique woven carpet symbolizes life, for it "retells" the archetypal story of creation. Speaking of this cosmogonic aspect of this novel, Massaud Moisés concludes that "it is not a matter of eight themes, but of one theme with variations."[63] In addition, the carpet is the point where the beginning and the end of the magical spiral converge, the point which contains the "curve of life" in its totality. Along with signifying love and life, this woven carpet containing the "calligraphy of leaves" (356) symbolizes the written text of aesthetic creation. In mentioning the polyphonic threads that this novel weaves into a "general design," José Paulo Paes describes *Avalovara* as "a novel in which...the various 'voices' of the story alternate until the final meeting; a kind of romanesque/novelistic (Since in Portuguese the word "novel" is "romance," Paes uses the adjective "romanesca," both meanings of which are applicable in this context) tapestry where individual threads of different colors come together to compose the general design."[64] In an article lamenting the gradual disappearance of the "Day of the Tailor" celebrated in Brazil on September 6, Osman Lins explains the relationship between a tailor and a writer which his personal life taught him:

> My interest in tailors, I admit, comes from my awareness of a certain parallel between the work of a writer and their work. But there are also other stronger and more personal reasons: my father was a tailor. The Alfaiataria Lins (The Lins Tailor Shop) was well known in the Pernambucan town of Vitória de Santo Antão, where he lived almost all of his life.[65]

Speaking of his analysis as "unraveling the woven fabric of ideas" in the collection of critical essays *Guerra Sem Testemunhas*, a text which, incidentally, he says is "conceived as concentric circles," Osman Lins spends a great deal of time and space describing the history of the writing surface, from clay tablets to papyrus roles composed of leaves which were superimposed on one another in a crisscross pattern "producing a kind of weaving warp;" to parchment, devised in the city of Pérgamo (whence the word "pergaminho") where the sale of papyrus was forbidden, which allowed the superimposition of sheets on one another, thereby giving form to the book as we know it today; and finally, to paper made from wood pulp mashed into a paste and spread on an absorbent tissue.[66] While modern-day critics play with the relationship between "text" and "textual" and "texture" and "tissue,"[67] Osman Lins incorporates the creative and textual power of weaving into the literary texts he elaborates. The seventh mystery of "Retábulo de Santa Joana Carolina," for example, begins with a verbal and visual hymn to the art of weaving (106), while *Avalovara* both begins *and* ends with the primordial text and central space of the woven carpet. There, through the cosmological dynamics of the narrative spiral, the eight letters on a magic square have been incorporated into the curve of life.

Given the cosmic direction of the spiral narrative converging on the woven carpet, circularity in *Avalovara* is fundamentally focused on a primordial and ultimate center. By finally weaving the union of Abel and ȱ into the carpet, furthermore, this spiral actively assumes its role as "The Figure in the Carpet," as Henry James called the motivating principle of narrative in his 1896 short story. When compared with *Absalom, Absalom!* and *Cien años de soledad*, then, *Avalovara* appears to be the most centered of the three texts I have been analyzing. The narrative cosmology of this novel can, however, be broken up by the playful reader who might choose to read all the "T" sections, for example, in succession, thereby creating the story of Cecilia and Abel seen separately from the other stories. Lins himself describes the ludic dimensions of his text by observing that the reader can begin by reading all of the "S" sections, etc. etc.[68] Up to this point, for instance, I have not yet discussed the "P" sections of *Avalovara*. Indeed, the "S" and "P" sections are perhaps the two letters of the magic text which can most readily be read separately as autonomous stories, because they are so deliberately metafictional in nature. While the ten "S" sections recount the invention of "The Spiral on a Square" by the Roman slave Loreius, the ten "P" sections tell the story of Heckethorn's attempts to create a magical clock which will simultaneously play all of Scarlatti's musical compositions when it strikes the hour. Entitled "O Relógio de Julius Heckethorn" ("Julius Heckerthorn's Clock"), these sections invent the fantastic timepiece which is a symbol of modern mechanical/temporal/aesthetic convergence and harmony. While these letter sections are autonomous to a point, the decentering of narrative discourse such a sectional reading would produce, however, limits the narrative to a letter within a square. Ultimately, such a reader discounts the essential circularity of the narrative spiral, thereby destroying the cosmology created by *Avalovara*. While the decentering of narrative discourse is produced by the proliferation of ripple voices in *Absalom, Absalom!*, and by the spinning off-center of the gyrating wheel in *Cien años de soledad*, in a text as deliberately conceived as *Avalovara*, narrative decentering, while always present as a possibility, will only occur through the willful act of a playful reader.

Notwithstanding this "play of Lins' spiral on a square," the discourse of *Avalovara* is decentered in yet another fundamental respect. The overwhelming desire for fulfillment which drives Abel and the reader to the narrative "N," the center of the spiral on a square, is in constant tension with the collective and cosmic dimensions of a text which expands and refracts its focus beyond the individual human being and beyond life on this earth. Instead of focusing on a character as an individual creation, therefore, Lins' *Avalovara* creates character/cities, collective, polyphonic characters whose lives take on the universal rhythms of the cosmos. Anatol Rosenfeld speaks of "multiple focal perspectives" and describes the breakdown of "anthropocentrism" in Lins' fiction, seen in relation to the cosmic dimensions of this writer's work.

> As he is integrated among a higher order of infinite dimensions, the human being gains greatness and at the same time loses it. He attains it through being seen in relation to a higher order; he is an important part of an harmonious whole, deriving from it integrity and valor. However, since he is a mere particle of an immense universe, he ceases being the center of things and hence loses stature. Osman Lins's personal vision is decidedly different from the anthropocentrism evident in traditional psychological novels.[69]

Clearly indicating his post-humanist world view, Osman Lins describes his work in relation to the "a-perspective vision" of the Middle Ages as contrasted to the specific perspectivity of the Renaissance. The Middle Ages, says he, were

> neither anthropomorphic nor anthropocentric, but theocentric, so that the artists, as a reflection of their medieval world view, tended to see things as if they were not fixed in one place. That led to a much richer world view since it didn't limit life to our carnal condition. Then the nineteenth century novel gave new emphasis to the Renaissance world-view. My contact with art and especially medieval works, reinforced the tendency to see things in an a-perspective manner which I already had even before traveling. With respect to the novel, this view offers much richer possibilities, especially in terms of narrative focus and vision. *Avalovara* offers an a-perspective vision which doesn't focus on one individual...but tries to see things globally.

> But I don't consider this to be a preoccupation only I have. I find this return to a-perspectivism to be a characteristic, perhaps the dominant characteristic, of contemporary art.

Finally, Lins credits "Faulkner and certain works of Virginia Woolf"[70] with initiating the shift to this a-perspective narrative, as his own literary production contributes to a post-humanist perspective on and expression of the modern de-centered world we inhabit.

CHAPTER VII

"THE WORLD IS ROUND"

Ripples, a wheel and a spiral, all images evolving from one of the most ancient visual and conceptual paradigms elaborated by humans: the circle. "Perhaps the history of the world is the story of a few metaphors," Jorge Luís Borges postulates in "The Sphere of Pascal,"[1] an essay which considers the evolution of a circular spherical configuration which signified *perfection* in Plato, *being* in Parmenides, *God* in the Middle Ages, the *universe* and *human existence* in the Renaissance and *existential despair* in Pascal.[2] While focusing specifically on this "metamorphoses of the circle," the title of his important study from 1966, Georges Poulet analyzes "the changes of meaning to which (the circle) has never ceased to adapt itself in the human mind." After emphasizing that it is a form which can take on different interpretations, Poulet goes on to explain that "these changes of meaning coincide with corresponding changes in the manner by which human beings represent to themselves that which is deepest in themselves, that is to say, the awareness of their relationship with the inner and the outer worlds."[3]

When in *Guerra Sem Testemunhas* Osman Lins begins by speaking of his work as being "similar to that of the old navigators who went in search of adventure and a route to the Indies,"[4] this Brazilian writer clearly relates the creation of a literary text to the discovery of a *new world*. Indeed, the elaboration of a novel does imply the discovery and creation of a *new world of literary expression and anticipated fulfillment*. Mirroring the sixteenth-century experience of global circumnavigation which proved that, in popular terms, "the world is round," as well as the "discovery" and "invention" of the "New World" of America, William Faulkner, Gabriel García Márquez and Osman Lins create *circular new worlds* through the narrative elaboration of *Absalom, Absalom!*, *Cien años de soledad* and *Avalovara*, three novels of the Americas that attest to the technical experimentation and thematic vitality of twentieth-century narrative discourse. Most fundamentally, these novels are formed and informed by circularity, a geometric configuration long utilized by human beings to elucidate and describe self in relation to the world. The different versions of circularity utilized by these twentieth-century American authors express, of course, their particular perspectives on living in this century and in this hemisphere.

Very basically, the circle is a complete round figure which has traditionally symbolized totality of being. Shaped, as its definition describes, by "a curved line every point of which is equally distant from the point at the center," the circumference and the form it creates unite various equidistant points on a plane into a total unit revolving around a center. The dynamics of this circumference and its center is such, that the circular shape thus formed is equally capable of concentration and expansion. Through the dynamics of a shape which implies both a totality and unlimited expansion, these three novelists of the Americas express their personal and aesthetic desire for collective collaboration and creation. While the narrative ripple pattern of *Absalom, Absalom!*'s multiple voices recreates the human psychic process of *collective narrative elaboration*, the gyrating wheel of *Cien años de soledad* spins *collective stagnation and forgetfulness* into oblivion, and the spiral on a square of *Avalovara* motivates the *collective experience of cosmic and aesthetic order and creation*. The desire for joining and passing on in *Absalom, Absalom!*, for deciphering and not forgetting in *Cien años de soledad*, and for cosmic ordering and fulfillment in *Avalovara* all reinforce the collective dimension of three narratives which give voice to *America as collaborative creation*. Taking on the role of communal storytelling through their respective texts, each of these authors rejects the role of individual novelist within the linear-directed logocentric world of paternal authority. Living in a modern decentered world or, as Edward Said puts it, "in a circle without a center," these authors create literary worlds which collect and expand and reflect collaborative desire and "communal aims."[5]

As might be expected from a text expressing the reality of the United States, a country wholeheartedly dedicated to individual fulfillment and modern progress, the circularity of *Absalom, Absalom!* is metaliterary in nature and struggles constantly to comprehend the linearity of Thomas Sutpen's individual paternal design. In effect, the polyphonic circularity of narrative discourse in *Absalom, Absalom!* joins and connects American voices into a collective ripple pattern obsessed with innocence lost and a dream unfulfilled. True to North American literary tradition, William Faulkner contends with the reality and outcome of the so-called "American dream," to many "the last and greatest of human dreams," as Nick Carroway puts it at the end of *The Great Gatsby*. Through the pages of *Absalom, Absalom!* Faulkner achieved his most eloquent expression as a writer of the twentieth century and as a citizen of the Americas. Simultaneously, he opened up a new world of collective literary expression to North American literature.

Characteristically equating the United States with "America" and the writer with "he," Sacvan Bercovitch describes the role of the writer in the United States in the following manner:

> American writers have tended to see themselves as outcasts and isolates, prophets crying in the wilderness. So they have been, as a rule: *American* Jeremiahs, simultaneously lamenting a declension and celebrating a national dream... What distinguishes the American writer...is his *refusal* to abandon the national covenant... His identification with America as it ought to be impels the writer to withdraw from what is in America. When he retreats into his art, however, it is characteristically to create a haven for what Thoreau called "the only true America." In effect, the ideals that prompt his isolation enlist individualism itself, aesthetically, morally and mythically, into the service of society.[6]

As an individual and as a writer, William Faulkner *is* "crying in the wilderness" for what is perhaps ""the only true America," an elusive dream which shall always lure the human imagination and will. But, in contrast to the other well-known writers of his generation, F. Scott Fitzgerald and Ernest

Hemingway, William Faulkner went beyond the portrayal of solitary individual characters. His experimentation with narrative technique and structure led him to create the polyphonic circularity of *Absalom, Absalom!*'s ripple pattern, at once a *collective lament* for a dream unfulfilled and an *affirmation of collective collaboration and creation*. Through the dynamics of narrative ripples, the predominant preoccupation of the North American literary psyche with loss of innocence, becomes the discovery of collective aesthetic expression and creation.

Within twentieth-century Latin American literature, the predominant search for identity has led quite naturally to narrative as collective expression and creation. Given this all-engrossing search for cultural and historical identity in the face of socio-political and literary dominance by other more forceful and more defined cultures of the Western world, the new writers of Latin America have come closest "to understanding the importance of collective creation in literature,"[7] in the words of "the translator of Latin America into English," Gregory Rabassa. Traditionally considered marginal to Western literary expression, Latin American narrative has certainly come of age within modern world literature by raising a fantastically hearty collective voice. Among the writers of Spanish and Portuguese America, Gabriel García Márquez is perhaps the best-known, and his *Cien años de soledad* is undoubtedly the most celebrated novel of Latin America. Written by an author who affirms that "every good novel is *una adivinanza del mundo*"[8] - a prophecy, a prediction, a guess, a conjecture of the world - *Cien años de soledad* is a prophecy of and for the world of Macondo, a prophetic warning to races condemned to one hundred years of solitude. Very simply, its gyrating wheel spinning off-center symbolizes the collective experience of Latin America, trapped within a vicious circle of exploitation and frustration and forgetfulness. Through this novel then, circularity becomes an image of entrapment and stagnation, leading to final destruction and annihilation. In addition, the repetitive cyclical movement of this narrative wheel recounts the *collective history of Latin America*, not according to the chronological and linear paradigm of Western historiography, but according to the periodic cyclical rhythm of the natural world. So dominant is this cyclical movement, that the ultimate apocalyptic destruction of Macondo becomes a prophecy to future generations as it suggests the possibility of renewal and another cycle of civilization. In the end, the fanciful circular world of Macondo created by Gabriel García Márquez voices a *collective warning to Latin America*, to races living vicious cycles of historical forgetfulness and cultural stagnation.

Following the rhythm of the natural world, the Brazilian writer Osman Lins also adopts cyclical circularity to shape and structure his novel *Avalovara*. While the gyrating wheel of *Cien años de soledad* proves to be radically destructive in its wiping Macondo from the face of the earth, however, Lins narrative spiral traces the "curve of life," a vital path leading to *collective creation and fulfillment*. Perhaps the most ambitious, and certainly the most experimental in expressing collective literary aspirations, this writer goes so far as to populate his novel with synthetic character/cities that I call "polyphonic collective characters." In both *Cien años de soledad* and *Avalovara*, the search for identity is patterned after natural cyclical movement and leads to collective literary expression and cultural enlightenment. The ultimate outcome of *Avalovara*'s spiral trajectory, however, takes on the constructive and creative dimensions of cosmic order, while the gyrating wheel of *Cien años de soledad* is apocalyptic and destructive in its vicious circularity. The symmetrical image of ☯ and of the spiral on a square clearly indicate the constructive emphasis of *Avalovara*, as the off-center diagram of the gyrating wheel I propose illustrates the destructive dimensions of *Cien años de soledad*.

While *Cien años de soledad* stems from García Márquez's existential preoccupations and *Avalovara* from Lins' cosmic aspirations, both create fantastic worlds that revitalize metaphysical and ontological issues and doubts. Emphasizing human psychic processes of understanding and interpretation, Faulkner's expanding narrative ripples in *Absalom, Absalom!* eloquently reflect modern epistemological concerns. Also concerned with epistemology, both *Cien años de soledad* and *Avalovara* link the human search for knowledge and understanding to the ultimate enlightenment coinciding with the simultaneous instant of ontological realization. Uniting both beginning and end, the first and the last, Genesis and Apocalypse, the fantastic narrative spiral of *Avalovara* and the gyrating wheel of *Cien años de soledad* recreate *collective totality of being through natural cyclical movement*, i.e. the totality of a circle - be it a concentrated point or an expansive circumference - is joined to the cyclical pattern traced by a revolving circle. Simultaneity and revolution; the circle as totality of being and the circle as cyclical change; the fantastic narrative spiral and gyrating wheel incorporate into themselves the collective trajectories of the modern metaphysical and social issues confronting the Americas in the twentieth century.

Along with collective cultural aspirations, the circularity of these novels reflects narrative design and desire in relation to beginnings and endings. Analyzing the role of "beginnings" in narrative creation and elaboration, Edward Said observes that "form and representations of narrative fictions are based upon a desire to mime the life processes of generation, flourishing and death."[9] The long-held focus on generation within the Western world has, of course, traditionally privileged and emphasized the role of the father and of paternal lineage as the source of being. Given the crisis of paternal authority and filiation which characterizes modern literature and thought, therefore, Faulkner, García Márquez and Lins have assembled their literary worlds in ways which contradict the authority of lineage, by adopting the more ancient circular paradigm of natural and cosmic processes, a paradigm which formed original perspectives on America and the New World. Consequently, Thomas Sutpen's linear design literally goes up in flames as *Absalom, Absalom!*'s narrative ripples expand indefinitely; the patriarch José Arcadio Buendía is tied to the chestnut tree in the front yard as the vicious cycle of one hundred years takes its course, and the two-dimensional convergence of the square palindrome is woven into the cosmic circular proportions of the magical narrative spiral of *Avalovara*. Very simply, the long-held emphasis on linearity has led to a re-adoption of the cyclical and spiral movement of nature and the cosmos, a trajectory which traces the cycle of the natural world: birth ---> development ---> death, and motivates the trajectory of literary creation: beginning ---> middle ---> ending. While in *Absalom, Absalom!* Clytie and Miss Rosa witness the genesis and participate in the final destruction of Sutpen's design and house, Aureliano in *Cien años de soledad* and Abel in *Avalovara* actually experience the enlightening moment of simultaneity which unites beginning and ending and which coincides with the final instant of narrative fulfillment.

In his 1967 study entitled *The Sense of an Ending*, Frank Kermode also unites beginnings and endings by stating very simply: "In a novel the beginning implies the end." Analyzing "our deep need for intelligible Ends," Kermode observes that since we humans live "*in medias rés*," we "need fictive concords with origins and ends to make sense of the middle." Paradigms of Apocalypse, which Kermode calls "concord(s) of imaginatively recorded past and imaginatively predicted future...achieved on behalf of us who remain 'in the middest,' lie under our ways of making sense of the world,"[10] according to this critic. Focusing on endings from a psychological perspective, Peter Brooks speaks of "narrative desire" in relation to "the anticipated structuring force of the ending" as he analyzes "the superimposition of the model of the functioning of the psychic apparatus on the functioning of the text."[11] Uniting the psychological and aesthetic function of endings, much of the writing of Jorge Luís Borges is concerned with the ultimate moment of being which is death; as Carmen del Rio phrases it: "Man writes in order to not die, but the origin and cause of his writing is precisely his mortality, the consciousness of his mortality."[12]

Indeed, the plotting of narrative circularity in the three texts I have been analyzing does end in death: Abel and O die in a final embrace as their relationship and text assumes orgasmic significance at the very end of *Avalovara*; Aureliano Buendía, as he finally deciphers his own destiny, is wiped from the face of the earth by the Apocalyptic winds that sweep through the last pages of *Cien años de soledad*; and, true to Faulknerian innovation and experimentation with narrative time and technique, Quentin Compson commits suicide in *The Sound & the Fury*, a novel published in 1929, seven years before *Absalom, Absalom!*. Moving from primordial chaos to an aesthetic struggle for order, these authors create textual significance through narrative circularity which leads back to chaos, i.e., the absence of order which is death. Actively participating in the aesthetic creation of plot and meaning in literary fictions, the circular narrative structures of these novels reflect, therefore, the archetypal story of creation and trace the paradigmatic cycle of creation: chaos ---> order ---> choas. In this way, they each retell the Story of Creation as they participate in the creation of literature and contribute to the aesthetic elaboration of a new world of human and literary expression and potential. Ultimately, beginning and ending coincide perfectly within the circle as geometric form and as narrative design.

Originating and ending in the "new world" of America, these twentieth century fictions not only recreate the archetypal trajectory of Genesis to Apocalypse, but also reflect the fall from grace and from Paradise retold within the first book of the Bible, as well as the initial hope that the American continents would fulfill the promise of the New Eden. The loss-of-innocence motif so characteristic of North American literature in general, and of *Absalom, Absalom!* specifically, expresses the experience and preoccupation of the United States in relation to the concept of America as the New Eden, the Promised Land lying to the West across the mysterious waters of the Atlantic. The Puritans' belief in elect nationhood stems from their staunch conviction that they were the people chosen by God to fulfill the promise of a New Jerusalem, to erect the city on a hill which would reinstate a new earthly Paradise "west of Eden." Once on North American soil, however, this utopian dream evolved from a spiritual aspiration to the secular "gospel of success" based on economic well-being and earthly progress. The sense of guilt which haunts the North American psyche springs from this materialization and secularization of a dream which was originally spiritual and utopian. Continuing the Jeremiad tradition within North American literature, the narrative ripple pattern of *Absalom, Absalom!* expresses a collective lament for a *Paradise lost* to inhumanity and inequality within the United States. *Cien años de soledad*, on the other hand, whimsically takes its characters to "the land no one had promised them" (27) and simultaneously offers an ironic portrayal of a *worn-out* American dream of a *Paradise unfulfilled*. Obviously more constructive in its perspective, *Avalovara* revives the figure of Abel, the second son of our fallen parents who was killed by his brother Cain, the builder of the first earthly city east of Eden.[13] Through the motivating force of the narrative spiral, i.e., the aesthetic curve of life, the writer Abel becomes, then, the "builder of new and unique cities *west of Eden*," the character/cities of the Old and New World populating the literary utopia of *Avalovara*, a vision of *Paradise fulfilled*. Perhaps only Brazil, the "colossus"[14] as John Crow calls this huge underdeveloped country of Latin America, could still produce a visionary portrait of America late in the twentieth century. The so-called "American Dream," popularly focused on the United States, becomes through these novels the "Dream of the Americas" looking to various and varied experiences of the New World five hundred years after its invention. In the end, this Dream of the Americas - haunted and obsessed, tired and worn-out, vigorous and creative - continues to lure and fascinate and inspire.

Woven together, these three novels create a literary tapestry portraying the experience of America five hundred years after its invention and discovery. In the end, Judith Sutpen's loom image in *Absalom, Absalom!* leaves us with "scratches," traces of what might have been; Amaranta in *Cien años de soledad*, meanwhile, weaves and unweaves the shroud of her eternal discontent and frustration; Abel and ♉ , in their turn, weave the cosmic pattern of aesthetic creation into their fantastic carpet: three textual images which point to the narrative and rhetorical significance of "ripples," a "gyrating wheel" and "a spiral on a square." A tragic lament, a frustrated warning and an inspired vision: such are the literary and social ramifications of circularity and visions of the New World in three twentieth-century novels of the Americas.

NOTES

1. Circularity, Linearity and America

1. Gabriel García Márquez, "Fantasía y creación artística en América Latina y el Caribe," *Texto Crítico*, 5.14 (1979): 4. I have translated all quotations from texts originally in Spanish & Portuguese included in this study. Except for the quotations taken from the novels I am analyzing, which I will include in both the original language and my own translation within the text of my analysis, these other quotations will appear, with few exceptions, only in translated form, although the source is listed here in the original language edition.

2. Gabriel García Márquez, *Cien años de soledad* (Buenos Aires: Editorial Sudamérica, 1976) 12. All subsequent quotations will be taken from this edition and incorporated into the text of this analysis.

3. Silvio Zavala, "Examen del título de la conmemoración del V centenario del descubrimiento de América," *Cuadernos americanos; nueva época*, 9.3 (Mayo-Junio 1988): 19.

4. Zavala, 18.

5. Edmundo O'Gorman, *The Invention of America* Bloomington: Indiana UP, 1961.

6. Leopoldo Zea, *La esencia de lo americano* (Buenos Aires: Editorial Pleamar, 1971) 9.

7. *Voyages of Discovery: Time-frame AD 1400-1500* (Alexandria Virginia: Time-Life, 1989) 12.

8. *Voyages*, 35-6.

9. Wilcomb E. Washburn, "The Meaning of 'Discovery' in the Fifteenth and Sixteenth Centuries," *The American Historical Review*, 68.1 (October 1962): 18.

10. Americo Vespucci, "Letter to Lorenzo Pietro di Medici, "*Mundus Novus*, trans. George Tyler Northrup (Princeton: Princeton UP, 1916) 1.

11. Octavio Paz, *El laberinto de soledad* (México: Fondo de Cultura Económica, 1950) 152.

12. O'Gorman, 61.

13. Sacvan Bercovitch, *The American Jeremiad* (Madison, Wisconsin: U of Wisconsin P, 1978) 148.

14. Leopolo Zea, *América en la consciencia de Europa* (México: Los Presentes, 1955) 98.

15. Russel B. Nye, *This Almost Chosen People: Essays in the History of American Ideas* (Michigan State UP, 1966) 50 & 45.

16. Quoted in José Luis López-Schümmer, "El Descubrimiento como mito," *Cuadernos Americanos: nueva época*, 9.3 (Mayo-Junio 1988): 23.

17. López-Schümmer, 26 & 24-5.

18. David W. Noble, *The Eternal Adam & the New World Garden* (New York: George Braziller, 1968) xi.

19. López-Schümmer, 24.

20. Paz, 85.

21. Arnold Chapman, "Pampas & Big Woods: Heroic Initiation in Güiraldes & Faulkner," *Comparative Literature*, 11 (1959): 76.

22. John S. Crow, *The Epic of Latin America* (Garden City, New York: Dobleday, 1971) 143.

23. Roderick Nash, *Wilderness & the American Mind* (New Haven & London: Yale UP, 1967) 25.

24. Bercovitch, 289.

25. Crow, 839-40

26. Bercovitch, 110.

27. Sacvan Bercovitch, *The Puritan Origins of the American Self* (New Haven & London: Yale UP, 1975) 145.

28. F. Scott Fitzgerald, *The Great Gatsby* (New York: Charles Scribner's 1925) 182.

29. Alexis de Tocqueville, *Democracy in America* (New York: Alfred A. Knopf, 1951) 20-1.

30. St. Jean de Crèvcoeur, "Letters from an American Farmer: III," *The Norton Anthology of American Literature*, Vol 1 (New York & London: W. W. Norton, 1979) 441-2.

31. Leopoldo Zea, *América en la historia* (México & Buenos Aires: Fondo de Cultura Económica, 1957) 19-20. Along with this fundamental difference in perspective, many other factors have, of course, contributed to the differences existant between Latin America

and North America, a topic to which I will dedicate future attention and study.

32. Perry Miller, *Errand into the Wilderness* (Cambridge & London: Harvard UP, 1956) 1-15.

33. John Winthrop, "A Model of Christian Charity," *The Norton Anthology of American Literature*, Vol 1 (New York & London: W. W. Norton, 1979) 24. Winthrop's words are, of course, modeled on the Biblical imagery which singled out the chosen people as proof that God's Divine Plan was being fulfilled here on earth. See, for example, Matthew 5:14-6 "Ye are the light of the world. A city that is set on a hill cannot be hid. Neither do men light a candle, and put it under a bushel, but on a candlestick; and it giveth light unto all that are in the house. Let your light so shine before men, that they may see your good works and glorify your Father, which is in heaven."

34. Russell B. Nye, *The Almost Chosen People: Essays in the History of American Ideas* (Michigan State UP, 1966) 51.

35. Francis Murphy, "Early American Literature, 1620-1820: Introduction" *The Norton Anthology of American Literature*, Vol 1 (New York & London: W. W. Norton, 1979) 2. Murphy goes on to affirm that "Both in the nineteenth century and in the twentieth, Americans have seen themselves as a 'redeemer nation' without, of course, possessing Bradford's Christian ideas."

36. Frederick Jackson Turner, *The Frontier in American History* (New York: Henry Holt, 1921)2-3. So fundamental is this frontier dynamic to the North American psyche, that many critics would agree with Perry Miller's affirmation that "*the* American theme" is that "of Nature versus civilization." Miller, 205.

37. James D. Bennett, *Frederick Jackson Turner* (Boston: Twayne, 1975) 95 & 99. Annette Kolodney offers a feminine perspective on the North American frontier as she contrasts the male metaphor - forest, wooded wilderness - to the female version of the national metaphor - open prairie and garden - in her study *The Land Before Her*, and affirms: "I would have had women's fantasies take the west rather than the psychosexual dramas of men intent on possessing a virgin continent. In the women's fantasies, at least, the garden implied home and community, not privatized erotic mastery." *The Land Before Her: Fantasy & Experience of the American Frontiers, 1630-1860* (Chapel Hill & London: U of North Carolina P, 1984) xxiii. Locating this fantasy of virgin soil in the Old World psyche, David W. Noble speaks of the "European dream of redemption in the virgin land of America." Noble, x.

38. William Humphrey, *Ah Wilderness! The Frontier in American Literature* (El Paso: Texas Western P, 1977) 15.

39. George Wolfskill & Stanley Palmer, eds., *Essays on Frontiers in World History* (Austin, Texas: U of Texas P, 1981) x.

40. Emilio Willems, "Social Change on the Latin American Frontier," *The Frontier: Comparative Studies*, eds. David Harry Miller & Jerome O. Steffen, (Norman: U of Oklahoma P, 1977) 259 & 262.

41. Crow, 144 & 145.

42. Crow, 837-8.

43. Bercovitch, *The American Jeremiad*, 163-4.

44. Bercovitch, *The Puritan Origins of the American Self*, 147.

45. Bercovitch, *The American Jeremiad*, 94 & 95.

46. Bercovitch, *The American Jeremiad*, 69.

47. Bercovitch, *The American Jeremiad*, 124 & 125.

48. As an inscription for the tombstone of his younger brother who died in an airplane crash on November 10, 1935, William Faulkner chose the epitaph he had given John Sartoris in the first of his Yoknapatawpha novels "I bare him on eagles' wings and brought him unto me." David Minter, *William Faulkner: The Writing of a Life* (Baltimore: John Hopkins P, 1980) 151.

49. Nye, 89.

50. Nash, 40.

51. Bercovitch, *The American Jeremiad*, 93-4.

52. Zea, *América en la historia*, 57.

53. Nye, 20-1.

54. Nye, 40.

55. Miller, 235.

56. Zea, *América en la conciencia de Europa*, 87 & 89-90. for an analysis of the concept of progress as an interpretation of history and a philosophy of action in the world and in North America, see J. B. Bury, *The Idea of Progress: An Inquiry into its Growth and Origin*. New York: Macmillian, 1932.

57. Bercovitch, *The American Jeremaid*, 20 & 28. A Canadian immigrant, Bercovitch describes, on page 11, his astonishment at the pronounced sense of mission he encountered in the cultural and literary expression

of the United States, "a country that," as he puts it, "could read its destiny in its landscape." This scholar explains his fascination with the "jeremiad," the Puritan sermon rhetoric of exhortation, and describes his immigrant's perspective in the following manner. "..what first attracted me to the study of the jeremiad was my astonishment, as a Canadian immigrant, at learning about the prophetic history of America. Not of North America, for the prophecies stop short at the Canadian and Mexican borders, but of a country that, despite its arbitrary territorial limits, could read its destiny in its landscape, and a population that, despite its bewildering mixture of race and creed, could believe in something called the American mission, and could invest that patent fiction with all the emotional, spiritual and intellectual appeal of a religious quest. I felt like Sancho Panza in a land of Don Quixotes."

58. Nye, 205.

59. Turner, 38.

60. Nye, 206.

61. Bennett, 100.

62. Fitzgerald, 182.

63. Nash, 82.

64. Miller, 235 & 236.

NOTES

2. Voices of America

1. Robert G. Collmer, "When 'Word' Meets *Palabra*: Crossing the Border with Literature," *William Faulkner: Prevailing Verities and World Literature*: Proceedings of the Comparative Literature Symposium (Lubbock, Texas Tech UP, 1973) 161.

2. Harley d. Oberhelman, "Faulknerian Techniques in Gabriel García Márquez's Portrait of a Dictator," *Ibero-American Letters in Perspective*: Proceedings of the Comparative Literature Symposium, eds, Wolodymer T. Zyla & Wendell M. Aycock (Lubbock, Texas Tech UP, 1979) 172.

3. James E. Irby, "La influencia de William Faulkner en cuatro narradores hispanoamericanos," Master's Thesis: Universidad Nacional Autónoma de Mexico, 1956; and John Brushwood, "Importancia de Faulkner en la novela latinoamericana," *Letras Nacionales* 31 (1976): 7-14.

4. Katalin Kulin, "Reasons and Characteristics of Faulkner's influence on Modern Latin American Fiction," *Acta Litteraria: Academie Scientiarum Hungaricae* 13 (1971) 349.

5. Carlos Fuentes in an interview with Christopher Sharp in *W.* Supplement to *Women's Wear Daily* (29 Oct - 5 Nov 1976): 9.

6. Carlos Fuentes in an interview with Jonathan Tittler in *Diacritics* 10.3 (Fall 1980): 52.

7. Carlos Fuentes, *La nueva novela en hispanoamérica* (Mexico: Joaquin Mortiz, 1969) 19.

8. Gabriel García Márquez & Mario Vargas Llosa, *La novela en América Latina: Diálogo* (Lima: Ediciones Universidad Nacional de Engeniería, 1968) 52-3.

9. Luis Harss, *Los nuestros* (Buenos Aires: Editorial Sudamericana, 1969) 396.

10. For further discussion of García Márquez's participation in the Barranquilla Group, see Jacques Gilard, "García Márquez, le Groupe de Barranquilla et Faulkner," *Cahiers du Monde Hispanique et Luso-Brésilian* (Caravelle) 27 (1976): 159-70. The observation just cited is taken from page 161 of this article.

11. Raul Rodríquez Márquez, "Veinte años después," *Magazin Dominical de El Espactador*, Bogotá (October 1967): 2.

12. Later that same year, of course, Faulkner was indeed awarded the Nobel Prize for literature.

13. It is interesting to note that both of these writers worked on film scripts for a time, Faulkner in Hollywood and García Márquez in Mexico City.

14. Harley Oberhelman, *The Presence of Faulkner in the Writings of García Márquez* (Lubbock, Texas: Texas Tech UP, 1980) 23-4. For futher information on other North American writers that García Márquez discussed in this newspaper column, see Gilard, especially page 168. The names listed - John Steinbeck, Richard Wright, Truman Capote, Ernest Hemingway, William Saroyan, John Dos Passos, Edgar Allen Poe and Mark Twain - indicate the scope of Márquez's knowledge of and interest in North American literature.

15. Armando Durán, "Conversaciones con Gabriel García Márquez," *Sobre García Márquez*, ed. Pedro Simón Martínez (Montevideo: Biblioteca de Marcha, 1970) 33-4.

16. Mario Vargas Llosa, "García Márquez: De Arcata a Macondo," *Nueve asedios a García Márquez* (Santiago de Chile: Editorial Universitaria, 1972) 140.

17. Miguel Fernández-Braso, *Gabriel García Márquez: Una conversación infinita* (Madrid: Editorial Azur, 1969) 88.

18. Referring to critics with his characteristic playfulness, Márquez could be poking fun at this kind of "groping in the dark" when he says: "Critics are very serious men and seriousness stopped interesting me a long time ago. I really get a kick out of seeing them skidding in the dark." This classic "Márquezean" observation appears in Fernández-Braso, 89.

19. Octavio Corvalon, "Introducción," *Hacia las fuentes de García Márquez* Seminario de Literatura Comparada (Cuadernos de Letras: Universidad de Salta, 1979) 17-8.

20. García Márquez, "Fantasía y creación artística," 7.

21. Commenting on the impact that Márquez's grandparents had on the creation of Macondo and on Faulkner's experience of his grandmother, Florence Delay & Jacqueline de Labriolle say: "One knows how much that imaginary town owes to the stories told by a grandmother as gifted as Caroline Barr, Faulkner's 'Mamma,' and to the memories of a grandfather, a Civil War veteran, who appears periodically in his work." "Márquez: Est-il le Faulkner Colombien?" *Revue de Litterature Comparée* 47 (1973): 95.

22. Oberhelman, "Faulknerian Techniques," 174-5.

23. Delay & de Labriolle, 97.

24. Delay & de Labriolle, 95-6.

25. Delay & de Labriolle, 113.

26. Delay & de Labriolle, 111-2.

27. Delay & de Labriolle, 112.

28. Lois Parkinson-Zamora, "The End of Innocence: Myth & Narrative Structure in Faulkner's *Absalom, Absalom!* and García Márquez' *Cien años de soledad*, "*Hispanic Journal* 41 (Fall 1982): 24.

29. Parkinson-Zamora, 24.

30. Mark Frederic Frisch, "Parallels between William Faulkner and Four Hispanic American Novelists" *DAI* 46 (1985): 972-A. U of Michigan.

31. John S. Brushwood, *The Spanish American Novel: A Twentieth-Century Survey* (Austin & London: U of Texas P, 1975) 335.

32. William Faulkner, *Absalom, Absalom!* (New York: The Modern Library, Random House, 1936) 8-9. *All* of the quotations in this discussion of "voice" are taken from the second paragraph of this text, found on the second and third pages of the novel, i.e., pages 8-9. Also, all subsequent quotations will be taken from this edition and incorporated into the text of this analysis.

33. Mary E. Davis, "The Haunted Voice: Echoes of William Faulkner in García Márquez, Fuentes and Vargas Llosa," *World Literature Today* 59.4 (Autumn 1985): 231.

34. Carlos Fuentes, 30.

35. García Márquez, "Fantasía y creatión artística," 4.

36. Fernández-Braso, 95-7.

37. Delay & de Labriolle, 123.

38. In a future study, I would like to analyze García Márquez's narrative technique in relation with that of Virginia Woolf, especially in terms of their treatment of time and their use of fantasy.

39. Harass, 396-7.

40. William Kennedy, "The Yellow Trolley Car in Barcelona, and Other Visions: A Profile of Gabriel García Márquez," *The Atlantic Monthly* 231 (1973): 57.

41. Dorothy Tuck, *Crowell's Handbook of Faulkner* (New York: Thomas Y. Crowell, 1964) 14-5.

42. Harley Oberhelman, "García Márquez and the American South," *Chasqui* 5.1 (Nov 1975): 30.

43. Gregory Rabassa, "Osman Lins and *Avalovara*: The Shape and Shaping of the Novel," *World Literature Today* 53.1 (Winter 1979): 32.

44. Rabassa, 31.

45. Rabassa, 35.

NOTES

3. "Ripples Spreading on Water"

1.   David Wyatt, "Faulkner and the Burdens of the Past,"*Prodigal Sons: A Study in Authorship and Authority* (Baltimore & London: Johns Hopkins UP, 1988) 93.

2.   Michael Millgate, *The Achievement of William Faulkner* (New York: Random House, 1966) 154.

3.   John T. Irwin, "Doubling and Incest/Repetition and Revenge," *William Faulkner's Absalom, Absalom!*, ed Harold Bloom (New York: Chelsea House, 1987) 10.

4.   Deborah Robbins, "The Desperate Eloquence of *Absalom, Absalom!*," *The Mississippi Quarterly* 34.3 (summer '81): 32.1.

5.   David Krause, "Opening Pandora's Box: Re-reading Compson's Letter and Faulkner's *Absalom, Absalom! Centennial Review* 3.2 (1986): 374.

6.   David Minter, "Family, Region & Myth in Faulkner's Fiction," *William Faulkner's Absalom, Absalom!*, ed. Harold Bloom (New York: Chelsea House, 1987) 82.

7.   Stephen M. Ross has written a thought-provoking analysis of the monological tendencies of *Absalom, Absalom!*, of, in his words, "just how great the pressure is to transform all the discourse in the text into the monological, into a single oratorically derived overvoice." Comparing Sutpen's "design" to the novel's discourse, Ross says: "Just as Sutpen seeks to create a perfect unified 'design' in his land and lineage, so too the novel's discourse seeks to become single-voiced." This critic forgets, however, what happens to Sutpen's lineage in this novel. Just as Sutpen's linear design figuratively and literally "goes up in flames," so the dialogical dynamics and speculation of this novel's discourse ultimately erase any monological tendencies. "Oratory and the Dialogical in *Absalom, Absalom!*, *Intertextuality in Faulkner*, eds. Michel Gresset & Noel Polk (Jackson: UP of Mississippi, 1985) 73-86.

8.   David Minter, *William Faulkner: the Writing of a Life* (Baltimore: Johns Hopkins UP, 1980) 152; Albert J. Guerard, *The Triumph of the Novel: Dickens, Dostoevsky & Faulkner* (New York: Oxford UP, 1976) 339; and Millgate, 150.

9.   Olga W. Vickery, *The Novels of William Faulkner* (Louisiana State U, 1959) 28.

10.   Minter, *William Faulkner: The Writing of a Life*, 118-9.

11. Richard Chase, "Faulkner - The Great Years," *The American Novel & its Tradition* (New York: Gordeon Press, 1978) 217-8.

12. William Faulkner, *Light in August* (New York: Vintage Books, 1932) 246 & 248. Subsequent quotations from this novel are taken from this edition and will be incorporated into the text of this study.

13. Edmond L. Volpe, *Reader's Guide to William Faulkner* (New York: Farrar, Straus, 1964) 42.

14. Collmer, 163. Speaking of his experience in teaching Faulkner, Collmer adds that this writer's style "presented fewer problems to persons whose English was not native than to many persons of an English background."

15. Dorothy Tuck, *Crowell's Handbook of Faulkner* (New York: Thomas Y. Crowell, 1964) 14.

16. J. Hillis Miller, "The Two Relativisms: Point of View and Indeterminancy in the Novel *Absalom, Absalom!*. *Relativism in the Arts*, ed. Betty Jean Craige (Athens: U of Georgia P, 1983) 151.

17. Georges Poulet, *The Metamorphoses of the Circle* (Baltimore: Johns Hopkins UP, 1966) vii.

18. Poulet, 7.

19. John T. Matthews, *The Play of Faulkner's Language* (Ithaca & London: Cornell UP, 1982) 115.

20. Guerad, 338.

21. Hyatt H. Waggoner, *William Faulkner: From Jefferson to the World* (U of Kentucky P, 1959) 155.

22. Donald M. Kartiganer, "Toward a Supreme Fiction: *Absalom, Absalom!* in *Faulkner: New Perspectives*, ed. Richard H. Brodhead (Englewood Cliffs, New Jersey: Prentice Hall, 1983) 157.

23. Vickery, 87.

24. Peter Brooks, "Incredulous Narration: *Absalom, Absalom!*," *reading for the Plot: Design & Intention in Narrative* (New York: Alfred A. Knopf, 1984) 294.

25. For a stimulating discussion of the function of Bon's letter and reading/rereading in *Absalom, Absalom!*, please see: David Krause, "Reading Bon's Letter and Faulkner's *Absalom, Absalom!*," *PMLA*, 99 (1984): 225-239.

26. Jean Weisberger, *Faulkner & Dostoevsky: Influence and Confluence* (Athens: Ohio UP, 1974) 117.

27. Jacques Derrida, "Structure, Sign and Play in the Discourse of the Human Sciences," *The Structural Controversy*, eds. Richard Macksey & Eugenio B. Donato (John Hopkins UP, 1972) 264.

28. Irwin, 33-4 & 32.

29. Brooks, 311 & 312.

30. Theodore Andrea Cook, *The Curves of Life: An Account of Spiral Formations and Their Application to Growth in Nature, to Science & to Art* (New York: Dover, 1979) 224.

31. Krause, "Opening Pandora's Box," 365.

32. Warwick Wadlington, *Reading Faulknerian Tragedy*, (Ithaca & London: Cornell UP, 1987) 215-6.

33. Minter, *William Faulkner: The Writing of a Life*, 159.

34. Frederick L. Gwynn & Joseph L. Blotner, eds, *Faulkner in the University: Class Conferences at the University of Virginia: 1957-8* (Charlottesville, Virginia: U of Virginia P, 1959) 275.

NOTES

4. A "Design"

1. James A. Snead, *Figures of Division: William Faulkner's Major Novels* (New York: Methuen, 1986) xi.

2. Brooks, 301

3. William Faulkner, *Selected Letters of William Faulkner*, ed. Joseph Blotner (New York: Random House, 1977) 78-9; 84.

4. Minter, *William Faulkner: The Writing of a Life*, 150.

5. Lewis P. Simpson, Yoknapatawpha & Faulkner's Fable of Civilization," *The Maker and the Myth: Faulkner and Yoknapatawpha*, eds. Evans Harrington & Ann J. Abadie (Jackson: UP of Mississippi, 1978) 125.

6. Annette Kolodny, *The Land Before Her: Fantasy and Experience of the American Frontiers, 1683-1860* (Chapel Hill & London: U of North Carolina P, 1984) 5.

7. Nye, 204.

8. Krause, "Opening Pandora's Box," 366.

9. Matthews, 156.

10. Brooks, 301.

11. Nancy Blake, "Creation and Procreation: The Voice and the Name, or Biblical Intertextuality in *Absalom, Absalom!*," *Intertextuality in Faulkner*, eds. Michel Gresset and Noel Polk (Jackson: UP Mississippi, 1985) 133.

12. Gwynn & Blotner, 71.

13. Gary Lee Stonum, "The Fate of Design" in *William Faulkner's Absalom, Absalom!*, ed. Harold Bloom (New York: Chelsea House, 1987) 44. Stonum lists the various relationships to inherited material within this novel as: Sutpen trying to establish a dynasty, Charles Bon seeking the recognition of a father, Quenton Compson trying to tell about the South and the writer composing a novel.

14. Matthews, 145.

15. Brooks, 303.

16. Eric J Sundquist, "*Absalom, Absalom!* and the House Divided" in *William Faulkner's Absalom, Absalom!*, ed. Harold Bloom (New York: Chelsea House, 1987) 91.

17. Vickery, 94.

18. Irwin, 20-1; 18 & 19.

19. Simpson, 126.

20. Brooks, 311; 301-2.

21. Irwin, 22.

22. Millgate, 164; 158.

23. Guerad, 307.

24. David Williams, *Faulkner's Women: The Myth and the Muse* (Montreal & London: McGill-Queen's UP, 1977) 13.

25. Judith B. Wittenberg, "William Faulkner: A Feminist Consideration: in *American Novelists Revisited: Essays in Feminist Criticism* (Boston: G. K. Hall, 1982) 328.

26. Loren F. Schmidtberger, "*Absalom, Absalom!* What Clytie Knew," *The Mississippi Quarterly* 35.3 (summer '82): 259.

NOTES

5. A "Gyrating Wheel"

1. Quoted in Richard Adams, *Faulkner: Myth and Motion* (Princeton UP, 1968) 12.

2. Katalin Kulin, *Creación mítica en la obra de Gabriel García Márquez* (Budapest: Akadémia Kladó, Editorial de la Academia de Ciencias de Hungria, 1980) 12.

3. Lucila Inés Mena, *La función de la historia en Cien años de soledad* (Barcelona: Plaza & Jones, 1979) 137.

4. Vincenzo Bollettino, *Breve estudio de la novelística de García Márquez* (Madrid: Playor, 1973) 95.

5. Carlos Fuentes, *La nueva novela en hispanoamérica*, 30.

6. Karl Löwith, *Meaning in History* (Chicago: U of Chicago P, 1949) 19.

7. Hayden White, *Tropics of Discourse: Essays in Cultural Criticism* (Baltimore, Maryland: Johns Hopkins UP, 1978) 5 & 216.

8. Mario Vargas Llosa, *García Márquez: Historia de un deicidio* (Barcelona Barral Editores, 1971) 598-9. For examples and an analysis of repetition in *Cien años de soledad*, see especially pages 598-607.

9. Josefina Ludemar, *Cien años de soledad: una interpretación* (Buenos Aires: Editorial Tiempo Contemporaneo, 1972) 92.

10. Claudia Dreifus, "Interview: Gabriel García Márquez," *Playboy* 30.2 (Feb 1983): 74.

11. Raymond L. Williams, "El tiempo en la novela: observaciones en torno al tiempo en la novela colombiana contemporanea," *Explicación de Textos Literarios* 11.2 (1982-83) 15.

12. Robert Lewis Sims, *The Evolution of Myth in Gabriel García Márquez* (Miami: Ediciones Universal, 1981) 111.

13. Gaston Bachelard, *The Poetics of Space*, trans. Maria Jolas (Boston: Beacon Press, 1964) 7 & 15.

14. Sims, 111.

15. Michael Palencia-Roth, *Gabriel García Márquez: La linea, el círculo y las metamorfosis del mito* (Madrid: Editorial Gredos, 1983) 92.

16. Michael Wood, "Review of *One Hundred Years of Solitude*," *Colombia Forum* 13.3 (summer 1970): 162.

17. Fuentes, La nueva novela en hispano américa, 10.

18. Palencia-Roth, 96; D. P. Gallagher, "Gabriel García Márquez," *Modern Latin American Literature* (London: Oxford UP, 1973) 157; and Sims, 123.

19. Sims, 142 & Laurence M. Porter, "The Political Function of Fantasy in García Márquez," *Centennial Review* 30.2 (1986): 200.

20. René Jara Cuadra, *Las claves del mito en Cien años de soledad* (Chile: Ediciones Universidad de Valparaiso, 1972) 18.

21. Emir Rodríguez Monegal, "Novedad y anacronismo de *Cien años de soledad*," *Homenaje a Gabriel García Márquez*, Helmy F. Giacoman, ed (New York: Las Américas Publishing Co., Inc., 1972) 32 and Gregorio Salvador, *Commentarios estructurales a Cien años de soledad* (Las Palmas: Litografía Saavedra, 1970) 30.

22. J. E. Cirlot, *A Dictionary of Symbols* (New York: Philosophical Library, 1962) 148.

23. Cuadra, 13.

24. Vargas llosa, 550.

25. Zunilda Gertel, "Tres estucturas fundamentales en la narrative hispanoamericana actual," *Nueva Narrativa Hispanoamericana* 5 (enero y sept, 1975): 219.

26. Luis Harss and Barbara Dohmann, *Into the Mainstream* (New York: Harper & Row, 1967) 39.

27. Suzanne Jill Levine, "*Pedro Páramo* & *Cien años de soledad*: un paralelo," *Homenaje a Gabriel García Márquez*, ed. Helmy F. Giacoman (New York: Las Américas, 1972) 283.

28. Rodriguez Monegal, 16 & Dreifus, 172.

29. Aníbal González, "Translation and Genealogy: *One Hundred Years of Solitude*," *Gabriel García Márquez: New Readings*, eds. Bernard McGuirk & Richard Caldwell (Cambridge: Cambridge UP, 1987) 73.

30. Gene H. Belle-Villada, "García Márquez and the Novel," *Latin American Literary Review* 13.25 (Jan-June 1985): 21.

31. Roberto Gonzáles Echevarría, "*Cien años de soledad*: The Novel as Myth and Archive," *Modern Language Notes* 99.2 (March 1984): 358 & 369.

32. Iris M. Zavala, "*Cien años de soledad*: Crónica de Indias," *Homenaje a Gabriel García Márquez*, ed. Helmy F. Giancoman (New York: Las Américas, 1972) 205. Although García Márquez himself has said that the word Macondo comes from the name of a banana plantation in the region in which he grew up, Zavala goes on to say that "macondo" is the "popular word used in Colombia to indicate a heafty bombacacea tree, similar to the silk-cotton tree."

33. Graciela Maturo, *Claves simbólicas de García Márquez* (Buenos Aires: Fernando García Cambeiro, 1972) 116.

34. Patricia Drechsel Tobin, *Time and the Novel: The Genealogical Imperative* (Princeton UP, 1978) 188; 178; 183; 191 & 184.

35. René Jara and Jaime Mejía Duque, *Las claves del mito en García Márquez* (Valparaíso: Ediciones Universitarias de Valparaíso, 1972) 75.

36. Gabriel García Márquez, *El coronel no tiene quine le escriba* (México: Ediciones Era, 1961) 11 & 25-6.

37. Kulin, 187.

38. Gabriel García Márquez, "Los funerales de la Mama Grande," *Los funerales de la Mama Grande* (Barcelona: Plaza & Janes, 1976) 121 & 139.

39. Julio Ortega, "Exchange System in *One Hundred Years of Solitude*," *Gabriel García Márquez and the Powers of Fiction*, ed. Julio Ortega (Austin: U of Texas P, 1988) 5.

40. Gabriel García Márquez, "The Solitude of Latin America: Nobel Lecture, 1982," trans. Marina Castañeda, *Gabriel García Márquez and the Powers of Fiction*, ed. Julio Ortega (Austin: U of Texas P, 1988) 91.

41. Emir Rodríguez Monegal, "*One Hundred Years of Solitude*: The Last Three Pages," *Critical Essays on Gabriel García Márquez*, ed. George R. McMurray (Boston: G. K. Hall, 1987) 149.

42. Georges Poulet, *The Metamorphosis of the Circle*, (Baltimore: Johns Hopkins UP, 1966) xi.

43. Ricardo Gullón, "García Márquez o el olvidado arte de contar," *Homenaje a Gabriel García Márquez*, ed. Helmy F. Giacoman (New York: Las Américas, 1972) 149; Sims, 139 and Vargas Llosa, 500.

44. Fernández-Braso, 96.

45. José Antonio Bravo, *Lo real maravilloso en la narrativa latinoamericana* (Lima: Editoriales Unidas, 1978) 43.

46. Mario Vargas Llosa, "García Márquez: de Aracataca a Macondo," *9 asedios a García Márquez* (Santiago de Chile: Editorial Universitaria, 1969) 127.

47. Dreifus, 76.

48. Fernández-Braso, 61 & 59.

49. Gerald Martin, "On 'Magical' and Social Realism in García Márquez," *Gabriel García Márquez: New Readings* eds. Bernard McGuirk & Richard Caldwell (Cambridge: Cambridge UP, 1987) 104.

50. García Márquez, "Nobel," 89.

51. Dreifus, 176.

52. Rodriguez Monegal, "Novedad," 42 & 41.

53. Zunilda Gertel, *La novela hispanoamericana contemporanea* (Buenos Aires: Nuevos Esquemas, 1970) 157.

54. Octavio Paz, *El laberinto de la soledad* (México: Fondo de Cultura Económica, 1950) 18, 152 & 153.

NOTES
6. A "Spiral on a Square"

1. Osman Lins, *Evangelho na Taba: Novos Problemas Inculturais Brasileiros* (São Paulo: Summus, 1979) 179, 200, 173 & 223.

2. Anatol Rosenfeld, "The Creative Narrative Processes of Osman Lins," *Studies in Short Fiction* 8.1 (Winter 1971): 242.

3. João Paulo Paes, "*Avalovara*: A Magia de Osman." Guia, (São Paulo: Edições Melhoramentos, 1973) 4.

4. Lins, 207.

5. Esdras do Nascimento, "Em Cada Novo Livro, Toda a Nossa Vida," *O Estado de São Paulo*, Suplemento Literário, 24 de março de 1969.

6. Edla van Steen, "Osman Lins," *Viver e Escrever*, Vol 1 (Porto Alegre: L & PM Editores, 1982) 76.

7. Julia Cuervo Hewitt, "Além de *Avalovara*," *Luso-Brazilian Review* 21.1 (summer 1984): 1.

8. Lins, 167 & *Avalovara* (São Paulo: Edições Melhoramentos, 1973) 7. Early in the text itself, the protagonist passes "a statue of Dante Alighieri" in a park (20) and later, the text is said to "imitate, in terms of its principal points, an ancient morality poem." (73).
All subsequent quotations will be taken from this edition and incorporated into the text of this analysis.

9. Lins, *Evangelho*, 166.

10. Lins, *Evangelho*, 157.

11. Lins, *Evanhelho*, 166.

12. This passage goes on to evoke the transcendent power of a melody which recalls the ancient belief in the harmony and music of the spheres: "...muitas relações permanecem além de nosso alcance, como uma música que, meio adormecidos á margem de um rio, ouvimos, noite alta, cantada por alguém numa canoa que desce a correnteza. Nossa mente assegura-nos que a melodia continua, sem que os sentidos confirmem tal certeza (73) ("...many relationships remain beyond our reach, like a melody which, half asleep on the banks of a river, we hear in the middle of the night, sung by someone in a boat going down river. Our mind assures us that the melody continues, while our senses fail to confirm our certainty.")

13. Cook, viii, 37-8 & 407.

14. Donald Atkinson, "The Origin and Date of the 'Sator' Word-Square," *The Journal of Ecclesiastical History* 2.1 (Jan-April 1951): 1 & 2.

15. *Encyclopedia Britannica* "Magic Square," 1989 edition.

16. Atkinson, 2-3.

17. J. Gwyne Griffiths, "'Arepo' in the Magic 'Sator' Square," *The Classical Review* 21 (1971): 7 & 8.

18. Walter O. Moeller, *The Mithraic Origin & Meanings of the Rotas-Sator Square* (Leiden, Netherlands: E. J. Brill, 1973) preface & 9.

19. Moeller, 13.

20. Ana Luiza Andrade, *Osman Lins: Crítica e Criação* (São Paulo: Editora Hucitec, 1987) 176.

21. In conversation with Gregory Rabassa, who translated both *Avalovara* and *Cien años de soledad* into English, this translator pointed out the fact that the letter "N," along with the letter "M," is at the middle of the 26-letter alphabet we use in English.

22. Lins, *Evangelho*, 142.

23. Candace Slater, "A Play of Vocies: The Theater of Osman Lins," *Hispanic Review* 49.3 (summer 1981): 291.

24. Paes, 2.

25. Lins, *Evangelho*, 176 & 175.

26. Regina Igel, "*Avalovara*: Arquétipos e a técnica de prefiguração, "*Luso-Brazilian Review* 20.2 (winter 1983): 223.

27. Lins, *Evangelho*, 175 & 165.

28. Lins, *Evangelho*, 174.

29. Lins, *Evangelho*, 23.

30. Lins, *Evangelho*, 218.

31. Lins, *Evangelho*, 266.

32. Rabassa, 33.

33. Lins, *Evangelho*, 220-1.

34. Lins, *Evangelho*, 140-1.

35. Lins, *Evangelho*, 169.

36. Osman Lins, *Nove, Novena* (São Paulo: Edições Melhoramentos, 1966) 209. Subsequent quotations will be taken from this edition and incorporated into the text of this analysis.

37. Andrade, 157.

38. van Steen, 75.

39. Slater, 75.

40. Osman Lins, *Guerra Sem Testemunhas: O Escritor, sua Candição e a Realidade Social* (São Paulo: Atica: 1974) 121.

41. Lins, *Evangelho*, 141.

42. Rosenfeld, 237.

43. van Steen, 79. As an aside, it is interesting to note that Gabriel García Márquez playfully observes that he became a writer since he was "unsuccessful at becoming a magician."

44. Lins, *Evangelho*, 252.

45. Rosenfeld, 233.

46. Lins, *Evangelho*, 213.

47. Rosenfeld, 232.

48. Fustel de Coulanges, *The Ancient City: A Study on the Religion. Laws and Institutions of Greece and Rome* (Boston: Lothrop, Lee & Shepherd, 1901) 180 & 181.

49. van Steen, 75.

50. Poulet, 350.

51. Daniel, 25. Speaking of Karl Jasper's principle of "round being," Gaston Bachelard quotes Jules Michelet and writes: "A bird, for Michelet, is solid roundness. It is round life... The bird, which is almost completely spherical, is certainly the sublime and divine summit of living concentration." *The Poetics of Space*, trans. Maria Jolas (Boston: Beacon Press, 1969) 237.

52. Ana Luisa Andrade, "Crítica e Criação: Síntese do Trajeto Ficcional de Osman Lins," *Revista Iberoamericana* 50.126 (Jan-March 1984): 125.

53. Lins, *Evangelho*, 132.
54. Andrade, *Osman Lins*, 228.
55. Lins, *Evangelho*, 85.
56. Lins, *Evangelho*, 90 & 91.
57. Daniel, 30 & 32.
58. Lins, *Evangelho*, 165.
59. Antônio Cândido,"A Espiral e o Quadrado" Introduction, *Avalovara* (São Paulo: Edições Melhoramentos, 1973) 10.
60. Lins, *Evangelho*, 180.
61. Alexandrino Severino, "Tempo e Espaço em *Avalovara*," *La Chispe* 81 (março de 1982): 312.
62. Cuervo-Hewitt, 4.
63. Quoted in Sérgio Luiz Prado Bellei, "A Leitura de *Avalovara*: Texto e Tentação Logocéntrica," *Romance Notes* 26.3 (spring 1986): 196.
64. Paes, 3.
65. Lins, *Evangelho*, 116.
66. Lins, *Guerra*, 21, 193 & 121-9.
67. Philip Norris, *Deconstruction: Theory and Practice* (London & New York: Methuen, 1982) 96.
68. Lins, *Evangelho*, 173.
69. Rosenfeld, 233.
70. Lins, *Evangelho*, 213-4.

NOTES
7. "The World is Round"

1. Jorge Luís Borge, "La esfera de Pascal," *Otras inquisiciones* (Buenos Aires: Emecé Editors, 1966) 13.

2. Harss, 122.

3. Poulet, vii.

4. Lins, *Guerra*, 13.

5. Edward Said, *Beginnings: Intention and Method* (New York: Columbia UP, 1985) 316 & xiv.

6. Berkovitch, *The American Jeremiad*, 131 & 182-3.

7. Rabassa, 35.

8. Fernández-Braso, 90.

9. Said, xiii.

10. Frank Kermode, *The Sense of an Ending: Studies in the Theory of Fiction* (New York: Oxford UP, 1967) 148, 8, 7 & 28.

11. Brooks, 37, 93 & 112.

12. Carman M. del Río, "Borges, la literatura y el tiempo: Hacia una estética para mortales," *Explicación de Textos Literários* 11.2 (1982-3) 59.

13. Jacques Ellul, *The Meaning of the City* (Grand Rapids, Michigan: William B. Eerdmans, 1970) 1.

14. Crow, 225.

BIBLIOGRAPHY

Adams, Richard P. *Faulkner: Myth and Motion*. Princeton UP, 1968.

Andrade, Ana Luiza. "Crítica e Criação: Síntese do Trajecto Ficcional de Osman Lins." *Revista Iberoamericana* 50.126 (Jan-Mar 1984): 113-27.

_____, *Osman Lins: Crítica e Criacão*. São Paulo: Editoria Hucitec, 1987.

Atkinson, Donald. "The Origin and Date of the 'Sator' Word-Square." *The Journal of Ecclesiastical History* 2.1 (Jan-April 1951): 1-18.

Bachelard, Gaston. *The Poetics of Space*. Trans. Maria Jolas. Boston: Beacon Press, 1964.

Belle Villada, Gene H. "García Márquez and the Novel." *Latin American Literary Review* 13.25 (Jan-June 1985): 15-23

Bennett, James D. *Frederick Jackson Turner*. Boston: Twayne, 1975.

Bercovitch, Sacvan. *The American Jeremiad*. Madison, Wisconsin: U of Wisconsin P, 1978.

_____, *The Puritan Origins of the American Self*. New Haven & London: Yale UP, 1975.

Blake, Nancy. "Creation & Procreation: The Voice & the Name, or Biblical Intertextuality in *Absalom, Absalom!*" *Intertextuality in Faulkner*. Eds. Michel Gresset & Noel Polk. Jackson: UP of Mississippi, 1985. 128-43.

Bollettino, Vincenzo. *Breve estudio de la novelistica de García Márquez*. Madrid: Playor S.A. 1973.

Borges, Jorge Luís. "La esfera de Pascal." *Otras inquisiciones*. Buenos Aires: Emecé Editores, 1966. 13-17.

Bravo, José Antonio. *Lo real maravilloso en la narrativa latinoamerican actual*. Lima: Editoriales Unidas, 1978.

Brooks, Peter. "Incredulous Narration: *Absalom, Absalom! Reading for the Plot: Design & Intention in Narrative*. New York: Alfred A. Knopf, 1984. 286-312.

Brushwood, John. "Importancia de Faulkner en la novela latinoamericana." *Letras Nacionales* 31 (1976): 7-14.

_____, *The Spanish American Novel: A Twentieth-Century Survey*. Austin & London: U of Texas P, 1975

Cândido, António. A Espiral e o Quardrado." Prefácio *Avalovara*. São Paulo: Edições Melhoramentos, 1973. 9-11.

Chapman, Arnold. "Pampas and Big Woods: Heroic Initiation in Güiraldes and Faulkner." *Comparative Literature*. 11 (1959): 61-77.

Chase, Richard. "Faulkner - The Great Years." *The American Novel and Its Tradition*. New York: Gordeon Press, 1978. 205-36.

Cirlot, J. E. *A Dictionary of Symbols*. New York: Philosophical Library, 1962.

Collmer, Robert G. "When 'Word' Meets *Palabra*: Crossing the Border with Literature." *William Faulkner: Prevailing Verities and World Literature*: Proceedings of the Comparative Literature Symposium. Eds. Wolodyme T. Zyla & Wendell M. Aycock. Lubbock, Texas: Texas Tech UP, 1979. 153-64.

Cook, Theodore Andrea. *The Curves of Life: an Account of Spiral Formations and Their Application to Growth in Nature, to Science & to Art*. New York: Dover, 1979.

Corvalan, Octavio. "Introducción." *Hacia las fuentes de García Márquez* Seminario de Literatura Comparada. Cuadernos de Letras: Universidad de Salta, 1979.

Crow, John S. *The Epic of Latin America*. Garden City, New York: Doubleday, 1971.

Cuadra, René Jara. *Las claves del mito en Cien años de soledad*. Chile: Ediciones Universitarias de Varparaíso, 1972.

Cuervo, Hewitt, Julia. "Além de *Avalovara*." *Luso-Brazilian Review*. 21.1 (Summer 1984): 1-11.

Daniel, Mary L. "Through the Looking Glass: Mirror Play in Two Works of João Guimarães Rosa & Osman Lins." *Luso-Brazilian Review*. 123.1 (Summer 1976): 19-34.

Davis, Mary E. "The Haunted Voice: Echoes of William Faulkner in García Márquez, Fuentes and Vargas Llosa. *World Literature Today*. 59.4 (Autumn 1985): 531-5.

de Coulanges, Fustel. *The Ancient City: A Study on the Religion, Laws and Institutions of Greece and Rome*. Boston: Lothrop, Lee & Shepard, 1901.

de Crèvcoeur, St. Jean. "Letters from an American Farmer: III." *The Norton Anthology of American Literature*, Vol 1. New York & London: W. W. Norton, 1979. 438-57.

de Tocqueville, Alexis. *Democracy in America*. New York: Alfred A. Knopf, 1951.

del Río, Carmen M. "Borges, la literatura y el tiempo: Hacia una estética para mortales." *Explicación de Textos Literarios* 11-2 (1982-3): 57-67.

Delay, Florence & Jacqueline de Labriolle. "Márquez: Est-il le Faulkner Colombien?" *Revue de Litterature Comparée* 47 (1973): 88-123.

Derrida, Jacques. "Structure, Sign and Play in the Discourse of the Human Sciences." *The Structural Controversy*. Eds. Richard Macksey & Eugenio B. Donato. Johns Hopkins UP, 1972. 247-72.

do Nascimento, Esdras. "Em Cada Novo Livro, Toda a Nossa Vida." *O Estado de São Paulo*. Suplemento Literário, 24 março de 1969.

Dreifus, Claudia. "*Playboy* interview: Gabriel García Márquez." *Playboy* 30.2 (Feb 1983): 65-178.

Durán, Armando. "Conversaciones con Gabriel García Márquez." *Sobre García Márquez*. Ed. Pedro Simón Martínez. Montevideo: Biblioteca de Marcha, 1970.

Ellul, Jacques. *The Meaning of the City*. Grand Rapids, Michigan, William B. Eerdmans, 1970.

Encyclopedia Britannica. "Magic Squares." 1989 edition.

Faulkner, William. *Absalom, Absalom!* New York: The Modern Library, Random House, 1936.

_____, *Light in August*. New York: Vintage Books, 1932.

_____, *Selected Letters of William Faulkner*. Ed. Joseph Blotner, New York: Random House, 1977.

Fernández-Braso, Miguel. *Gabriel García Márquez: Una conversación infinita*. Madrid: Editorial Azur, 1969.

Fitzgerald, F. Scott. *The Great Gatsby*. New York: Charles Scribner's & Sons, 1925.

Frisch, Marc Frederic. "Parallels between William Faulkner and Four Hispanic American Novelists." *DAI* 46 (1985): 972. University of Michigan.

Fuentes, Carlos. Interview with Christopher Sharp. *W*. Supplement to *Women's Wear Daily* (29 Oct - 5 Nov 1976): 9.

_____, Interview with Jonathan Tittler. *Diacritics* 10.3 (Fall 1980): 52.

_____, *La nueva novela en hispanoamérica*. México: Joaquin Mortiz, 1969.

García Márquez, Gabriel. *Cien años de soledad*. Buenos Aires: Editorial Sudamérica, 1976.

_____, *El coronel no tiene quien le escriba*. México: Ediciones Era, 1961.

_____, "Fantasía y creación artística en América Latina y el Caribe." *Texto Crítico* 5.4 (1979): 3-8.

_____, "Los funerales de la Mama Grande." *Los funerales de la Mama Grande*. Barcelona: Plaza & Janes, 1979.

_____, "The Solitude of Latin America: Nobel Lecture, 1982." *Gabriel García Márquez & the Powers of Fiction*. Ed. Julio Ortega. Austin: U of Texas P, 1988. 87-91.

_____ & Mario Vargas Llosa. *La novela en América Latina: Diálogo*. Lima: Ediciones Universidad Nacional de Engenieria, 1968

Gertel, Zunilda. *La novela hispanoamericana contemporanea*. Buenos Aires: Nuevos Esquemas, 1970.

_____, "Tres estructuras fundamentales en la narrativa hispanoamericana actual." *Nueva Narrative Hispanoamericana* 5 (enero y sept 1975): 215-27.

Gilard, Jacques. "García Márquez, le Groupe de Barranquilla et Faulker." *Cahiers du Monde Hispanique et Luso-Brésilien*. (Caravelle) 17 (1976): 159-70.

González, Aníbel. "Translation & Genealogy: *One Hundred Years of Solitude*." *Gabriel García Márquez: New Readings*. Eds. Bernard McGuirk & Richard Caldwell. Cambridge UP, 1987.

González Echeverría, Roberto. "*Cien años de soledad*: The Novel as Myth & Archive." *Modern Language Notes* 99.2 (March 1984): 358-80.

Griffiths, J. Gwyne. "Arepo' in the Magic 'Sator' Square." *The Classical Review* 21 (1971): 6-8.

Guerard, Albert J. *The Triumph of the Novel: Dickens, Dostoevsky & Faulkner*. New York: Oxford U Press, 1976.

Gullón, Ricardo. "García Márquez o el olvidado arte de contar." *Homenaje a Gabriel García Márquez*. Ed. Helmy F. Giacoman. New York: Las Américas, 1972. 143-70.

Gwynn, Frederick L. & Joseph L. Blotner, eds. *Faulkner in the University: Class Conferences at the University of Virginia: 1957-8.* Charlottesville, Virginia: U of Virginia P, 1959.

Harss, Luís. *Los nuestros.* Buenos Aires: Editorial Sudamericana, 1969.

_____ & Barbara Dohmann. "Alejo Carpentier, or the Eternal Return." *Into the Mainstream.* New York: Harper & Row, 1967.

Hillis Miller, J. "The Two Relativisms: Point of View and Indeterminancy in the Novel *Absalom, Absalom! Relativism in the Arts.* Ed. Betty Jean Craige. Athens: U of Georgia P, 1983. 148-70.

Humphrey, William. *Ah, Wilderness! The Frontier in American Literature.* El Paso: Texas Western P, 1977.

Igel, Reginá. "*Avalovara*: Arquétipos e a Técnica de Prefiguração." *Luso-Brazilian Review* vol 20, no 2 (Winter 1983): 223-31.

Irwin, John T. *Doubling & Incest/Repetition & Revenge: A Speculative Reading of Faulkner.* Baltimore & London: Johns Hopkins UP, 1975.

Jara, René & Jaime Mejia Duque. *Las claves del mito en García Márquez.* Valparaiso: Ediciones Universitarias de Valparaiso, 1972.

Kartiganer, Donald M. "Toward a Supreme Fiction: *Absalom, Absalom! Faulkner: New Perspectives.* Ed. Richard H., Brodhead. Englewood Cliffs, New Jersey: Prentice-Hall, 1983. 153-73.

Kennedy, William. "The Yellow Trolley Car in Barcelona and Other Visions: A Profile of Gabriel García Márquez." *Atlantic Monthly* 231 (1973): 50-8.

Kermode, Frank. *A Sense of an Ending: Studies in the Theory of Fiction.* New York: Oxford UP, 1967.

Kolodny, Annette. *The Land Before Her: Fantasy & Experience of the American Frontiers, 1630-1860.* Chapel Hill & London: U of North Carolina P, 1984.

Krause, David. "Opening Pandora's Box: Re-Reading Compson's Letter & Faulkner's *Absalom, Absalom!*" *Centennial Review* 30.2 (1986): 358-82.

_____, "Reading Bon's Letter & Faulkner's *Absalom, Absalom!*" *PMLA* 99 (1984): 225-39.

Kulin, Katalin. *Creación mítica en la obra de Gabriel García Márquez.* Budapest: Akadémiai Kiadó, 1980.

Levine, Suzanne Jill. "*Pedro Páramo* y *Cien años de soledad*: un paralelo." *Homenaje a Gabriel García Márquez*. Ed. Helmy F. Giacoman. New York: Latin American Publishing Co., Inc. 1972. 281-93.

Lins, Osman. *Avalovara*. São Paulo: Edições Melhoramentos, 1973.

_____, *Evangelho na Taba: Outros Problemas Inculturais Brasileiros* São Paulo: Summus Editorial, 1979.

_____, *Guerra Sem Testemunhas: O Escritor, Sua Condição e Sua Realidade Social*. São Paulo: Martins Editora, 1969.

_____, *Nove, Novena*. São Paulo: Edições Melhoramentos, 1966.

López-Schümmer, José Luís. "El Descubrimiento como mito." *Cuadernos Americanos: nueva época*. 9.3 (Mayo-Junio 1988): 21-6.

Löwith, Karl. *Meaning in History*. Chicago: U of Chicago P, 1949.

Ludemar, Josefina. *Cien años de soledad: Una interpretación*. Buenos Aires: Editorial Tiempo Contemporáneo, 1972.

Martin, Gerald. "On 'magical' & social realism in García Márquez." *Gabriel García Márquez: New Readings*. Eds. Bernard McGuirk & Richard Caldwell. New York: Cambridge U Press, 1987. 95-116.

Matthews, John T. *The Play of Faulkner's Language*. Ithaca & London: Cornell UP, 1982.

Maturo, Graciela. *Claves simbólicas de García Márquez*. Buenos Aires: Fernando García Cambeiro, 1972.

Mena, Lucila Inés. *La función de la historia en Cien años de soledad*. Barcelona, Plaza & Janes S.A. 1979.

Miller, Perry. *Errand Into the Wilderness*. Cambridge & London: Harvard UP, 1956.

Millgate, Michael. *The Achievement of William Faulkner*. New York: Random House, 1966.

Minter, David. "Family, Region & Myth in Faulkner's Fiction." *William Faulkner's* Absalom, Absalom! Ed. Harold Bloom. New York: Chelsea House Publishers, 1987. 75-89.

_____, *William Faulkner. The Writing of a Life*. Baltimore: Johns Hopkins UP, 1980.

Moeller, Walter O. *The Mithraic Origin & Meanings of the Rotas-Sator Square*. Leiden, Netherlands: E. J. Brill, 1973.

Murphy, Francis. "Early American Literature, 1620-1820: Introduction." *The Norton Anthology of American Literature*. Vol 1. New York & London: W. W. Norton, 1979. 1-10.

Nash, Roderick. *Wilderness & the American Mind*. New Haven & London: Yale UP, 1967.

Noble, David W. *The Eternal Adam & the New World Garden*. New York: George Braziller, 1966.

Norris, Phillip. *Deconstruction: Theory and Practice*. London & New York: Methuen, 1982.

Nye, Russel B. *This Almost Chosen People: Essays in the History of American Ideas*. Michigan State UP, 1966.

Oberhelman, Harvey D. Faulknerian Techniques in Gabriel García Márquez's Portrait of a Dictator." *Ibero-American Letters in Perspective*: Proceedings of the Comparative Literature Symposium. Eds. Wolodymyer T. Zyla & Wendell M. Aycock. Lubbock, Texas: Texas Tech Press, 1979. 171-81.

_____, "García Márquez and the American South." *Chasqui* 5.1 (Nov 1975): 29-38.

_____, *The Presence of Faulkner in the Writings of García Márquez*. Lubbock, Texas: Texas Tech Press, 1980.

O'Gorman, Edmundo. *The Invention of America*. Bloomington: Indiana UP, 1961.

Ortega, Julio. "Exchange System in *One Hundred Years of Solitude*." *Gabriel García Márquez & the Powers of Fiction*. Ed. Julio Ortega. Austin: U of Texas P, 1988. 1-16.

Paes, José Paulo. "Avalovara: A Magia de Osman." Guia. *Avalovara*. São Paulo: Edições Melhoramentos, 1973.

Palencia-Roth, Michael. *Gabriel García Márquez: La linea, el circulo y las metamorfosis del mito*. Madrid: Editorial Gredos, 1983.

Parkinson-Zamora, Lois. "The End of Innocence: Myth & Narrative Structure in Faulkner's *Absalom, Absalom!* and García Márquez' *Cien años de soledad*." *Hispanic Journal* 4.1 (Fall 1982): 23-40.

Paz, Octavio. *El laberinto de la soledad*. México: Fondo de Cultura Económica, 1950.

Porter, Laurence M. "The Political Function of Fantasy in García Márquez." *Centennial Review* 30.2 (1986): 196-207.

Poulet, Georges. *The Metamorphosis of the Circle*. Baltimore: Johns Hopkins UP, 1966.

Prado, Bellei, Sérgio Luiz. "A Leitura de *Avalovara*: Texto e Tentação Logo-céntrica." *Romance Notes* 26.3 (Spring 1986): 194-203.

Rabassa, Gregory. "Osman Lins & *Avalovara*: The Shape & Shaping of the Novel." *World Literature Today* 53.1 (Winter 1979): 30-5.

Robbins, Deborah. "The Desperate Eloquence of *Absalom, Absalom!*" *The Mississippi Quarterly*, 34.3 (Summer 1981): 315-24.

Rodríguez Márquez, Raúl. "Veinte años después." *Magazin Dominical de El Espectator.* Bogatá (Oct 1957): 2.

Rodríguez Monegal, Emir. "Novedad y anacronismo de *Cien años de soledad*." *Homenjae a Gabriel García Márquez*. Ed. Helmy F. Giacoman. New York: Latin American Publishing Co., 1972. 15-41.

_____, "*One Hundred Years of Solitude*: The Last Three Pages." *Crítical Essays on Gabriel García Márquez*. Ed. George R. McMurray. Boston: G.K. Hall, 1987. 147-52.

Rosenfeld, Anatol. "The Creative Narrative Processes of Osman Lins." *Studies in Short Fiction*. 8.1 (Winter 1979): 230-44.

Ross, Stephen M. "Oratory & the Dialogical in *Absalom, Absalom! Intertextuality in Faulkner*. Eds. Michel Gresset & Noel Polk. Jackson: UP of Mississippi, 1985. 73-86.

Said, Edward. *Beginnings: Intention and Method*. New York: Columbia UP, 1985.

Salvador, Gregorio. *Comentarios estructurales a Cien años de soledad*. Las Palmas: Litografia Saavedra, 1970.

Schmidtberger, Loren F. "*Absalom, Absalom!*: What Clytie Knew." *The Mississippi Quarterly* 35.3 (Summer 1982): 255-63.

Severino, Alexandrino. "Tempo e Espaço em *Avalovara. La Chispa* 81 (março 1982): 309-15.

Simpson, Lewis P. "Yoknapatawpha & Faulkner's Fable of Civilization." *The Maker & the Myth: Faulkner & Yoknapatawpha*. Eds. Evans Harrington & Ann J. Abadie. Jackson: UP of Mississippi, 1978. 122-45.

Sims, Robert Lewis. *The Evolution of Myth in Gabriel García Márquez*. Miami: Ediciones Universal, 1981.

Slater, Candace. "The Play of Voices: The Theater of Osman Lins.: *Hispanic Review*. 49.3 (summer 1981) 285-95.

Snead, James A. *Figures of Division: William Faulkner's Major Novels*. New York & London: Methuen, 1986.

Stonum, Gary Lee. "The Fate of Design." *William Faulkner's* Absalom, Absalom! Ed. Harold Bloom. New York: Chelsea House, 1987. 35-55.

Sundquist, Eric J. "*Absalom, Absalom!* and the House Divided." *William Faulkner's* Absalom, Absalom! Ed. Harold Bloom. New York: Chelsea House, 1987. 91-104.

Tobin, Patricia Drechsel. *Time & the Novel: The Genealogical Imperative*. Princeton UP, 1978.

Tuck, Dorothy. *Crowell's Handbook of Faulkner*. New York: Thomas Y. Crowell, 1964.

Turner, Frederick Jackson. *The Frontier in American History*. New York: Henry Holt, 1921.

van Steen, Edla. "Osman Lins." *Viver e Escrever* Porto Alegre: L & PM Editores, 1982. 69-83.

Vargas Llosa, Mario. "García Márques: de Aracataca a Macondo." *9 asedios a García Márquez*. Santiago de Chile: Editorial Universitaria, 1969. 126-46.

_____, *García Márquez: Historia de un deicidio*. Barcelona: Barral Editores, 1971.

Vespucci, Americo. "Letter to Lorenzo Pietro di Medici." *Mundus Novus*. Trans. George Tyler Northrup. Princeton: Princeton UP, 1916.

Vickery, Olga W. *The Novels of William Faulkner*. Louisiana State UP, 1959.

Volpe, Edmond L. *Reader's Guide to William Faulkner*. New York: Farrar, Straus & Co., 1964.

Voyages of Discovery: Time-frame AD 1400-1500. Alexandria, Virginia: Time-Life, 1989.

Wadlington, Warwick. *Reading Faulknerian Tragedy*. Ithaca & London: Cornell UP, 1987.

Waggoner, Hyatt H. *William Faulkner: From Jefferson to the World*. U of Kentucky P, 1959.

Washburn, Wilcomb E. "The Meaning of 'Discovery' in the Fifteenth and Sixteenth Centuries." *The American Historical Review*. 68.1 (October 1962): 1-21.

Weisberger, Jean. *Faulkner & Dostoevsky: Influence and Confluence.* Athens: Ohio UP, 1974.

White, Hayden. *Tropics of Discourse: Essays in Cultural Criticism.* Baltimore: Johns Hopkins Up, 1978.

Willems, Emilio. "Social Change on the Latin American Frontier." *The Frontier: Comparative Studies*. Eds. David Harry Miller & Jerome O. Steffen. Norman: U of Oklahoma P, 1977. 259-73.

Williams, Raymond L. "El tiempo en la novela: Observaciones en torno al tiempo en la novela colombiana contemporánea." *Explicación de textos literarios* 11.2 (1982-3): 11-28.

Winthrop, John. "A Model of Christian Charity." *The Norton Anthology of American Literature*, Vol 1. New York & London: W. W. Norton, 1979. 11-24.

Wittenberg, Judith Bryant. "William Faulkner: A Feminist Consideration." *American Novelists Revisited: Essays in Feminist Criticism*. Boston: G. K. Hall, 1982. 325-38.

Wolfskill, George & Stanley Palmer, eds. *Essays on Frontiers in World History*. Austin, Texas: U of Texas P, 1981.

Wood, Michael. "Review of *One Hundred Years of Solitude*." *Colombia Forum* 13.3 (Summer 1970): 160-5.

Wyatt, David. "Faulkner & the Burdens of the Past." *Prodigal Sons: A Study in Authorship & Authority*. Baltimore & London: Johns Hopkins UP, 1980. 72-100.

Zavala, Iris M. "*Cien años de soledad*: Crónica de Indias." *Homenaje a Gabriel García Márquez*. Ed. Helmy F. Giacoman. New York: Latin American Publishing Co., 1972. 199-212.

Zavala, Silvio. "Examen del título de la conmemoración del V centenario del descubrimiento de América." *Cuadernos americanos: nueva época* 9.3 (Mayo-Junio 1988): 14-20.

Zea, Leopoldo. *América en la consciencia de Europa*. México: Los Presentes, 1955.

_____, *América en la historia*. México & Buenos Aires: Fondo de Cultura Económica, 1957.

_____, *La esencia de lo americano*. Buenos Aires: Editorial Pleamar, 1971.